New Photography of the

Cat.

Written by

LUCY DAVIES

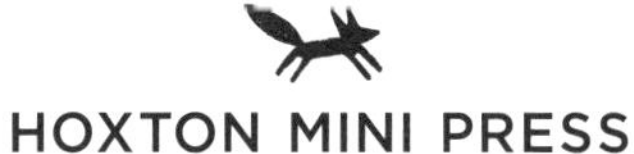

HOXTON MINI PRESS

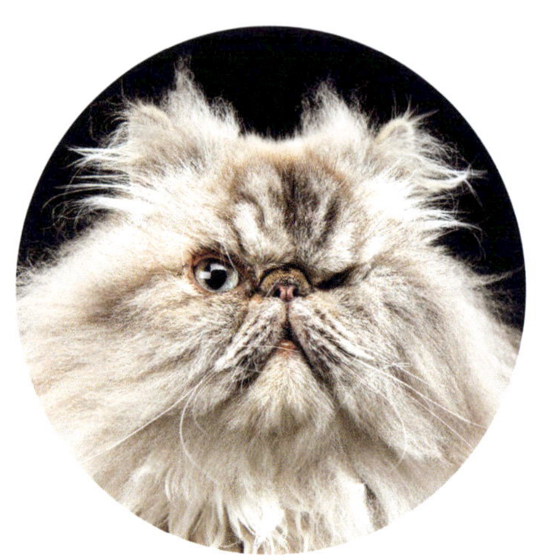

CONTENTS

Opposite: *The Regulator* by Carli Davidson, 2014

THE CREAM OF THE MODERN CAT

You're here, so I'm guessing you're a cat person. Or at the least, cat-curious. And you're in good company – science finds cat people to be smarter and more creative than their dog-owning equivalents. Also prone to worry, but we'll gloss over that.

Cats enliven a house – to the polymath Jean Cocteau, they were its 'visible soul'. They bestow their warm purring weight uncannily when and where needed and possess a playfulness that transcends any obvious purpose.

True, they are kind of mercurial, given to condescension, furniture parkour and clawing the curtains. Sure, they come with deeply specific riders concerning where they will sleep, what time breakfast ought to be served and which bowl they will eat it from. What was just so yesterday, might well not be today. No reason why!

Some of the greatest figures in history have chosen to overlook these foibles, however. Ernest Hemingway, for instance, named his after Hollywood stars; Queen singer Freddie Mercury telephoned to speak to Oscar, Tiffany, Delilah, Goliath, Miko, Romeo and Lily while he was away on tour, while President Abraham Lincoln let Tabby and Dixie eat at the table during state dinners.

'What greater gift than the love of a cat?' Charles Dickens said, whose own – Bob – used his paw to put out the candle the author was reading by if he wasn't receiving quite enough attention. The love was mutual. After Bob died, Dickens had said paw stuffed and turned into a letter opener (and he wrote a lot of letters).

Cats have always been irresistible to artists. Their intensely expressive eyes and agile bodies appear on the tomb walls of ancient Egypt, on Etruscan and Greek vases, Chinese scrolls, medieval manuscripts, in Leonardo's sketchbooks and Japanese watercolours. Things went a bit south with the Salem and Essex witch trials – when cats' association with paganism and dark magic made them objects of suspicion – but soon rallied. In the late 1800s, they were popular subjects for daguerreotypes and cabinet cards and even an early form of motion picture called the Kinetoscope (you can see the film, of boxing cats, on YouTube). Renoir painted with a cat on his lap (his work has been authenticated by cat hair trapped in the paint) and Matisse liked to keep his within stroking distance of the easel (not on record: how he made them stay there).

In fact, modernism bolstered cats' status immeasurably. Their aloofness chimed with the avant-garde spirit of independence; their ambulatory habits and fondness for preening made them natural flaneurs. The most bohemian nightclub in Paris was even named after them – Le Chat Noir. In the twilight years of the 19th century, this convivial Montmartre cavern was where Toulouse-Lautrec, Debussy and Verlaine hung out, and where painting and polemic converged.

Things took a somewhat less stylish turn with the trippy visions of Louis Wain, whose turn-of-the-century paintings of anthropomorphic cats (they play the tuba, pour tea, wear monocles and cravats) made him so famous in Britain that he could swap them for a haircut. His near contemporary, the photographer Harry Pointer, did much the same with a line in greeting cards. One captioned *The Old Batchelor* pictures a cat on a barrel with a bottle of gin and a glass. Lolz!

Actually, 'Lolz' is about right, because in Pointer's and Wain's pictures lie the first stirrings of today's cat memes, of 'Grumpy Cat' – the internet celebrity with resting scowl face – and 'Caturday', the one day a week when, by tradition, the internet interrupts its trolling to share pictures of cute, grammatically challenged cats.

Indeed, cats reign over cyberspace, and who could have foreseen that? Not even the World Wide Web's inventor, Tim Berners-Lee, who when asked to name a use of the internet that he had not anticipated, replied with one word: 'kittens'.

The projects in this book run the gamut of today's cativerse. Prepare to meet imaginary cats as tall as skyscrapers, cats wearing fur hats, cats who see their purpose in life as sitting staring out of windows. There are symmetrical cats, cat–human doppelgängers and cat houses so fabulous you'll want to move right in. Portraits of the alley cats of Istanbul and the communally owned cats of Singapore, of AI-generated cats and girls with cats that confront ye olde myth of the 'crazy cat lady'.

If you didn't identify as a cat person when you opened this book, it's quite possible you will by the time you finish it. It's disarming, it's irresistible, it's cat cajolery! But it's also more than that. Laced in these photographs is a portrait of a relationship, one that stretches back thousands of years but is still evolving. Cats are no less incomprehensible, but they still comfort in an age of uncertainty, an ideal of individual freedom. A lesson in living every day as if it were Sunday. As the novelist Colette so wisely said, 'time spent with a cat is never wasted.'

Lucy Davies, 2025

CHINESE WHISKERS
Marcel Heijnen

Think 'Hong Kong' and no doubt glassy skyscrapers and high-end malls come to mind. But in districts of the city such as Sai Ying Pun and Sheung Wan pockets of old-world Hong Kong remain, including many of the tiny, characterful mom-and-pop stores selling dried seafood, rice and herbal medicines.

Returning to the city in 2015 after an absence of 20 years, Dutch photographer Marcel Heijnen was struck by how many of these dusty, brightly coloured emporiums had their own resident cat. Shopkeepers share their space with these feline companions who blend into their surroundings, making themselves at home among the packets, jars and boxes. It's a quid pro quo arrangement because, in return, the cats keep rats and mice at bay and entice browsing customers inside. After starting his *Chinese Whiskers* series in Hong Kong, Heijnen continued to explore the shop cat phenomenon across the provinces of mainland China.

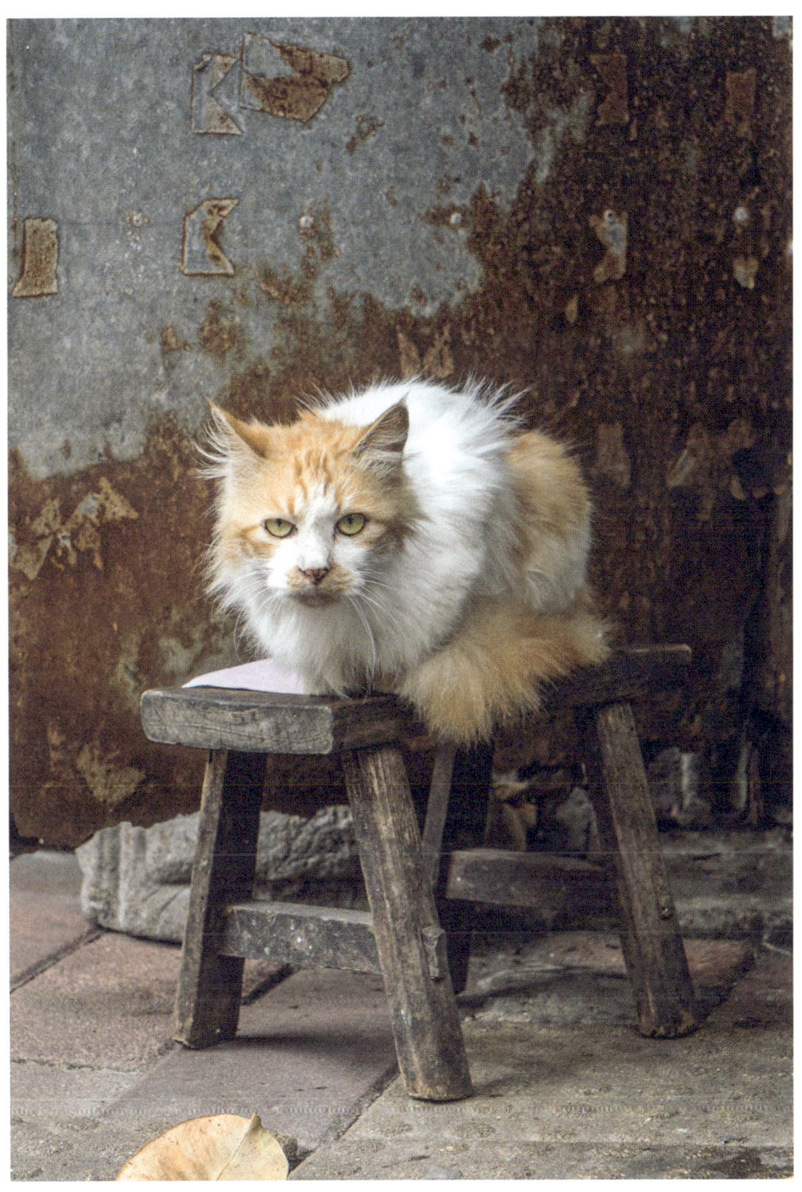

Fist of Furry, Guangzhou, 2018

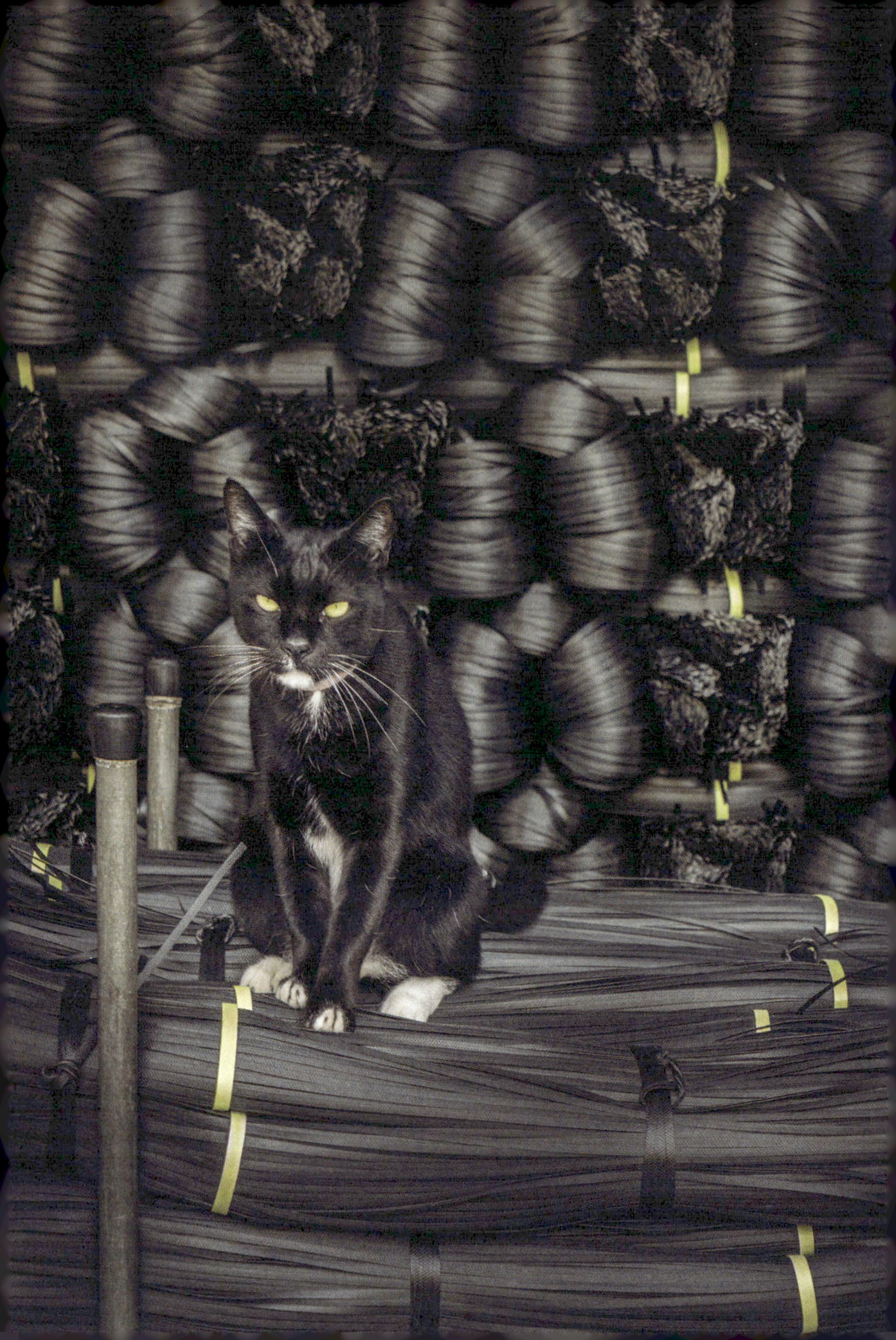

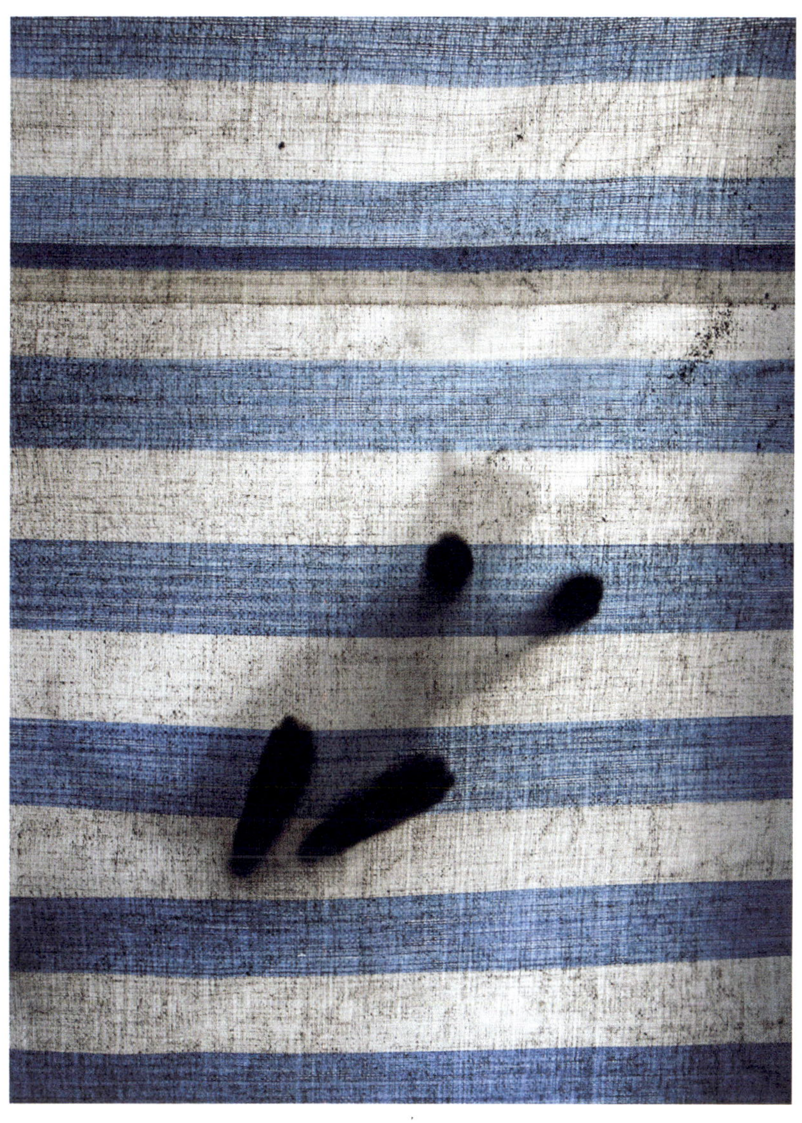

Above: *Paws for Thought, Hong Kong,* 2016
Opposite: *Black is the New Black, Hong Kong,* 2017

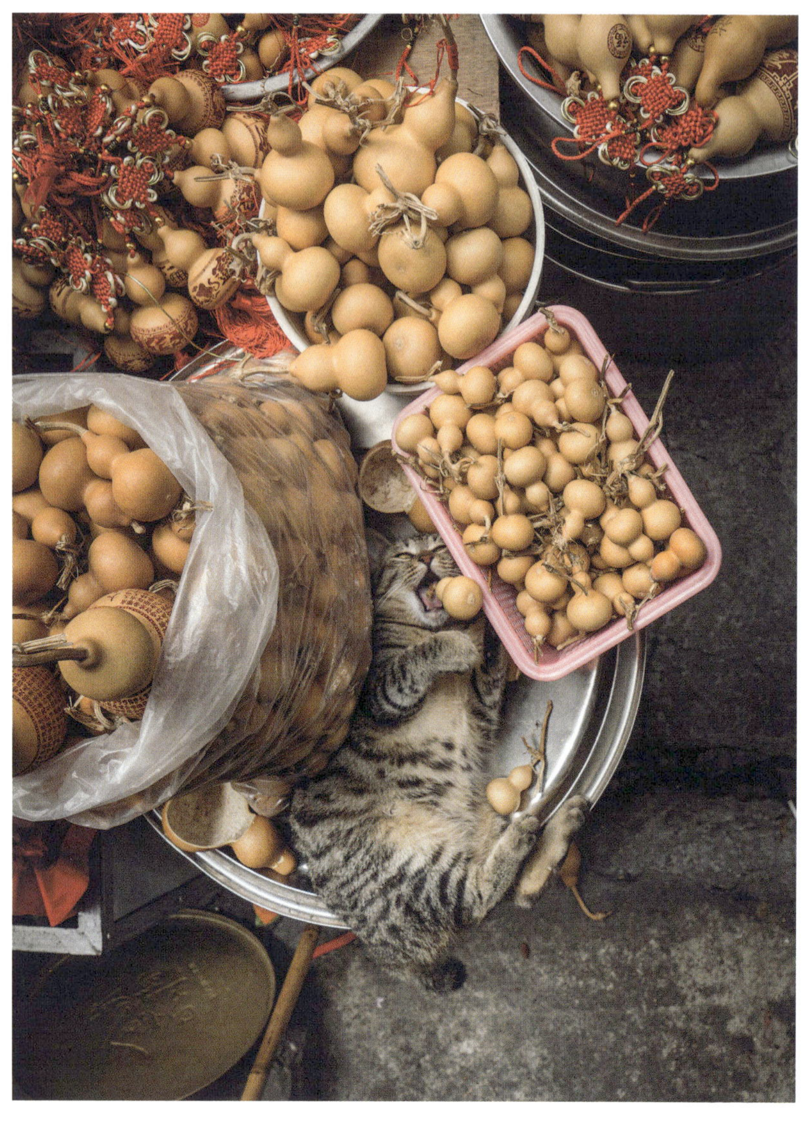

Above: *Falling Up*, *Guangzhou*, 2018
Opposite: *Basket Case*, *Guangzhou*, 2019

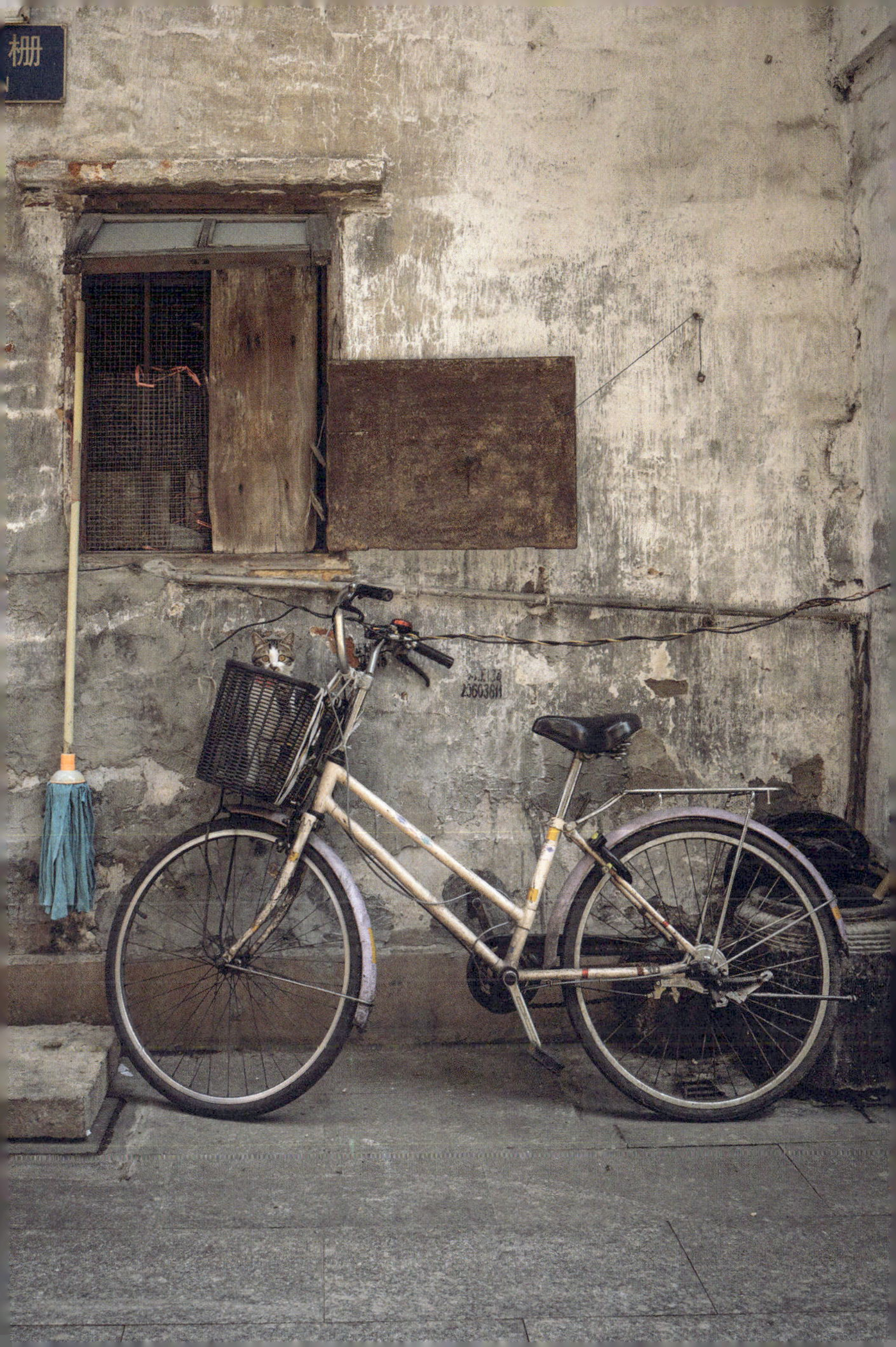
栅

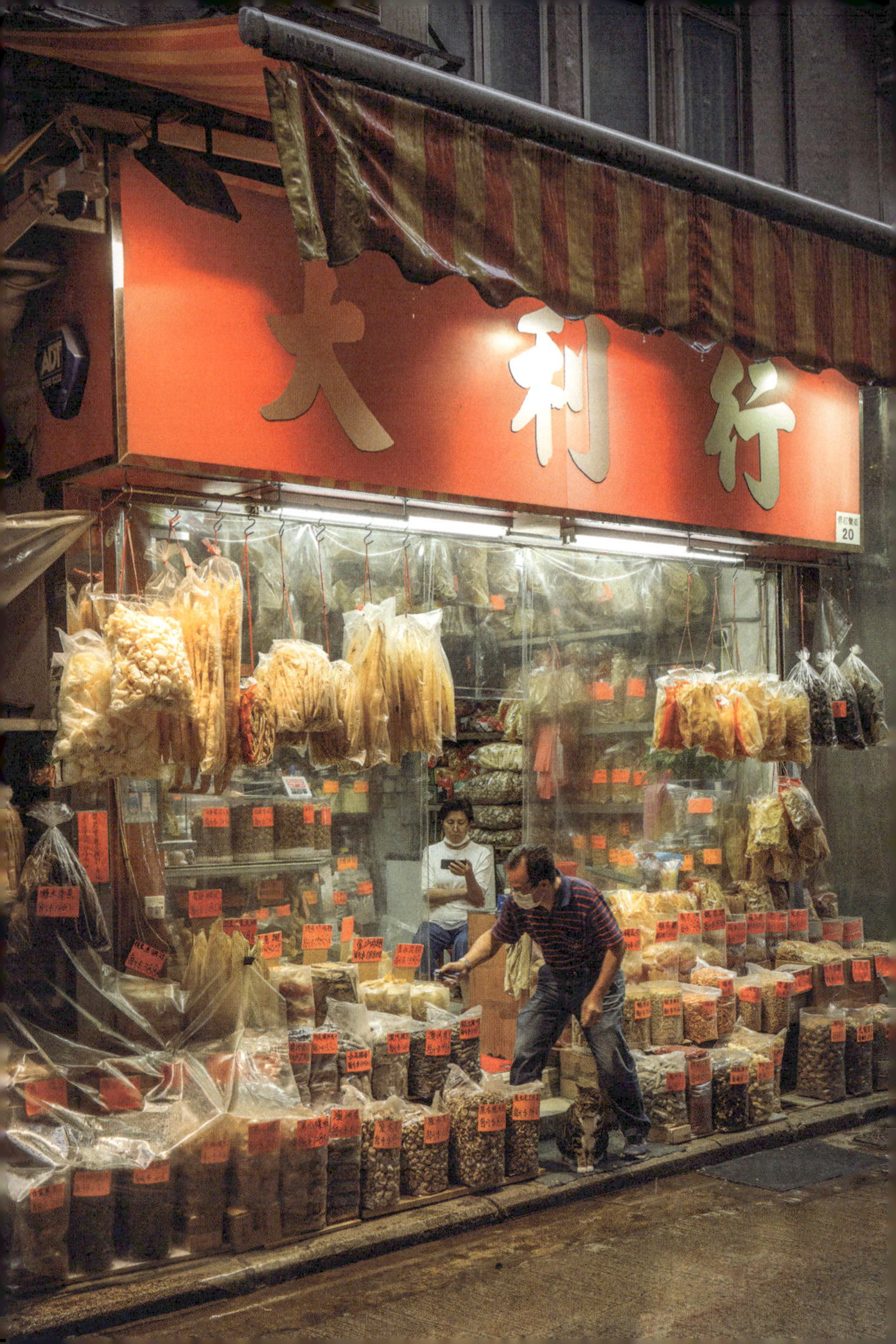
大利行
ADT
20

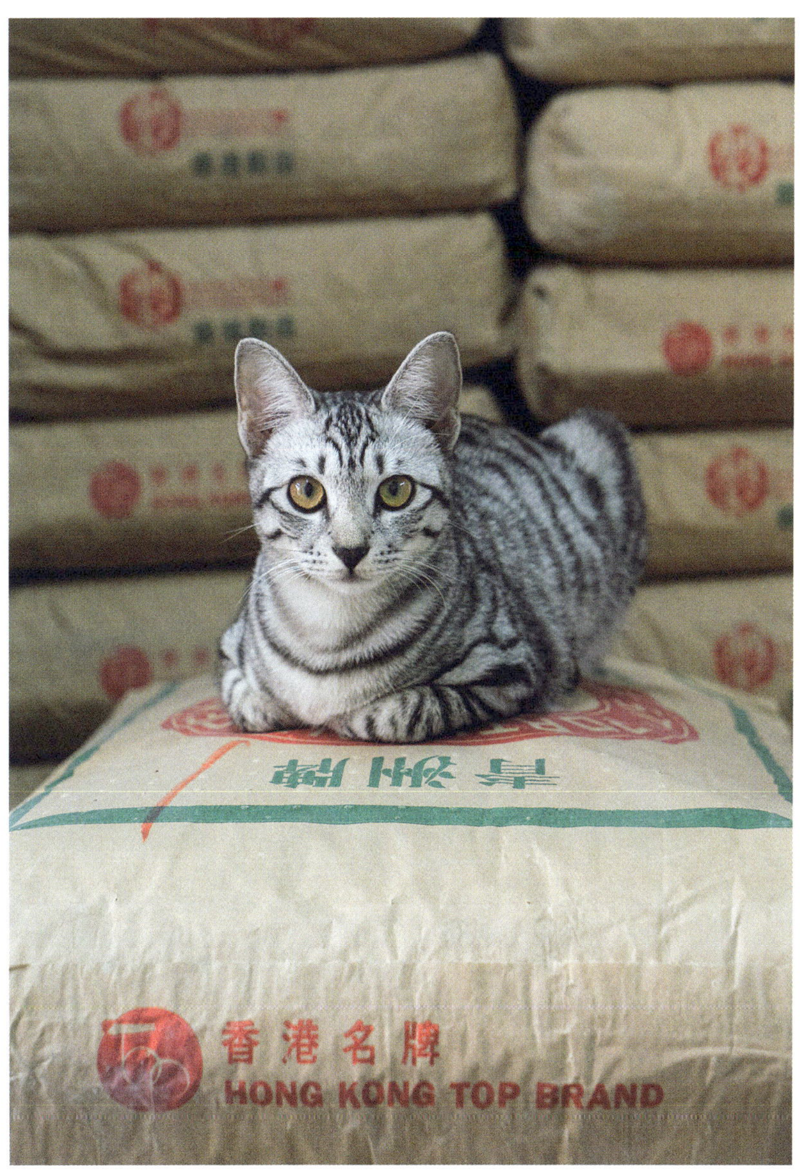

Above: *Hong Kong Top Brand, Hong Kong*, 2016
Opposite: *Fai Zai at Night, Hong Kong*, 2020

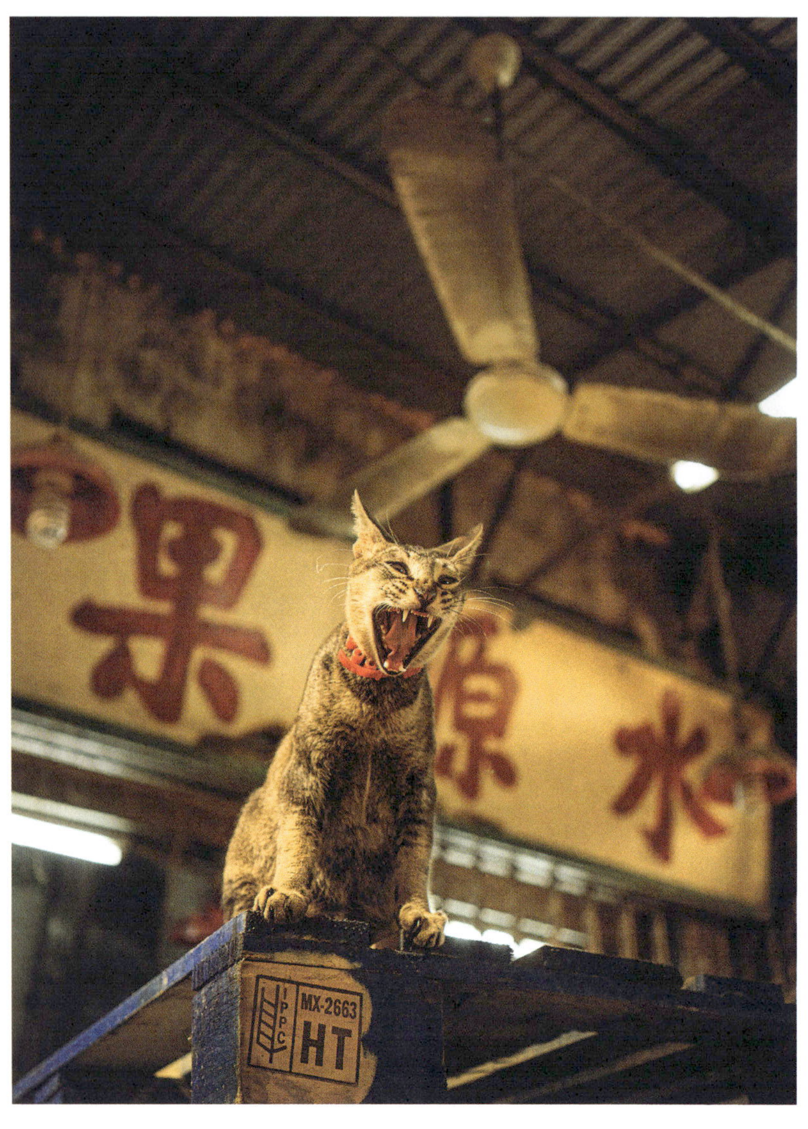

Above: *Yawn, Hong Kong*, 2021
Opposite: *Generation Gap, Shanghai*, 2017

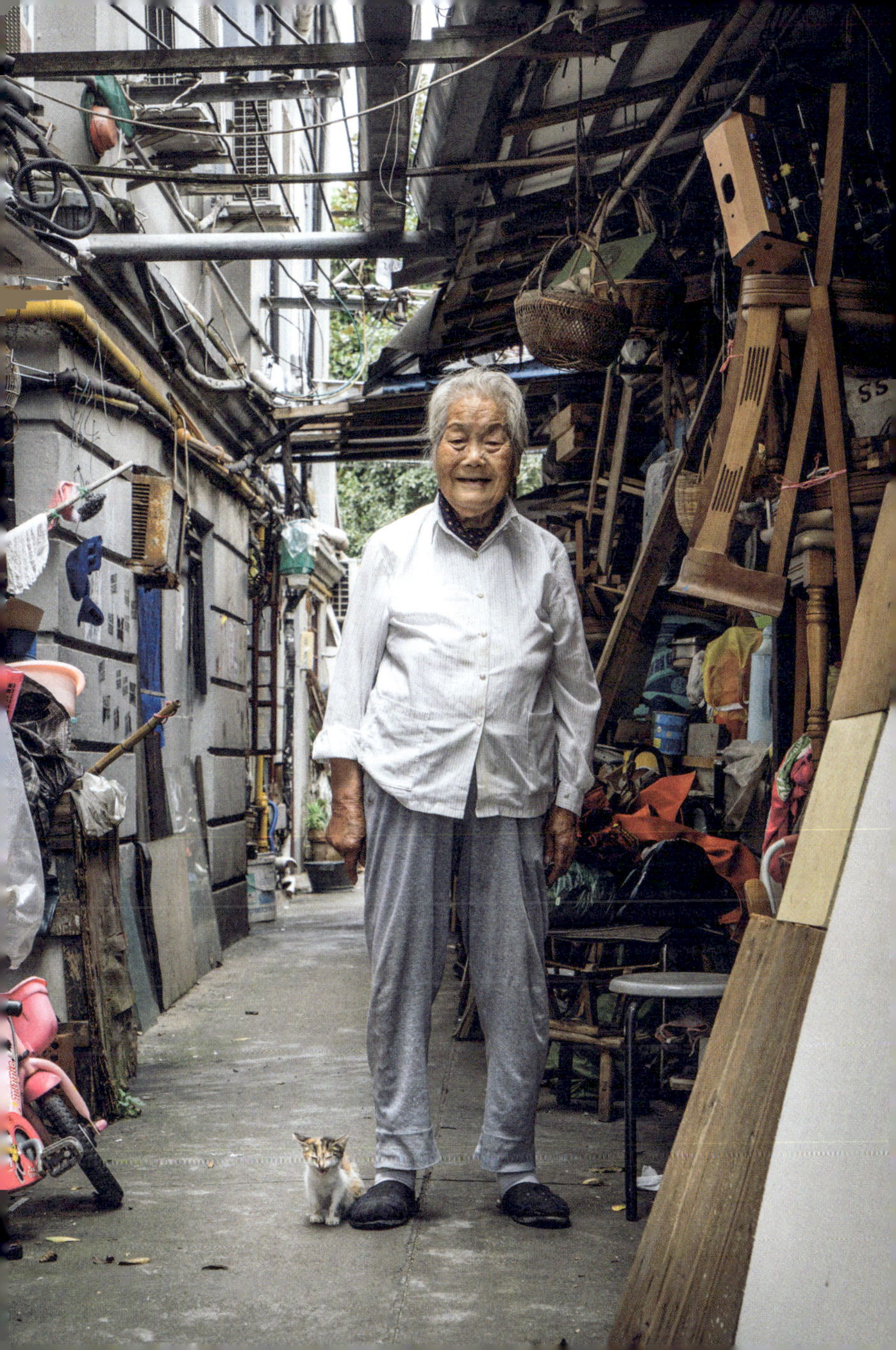

ANIMAL SOUL
Robert Bahou

What goes on between a cat's ears? You might devote your entire lifetime to that riddle and still be none the wiser, though photographer Robert Bahou doesn't seem to be daunted. He grew up around cats (along with dogs and horses), and from an early age became intrigued by the intricacies of their individual personalities. Could he capture that in a portrait?

It turned out to be easy, he says. 'They don't behave the way we do when faced with a camera. They don't adjust themselves, turn to their good sides, pull a prepared face, or hide anything. What's left is a truly honest moment between them and the camera.'

To capture the cats 'as themselves' he has some ground rules: no humour, no props, an empty black background. To get the cat to look at his lens, he sometimes uses a little fishing rod with a feather on it. His best pictures 'leave everything to the imagination,' he says. 'I can never say with certainty who an animal is. I don't think anybody can.'

Camila, 2015

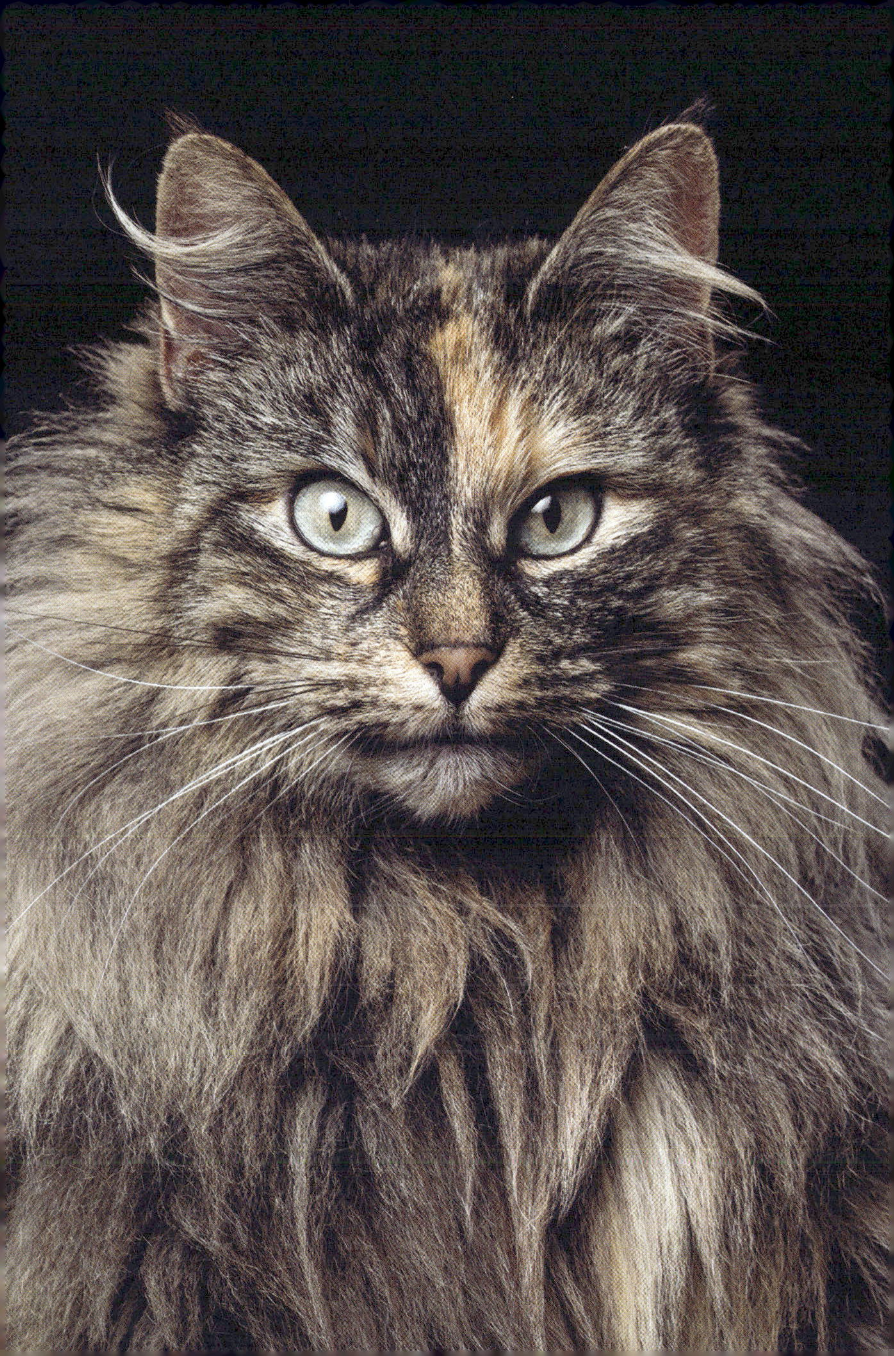

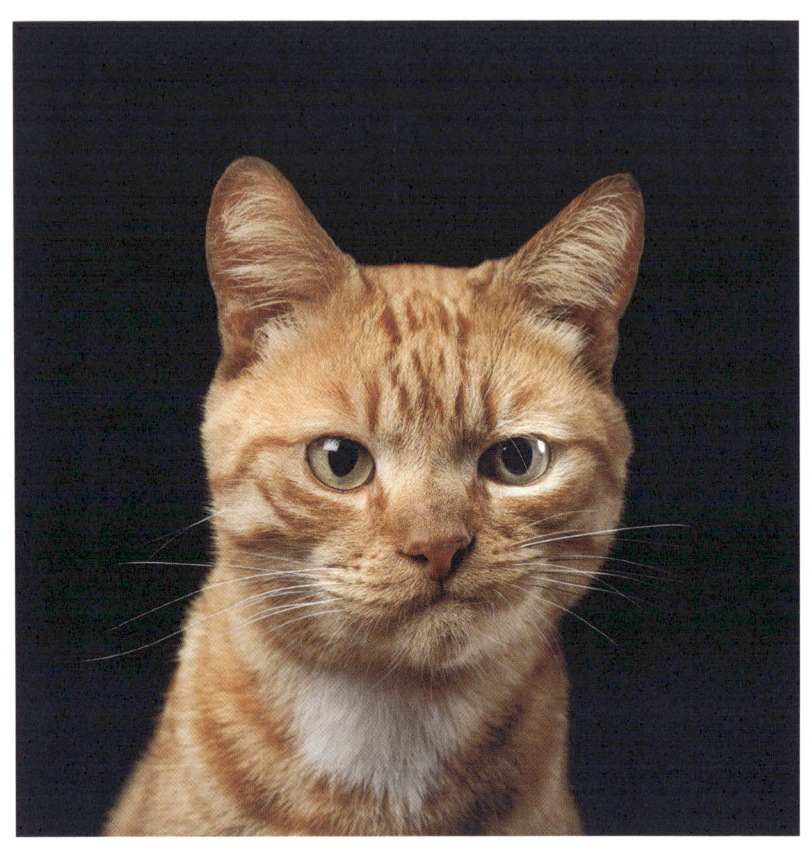

Scuba, 2014

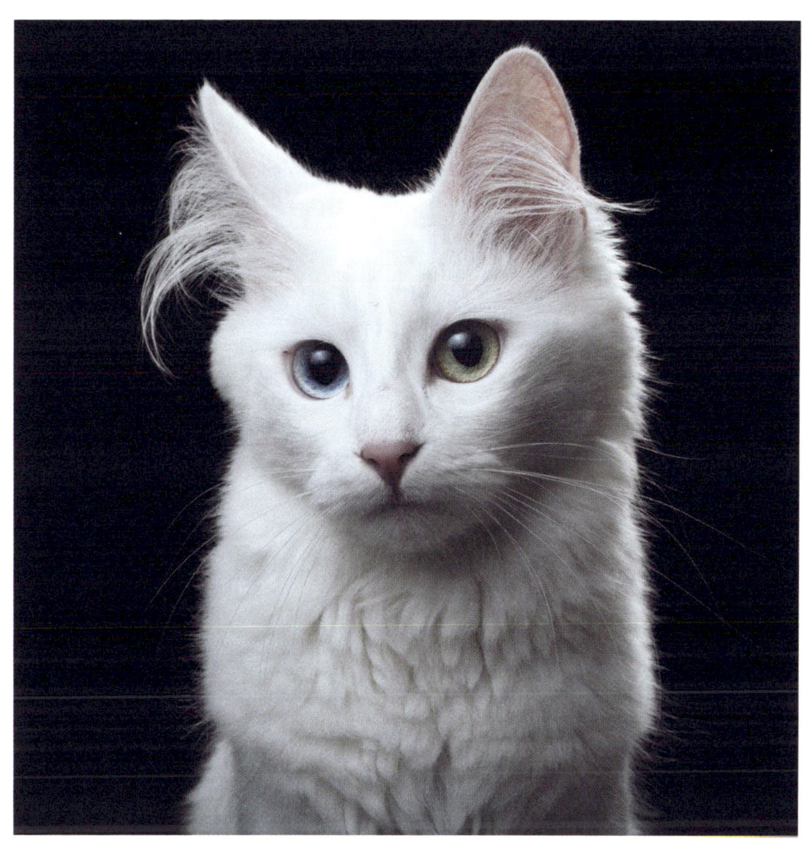

Smoke, 2015

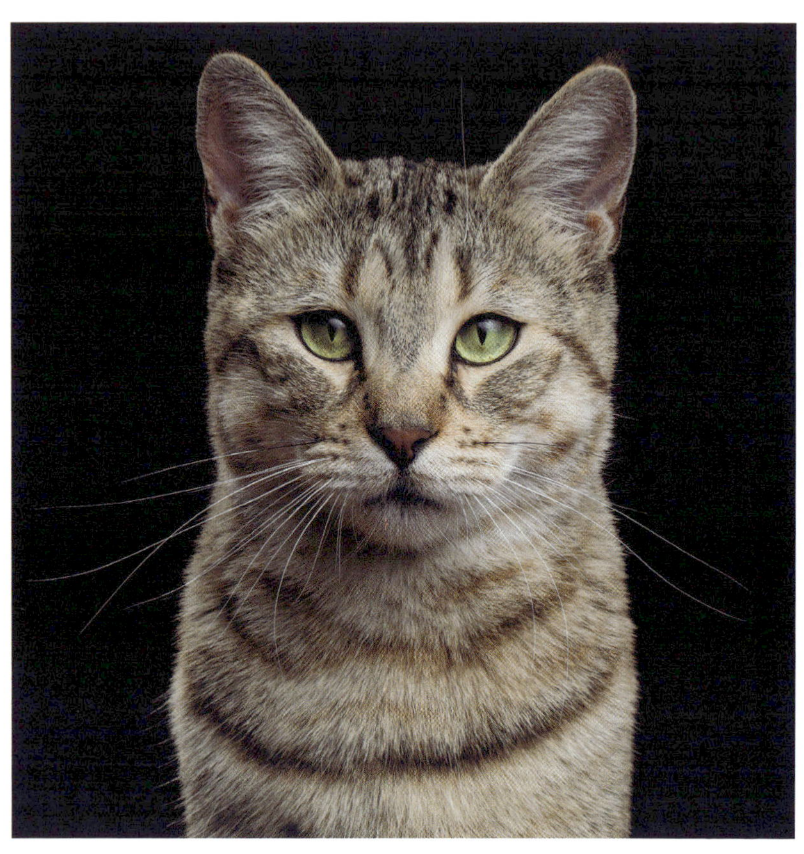

Above: *Eddie*, 2015
Opposite: *Joze*, 2015

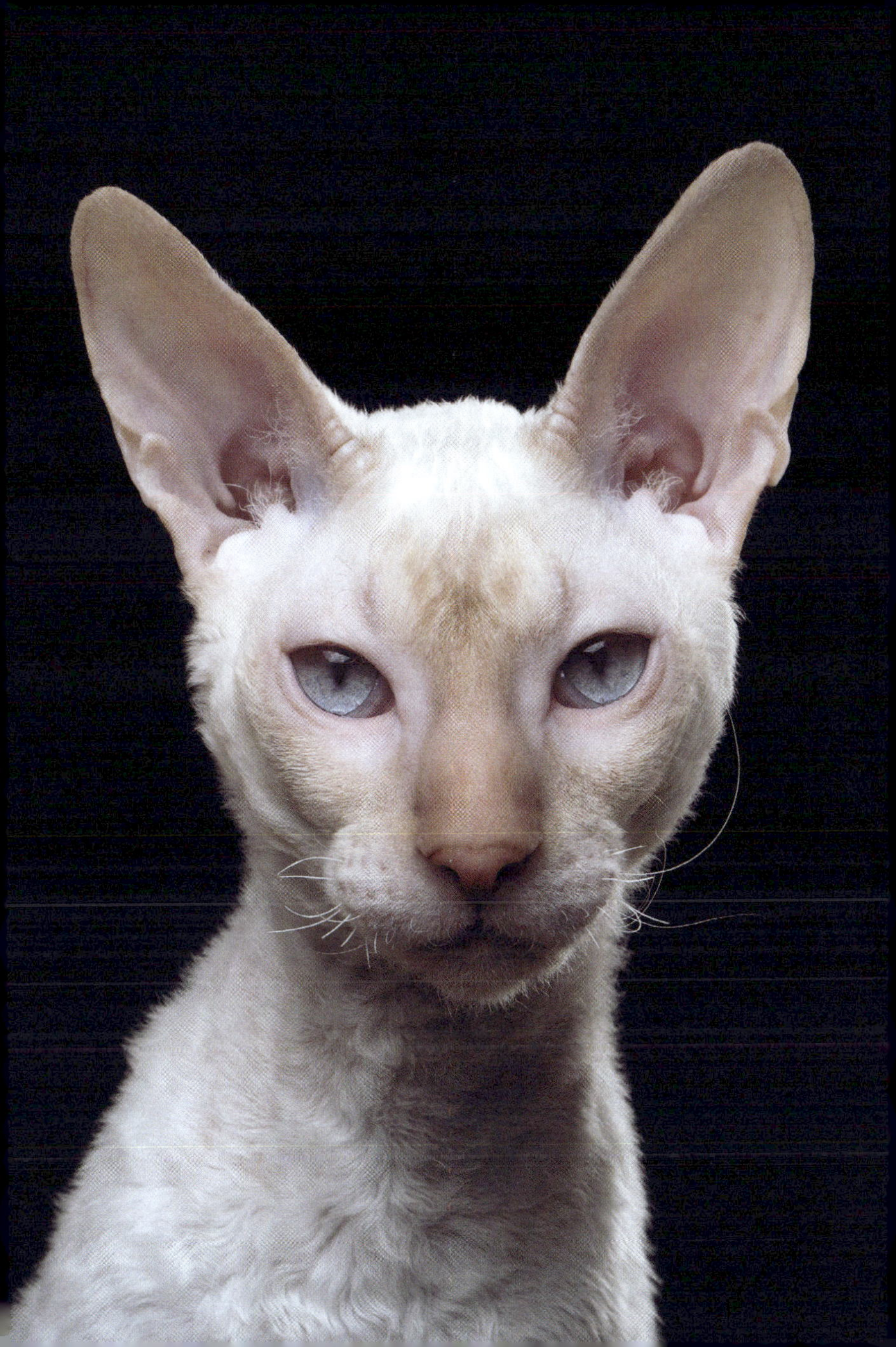

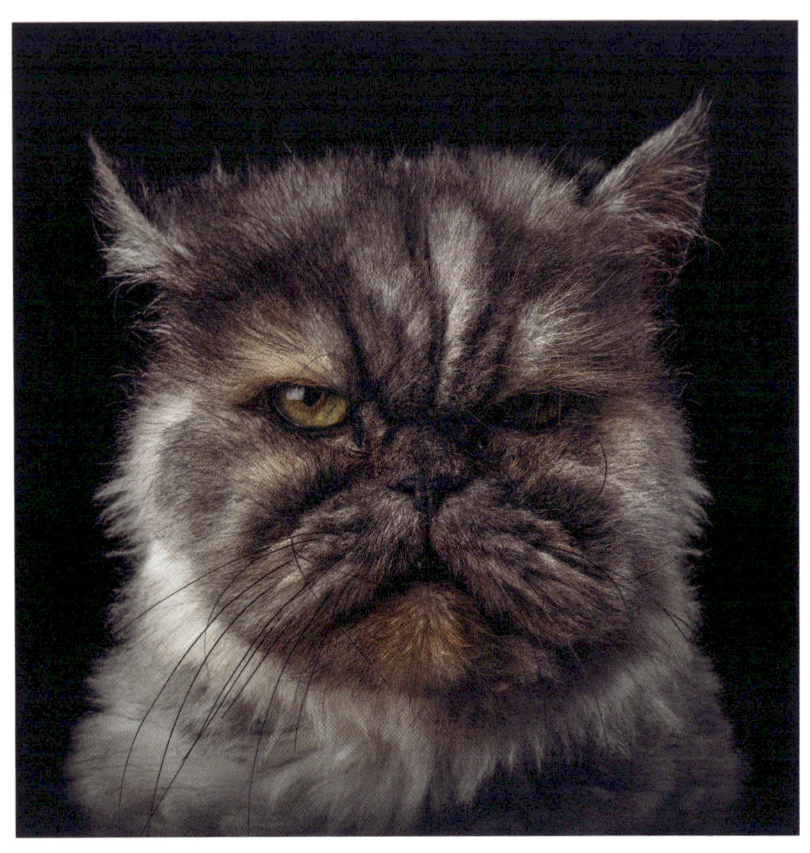

Gin, 2014

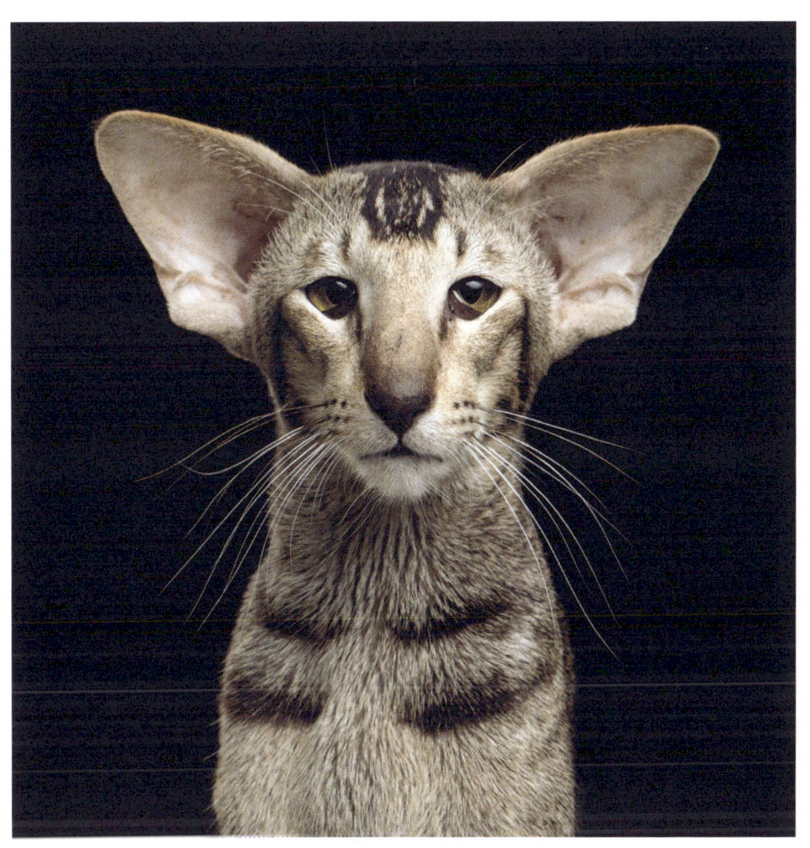

Wietje, 2015

SPHYNX CATS
Alicia Rius

To some, they may bear an uncanny resemblance to Gollum from *The Lord of the Rings*, but to photographer Alicia Rius, Sphynx cats are bright, joyful, very affectionate and quite social.

The first time the Los Angeles-based photographer encountered the congenitally hairless breed, she was mesmerised. 'It was so weird, I could feel the folds and the skin – everything. It was like a raw cat; something beautiful and awkward and rare. I became a bit obsessed.' Without 'fluffy and fancy coats', Sphynx cats show Rius their every emotion and sensation, she says. 'Everything is exposed, vulnerable. There's something disturbing yet eerie that makes me astonished every time I look at one of them.'

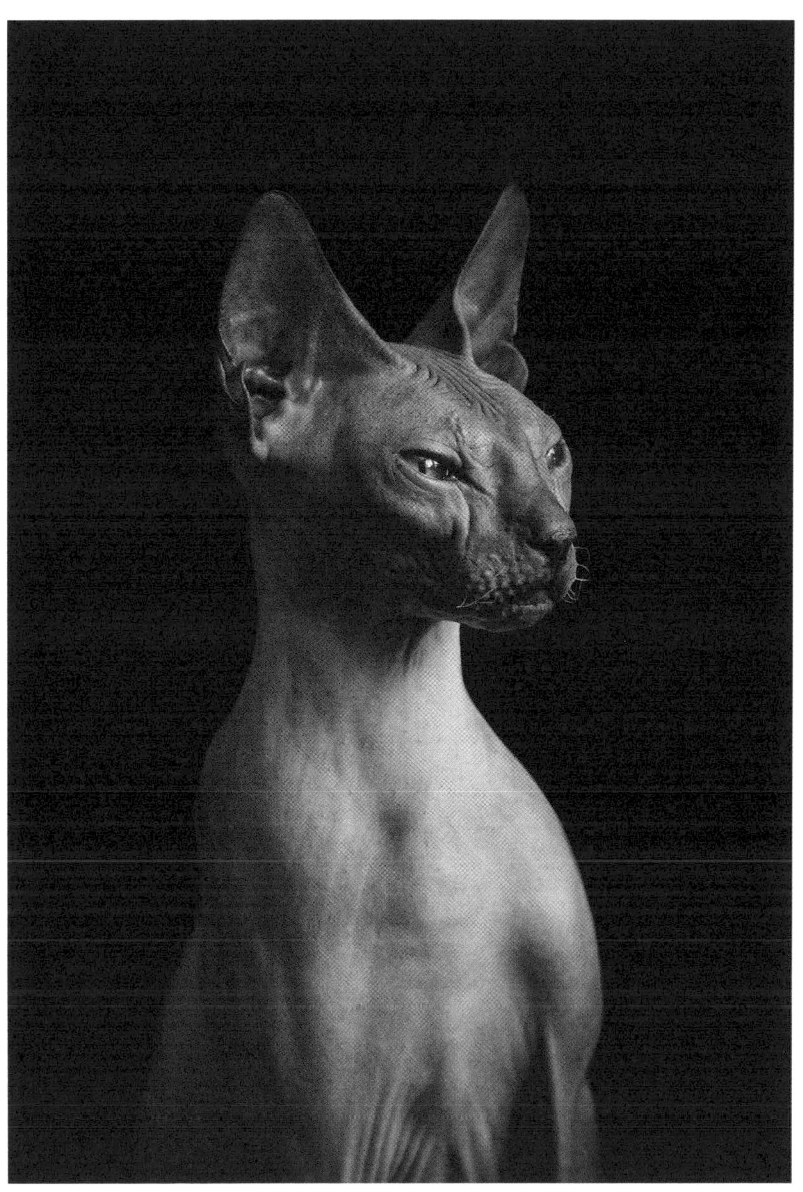

The Gaze, Los Angeles, 2015

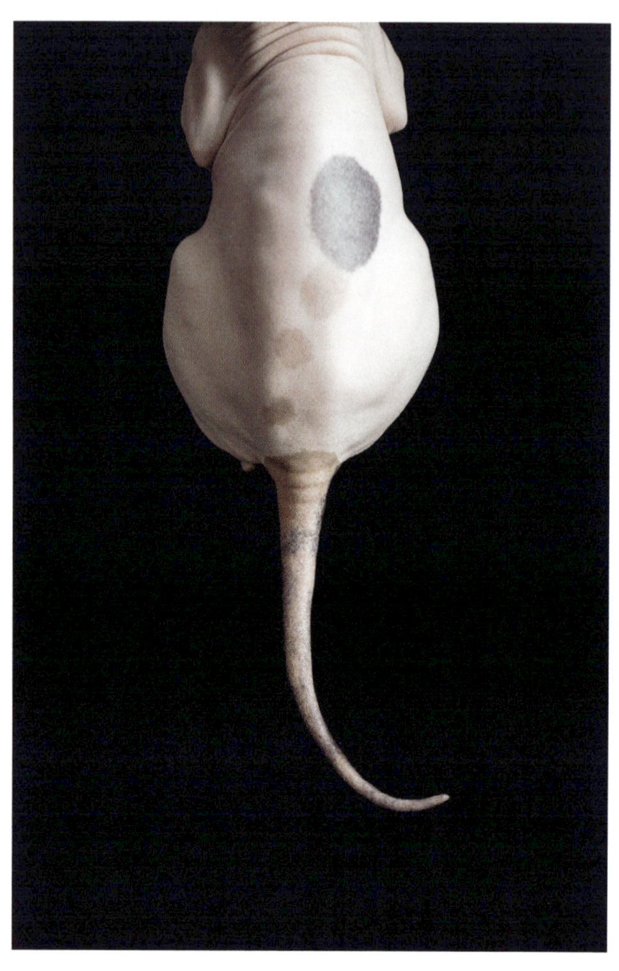

Above: *Tail, Los Angeles*, 2015
Opposite: *The Conductor, Los Angeles*, 2015
Overleaf: *Interrupted, San Francisco*, 2016

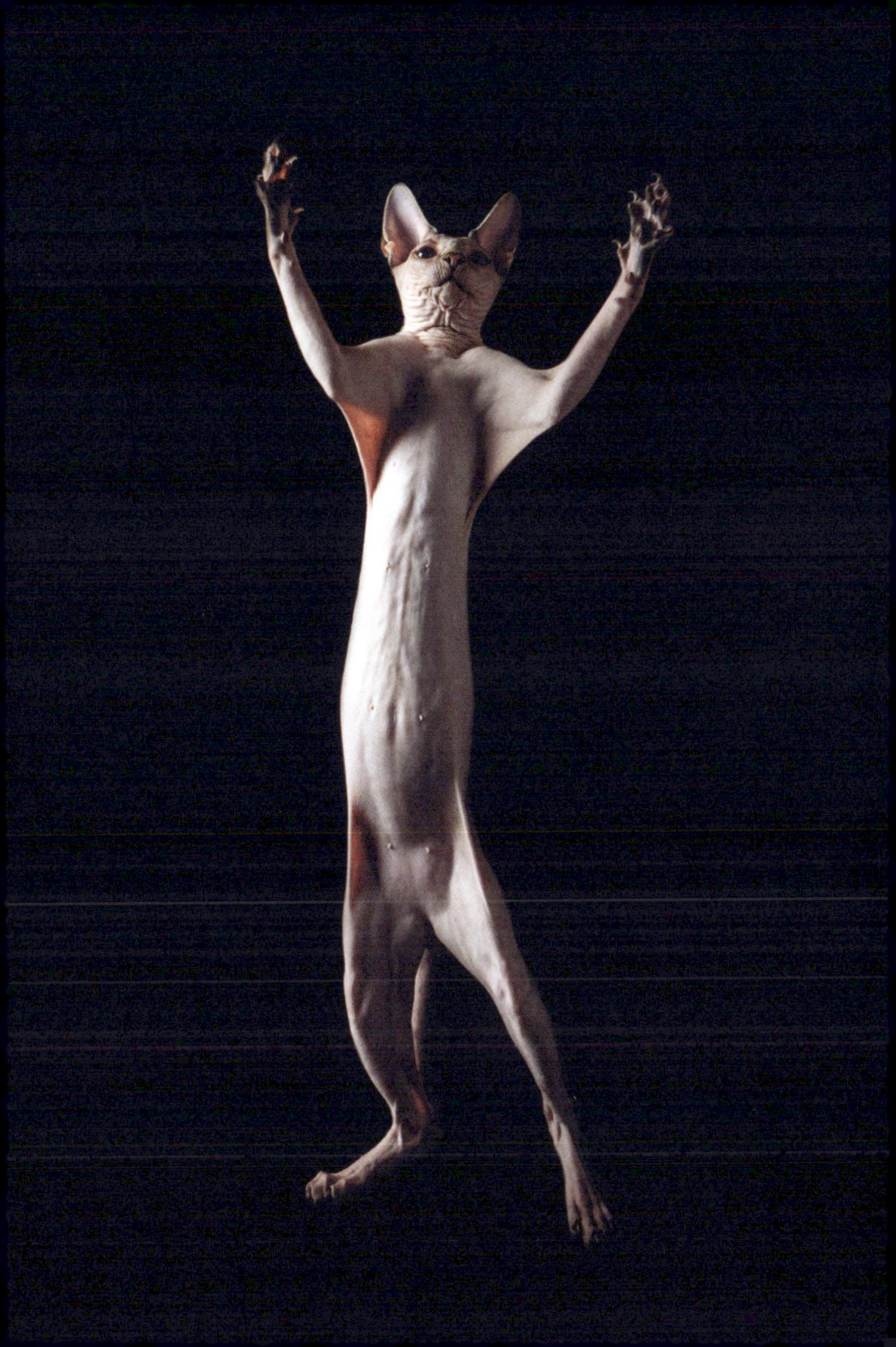

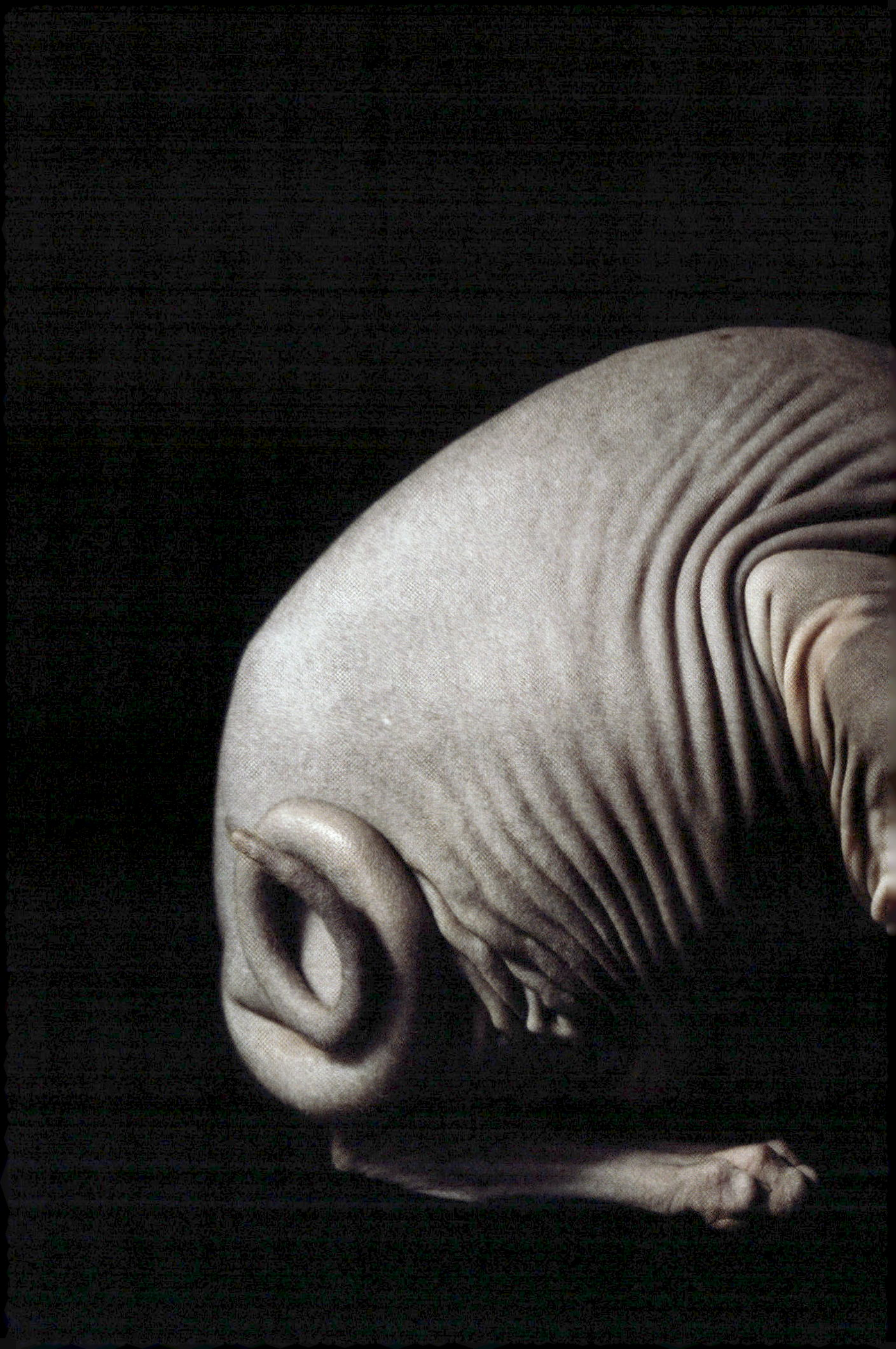

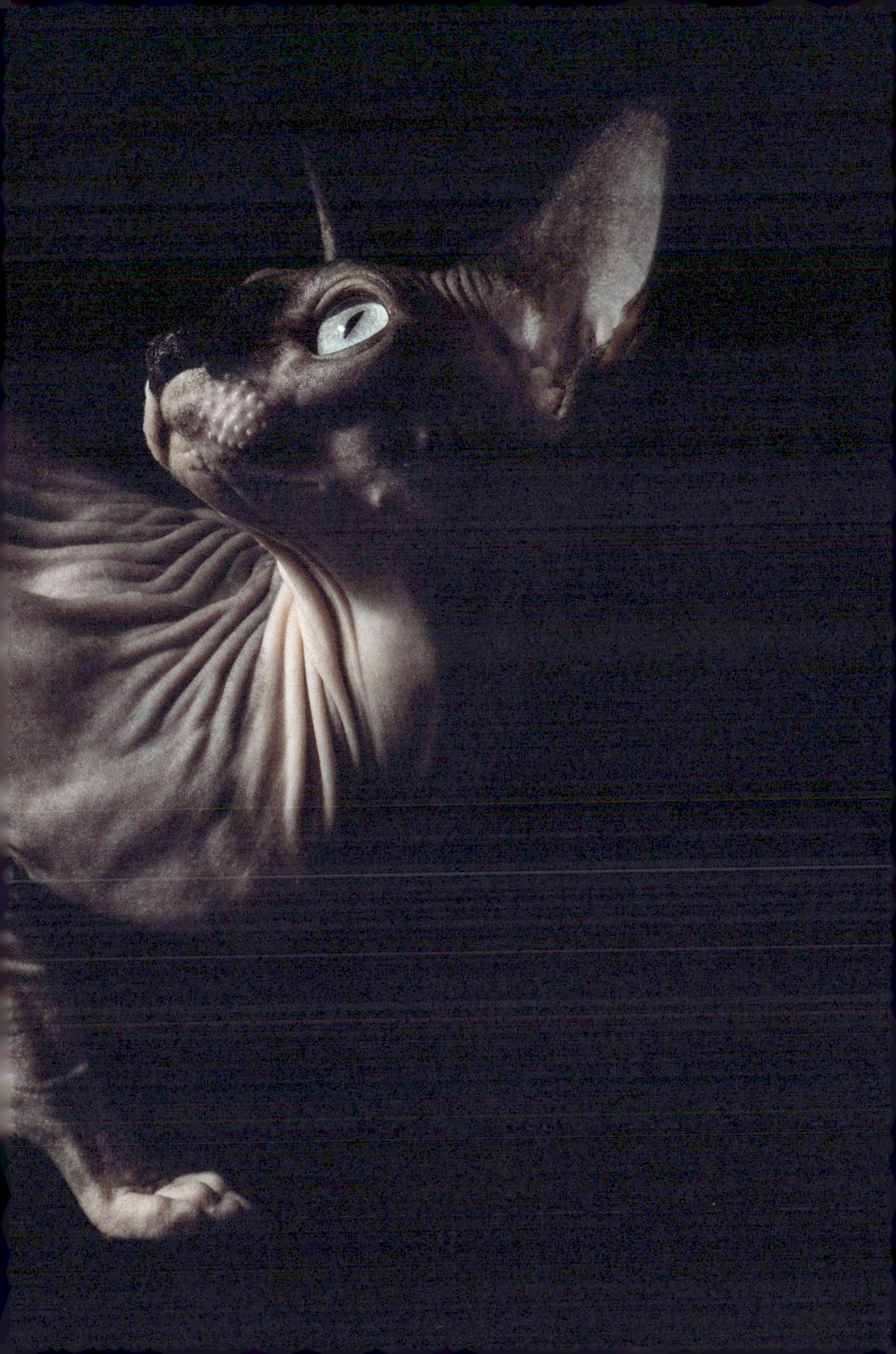

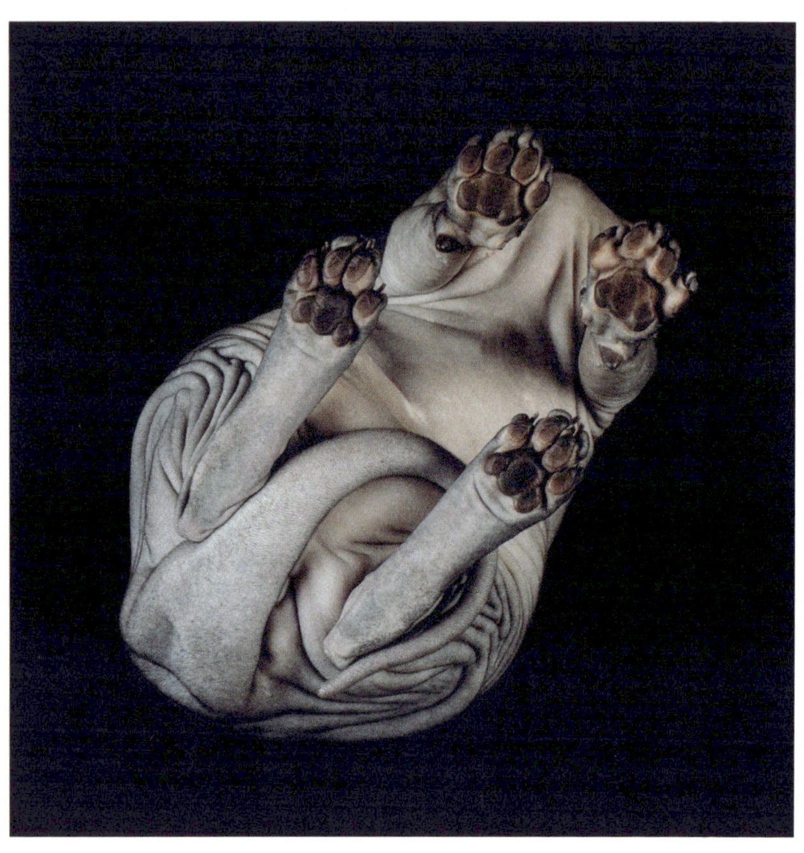

Underneath, Los Angeles, 2016

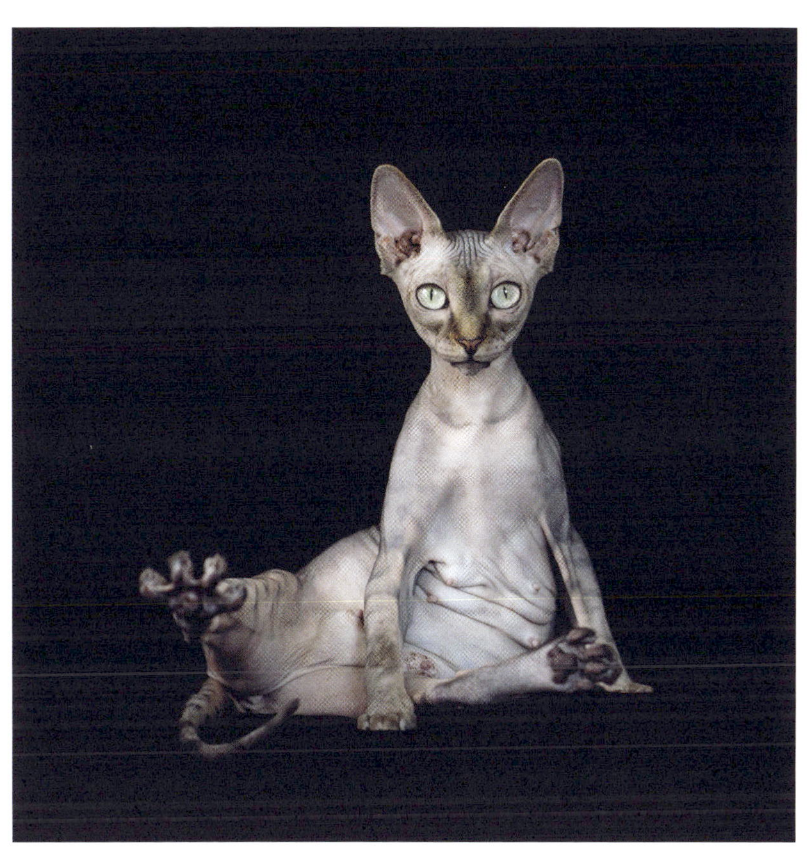

Staring, Long Beach, 2015

CHARLIE
Lola Dupre

Lola Dupre makes staggeringly intricate cut-paper collages in the old-fashioned way – with scissors and glue. Charlie is her cat, a 'complicated hero' whom she rescued in 2017 and began photographing for a series of collage portraits about two weeks later. The process helped both of them to bond.

'When rehoming a cat, it can often take several years before they settle into the new surroundings,' Dupre explains. 'In some of the earlier portraits you can pick up on some angst, a certain nervousness. After 36 portraits, I think we have come to an understanding.'

Dupre's technique – cutting several copies of the same image, then recombining them to stretch and warp it – was initially inspired by Jean-Paul Goude's cover art for Grace Jones's 1985 album *Slave to the Rhythm*. Over the years, she has applied it to fare as diverse as Vermeer's painting *Girl with a Pearl Earring* and the American comedian Larry David, but Charlie remains her primary muse. 'Cats make great subject matter because of the perfect, impossible forms they comfortably create,' she says. 'They defy gravity and expectation, changing forms in an almost liquid manner.'

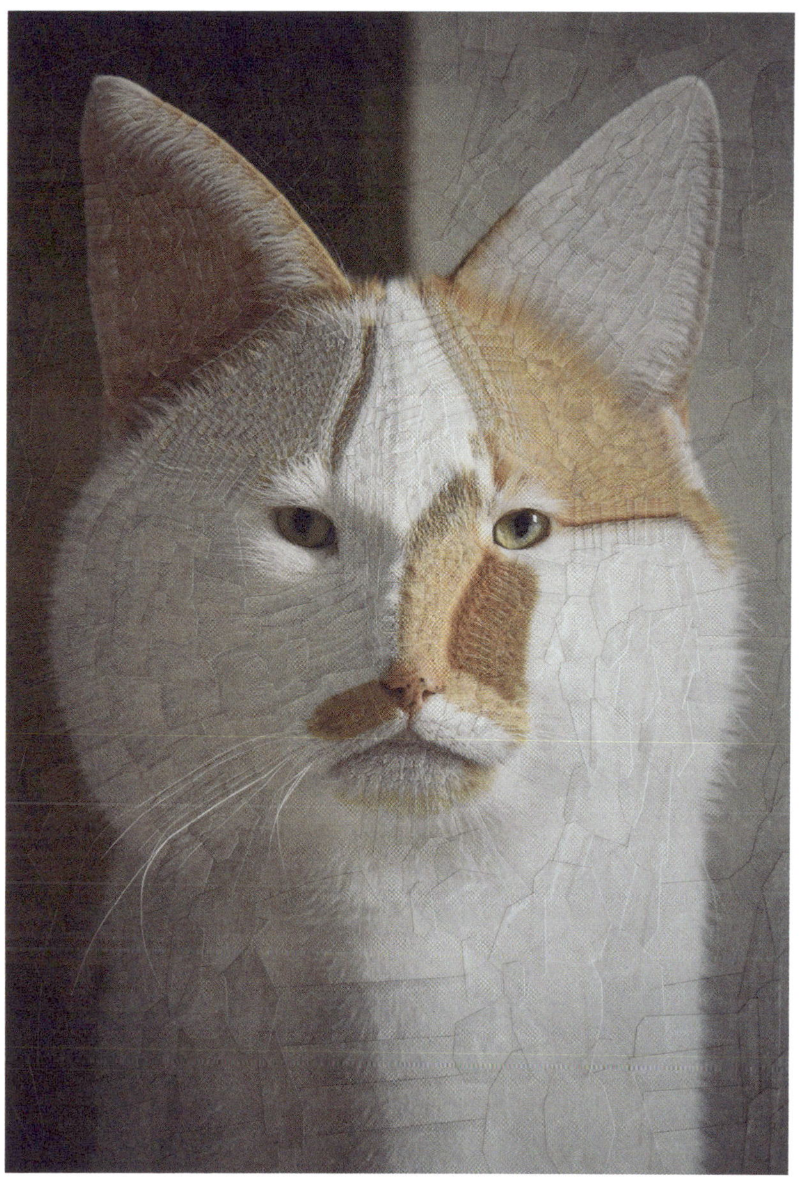

Charlie 35, The Moon Has Eyes, 2021

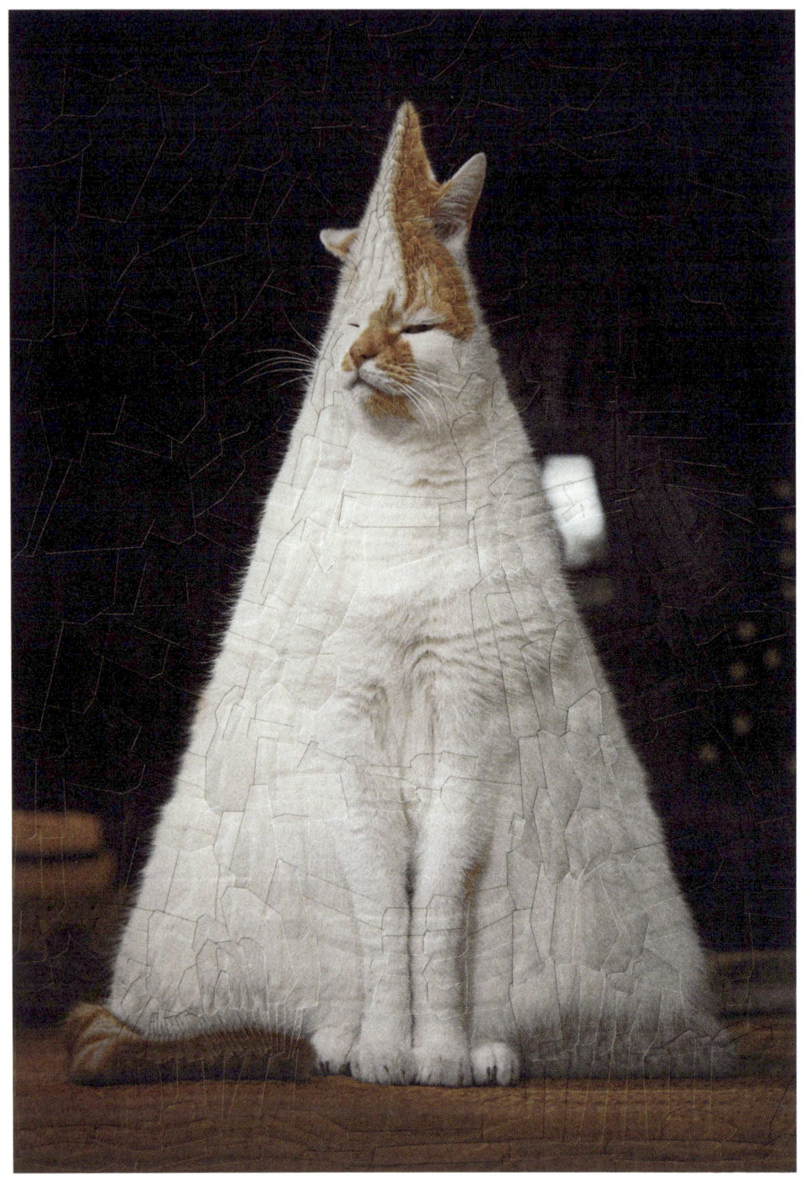

Charlie 27, 2020

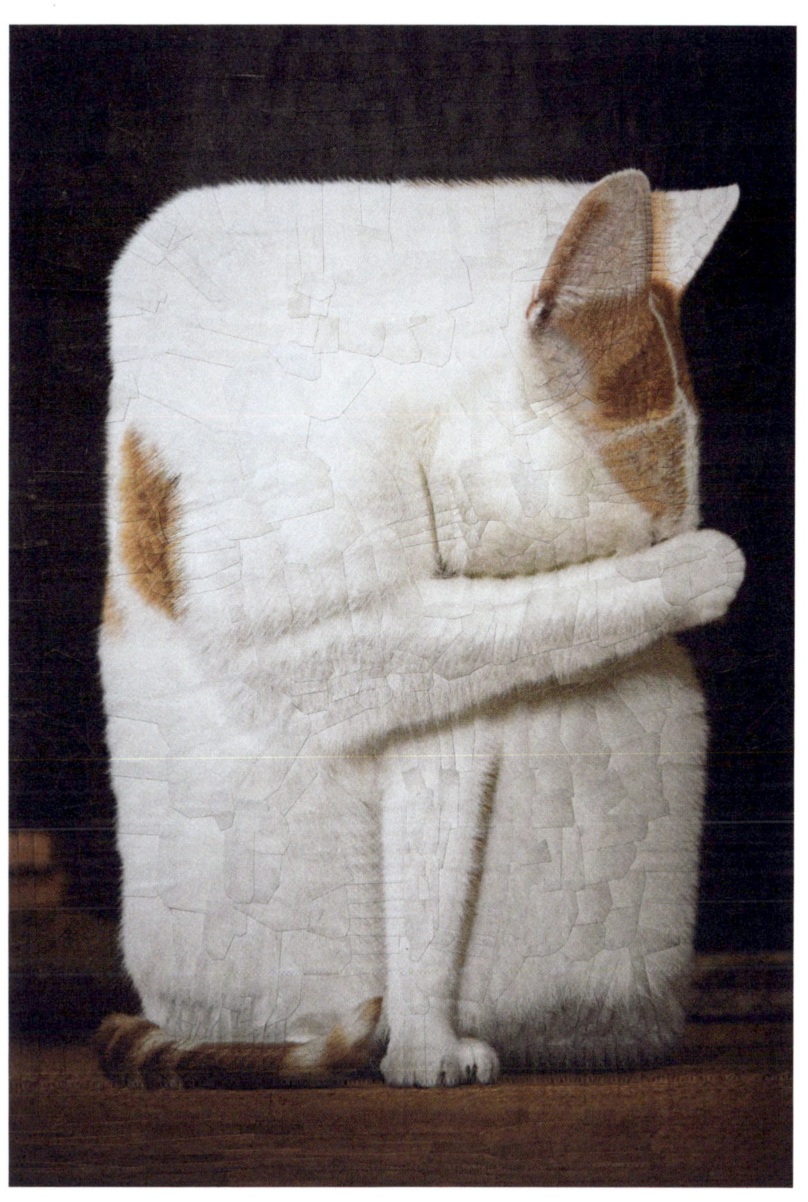

Charlie VIII, even softer, 2018

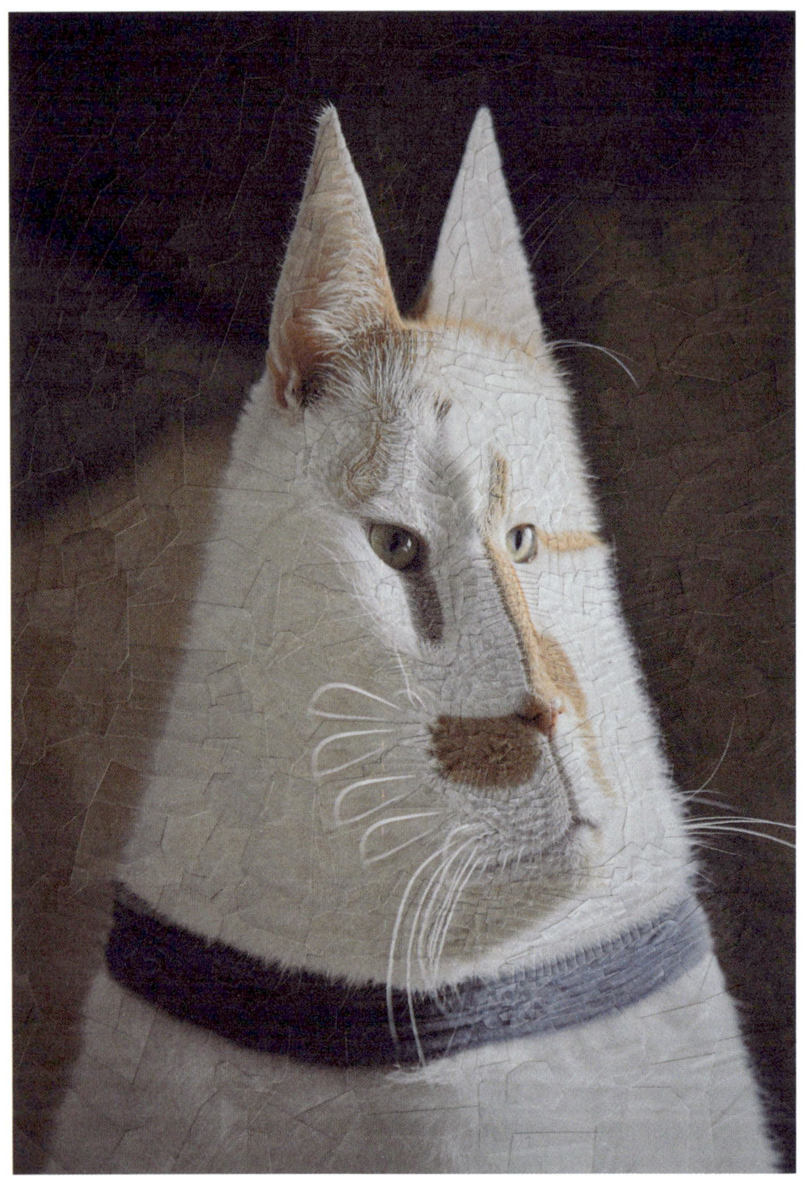

Charlie 26, 2020

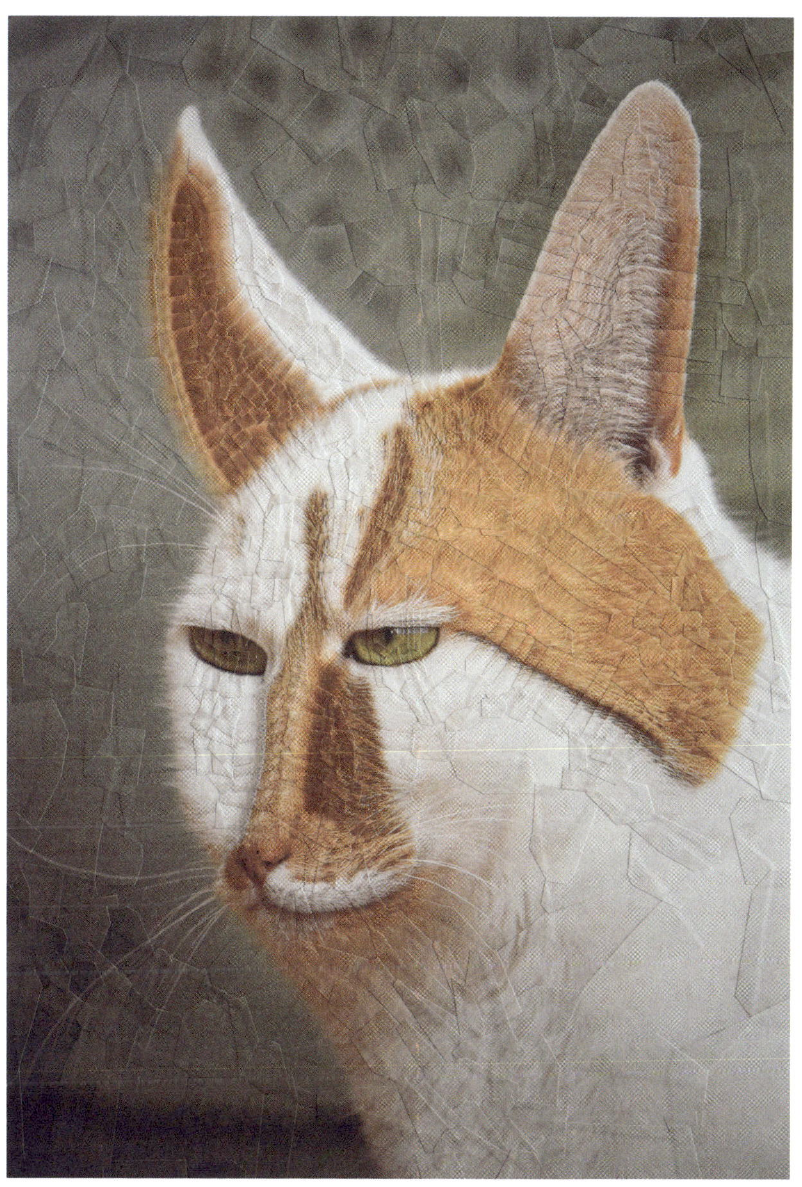

Charlie, Destroyer of Butterflies, 2018

FUR
Gerrard Gethings

Gerrard Gethings pairs humans with their doppelgängers – cat doppelgängers, that is. The idea began when he stumbled upon an internet meme of a cat that people thought looked like the character Ross Geller in *Friends*.

Gethings had already made photographs of people whose faces, attitude or hairstyle resembled dogs for a best-selling memory card game, but the Geller cat 'pushed me over the edge, into thinking there was something in it,' he says. The people in the photographs aren't the cats' owners. Gethings casts his cats first, then seeks a match based on markings, fur or facial expression. Instagram has sometimes helped, as when he posted a picture of a cat that looked, to him, like the *Harry Potter* character, Hagrid. 'This guy came back and said, "I look exactly like that." And he did.' (See p.44).

The cats were less helpful, some refusing to cooperate even when Gethings (who trained with the iconic portraitist Terry O'Neill) pulled out every trick and treat in the coaxing book. It was, he admits, 'quite demoralising'.

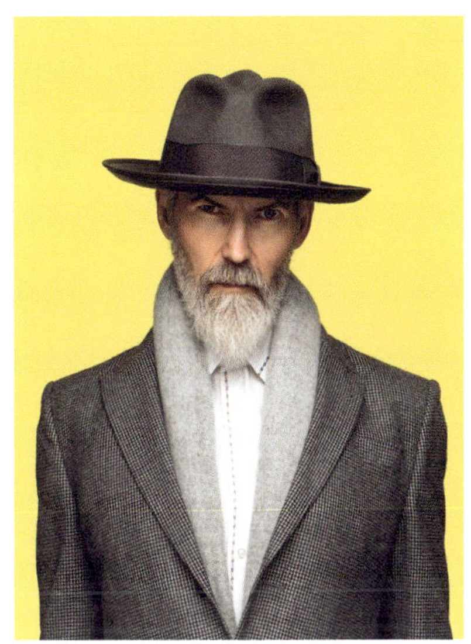

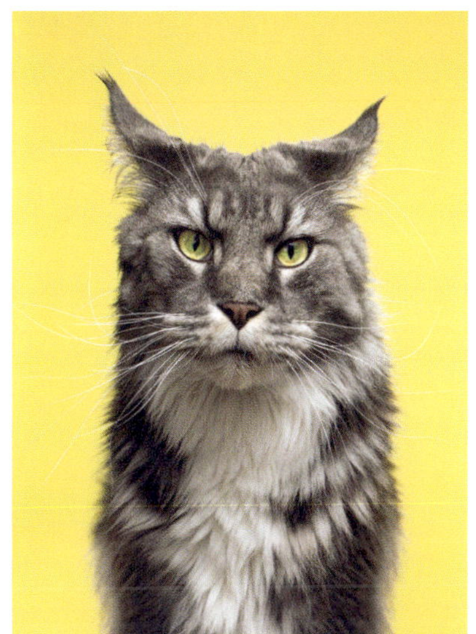

Left: *Dominic*, 2019
Right: *Merlin (Blue Tabby Maine Coon)*, 2019

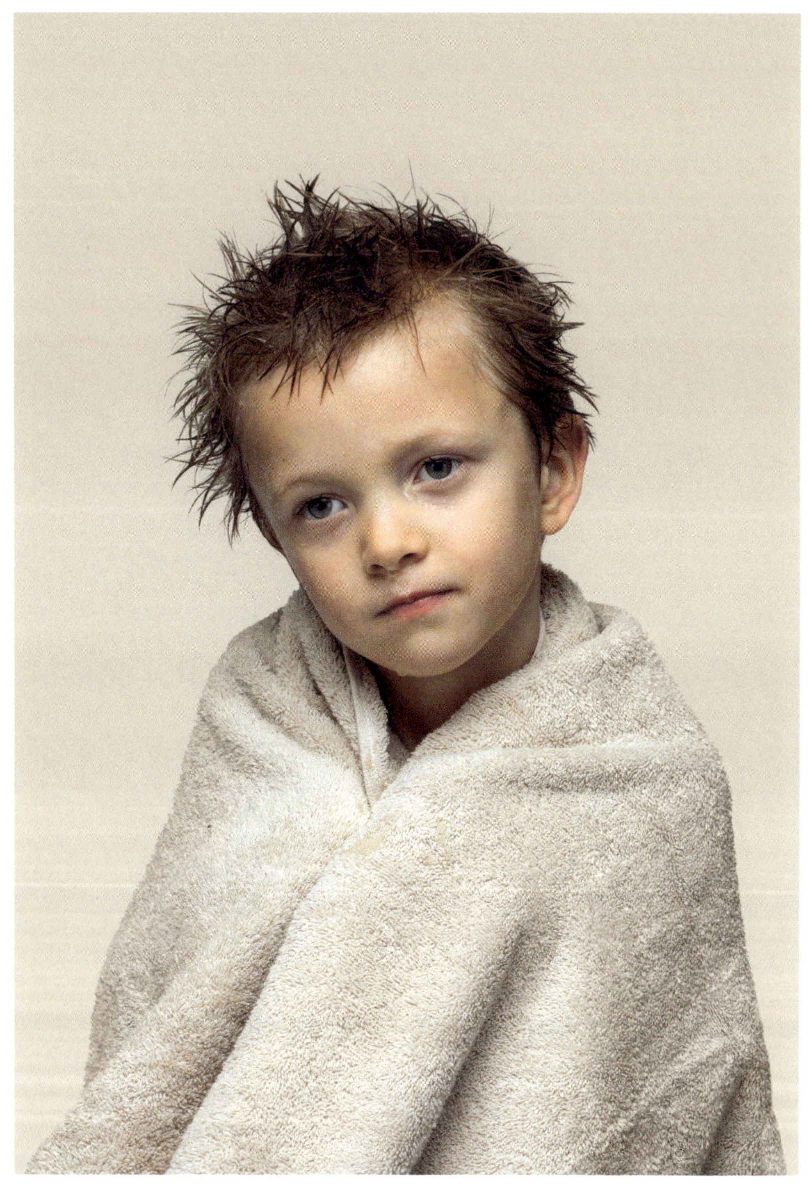

Arlo, 2019

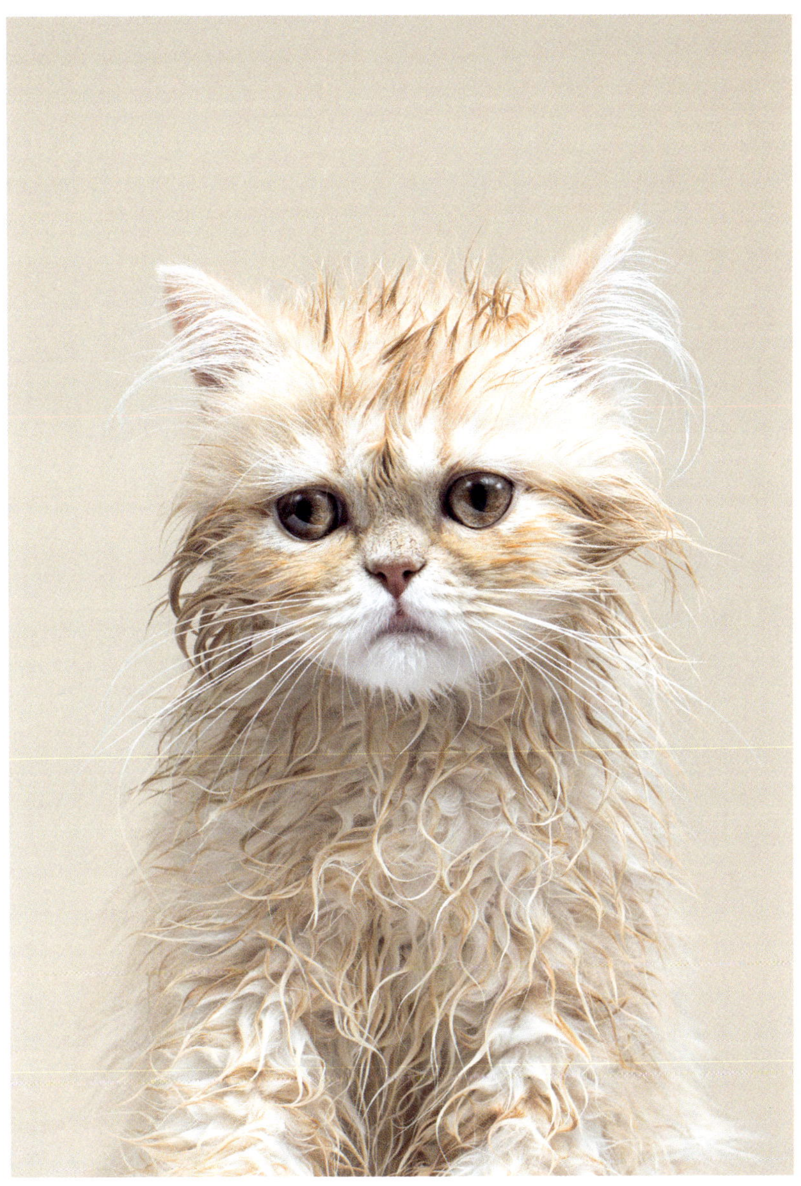

Buttercup (Cream Persian), 2019

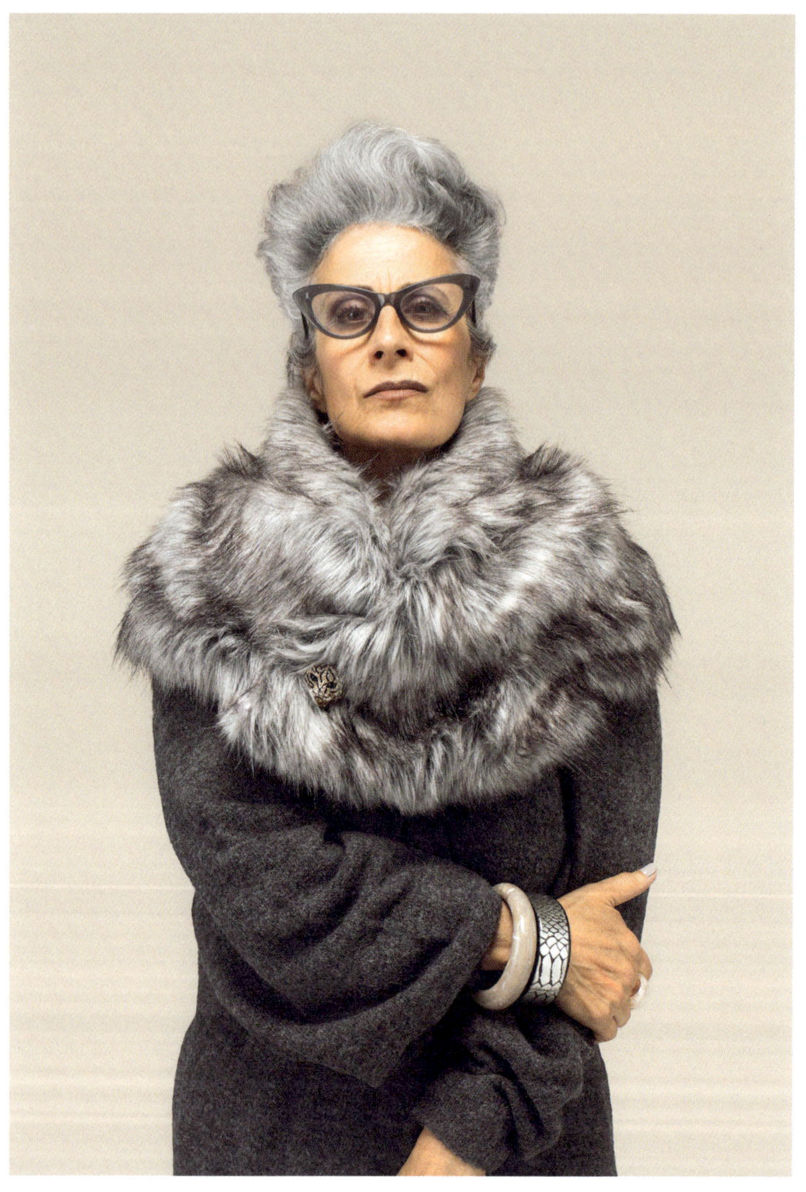

Marielle, 2019

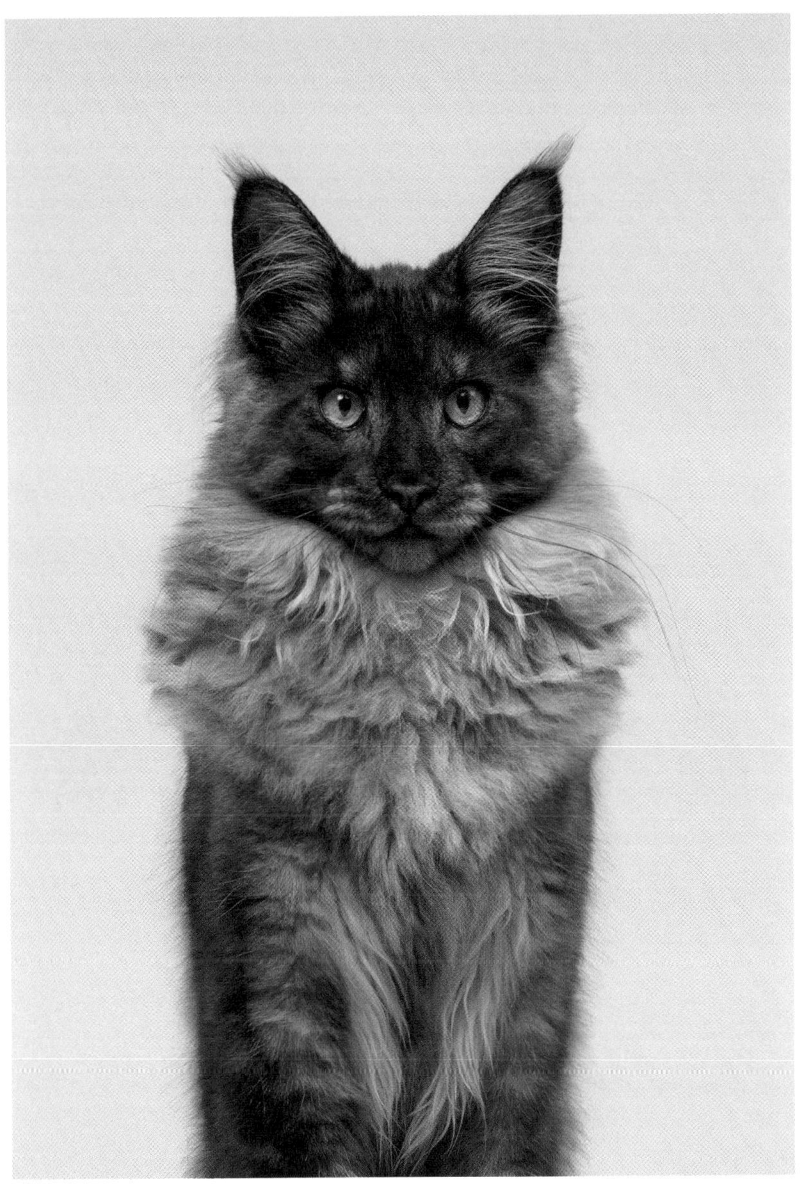

Jacques (Silver Maine Coon), 2019

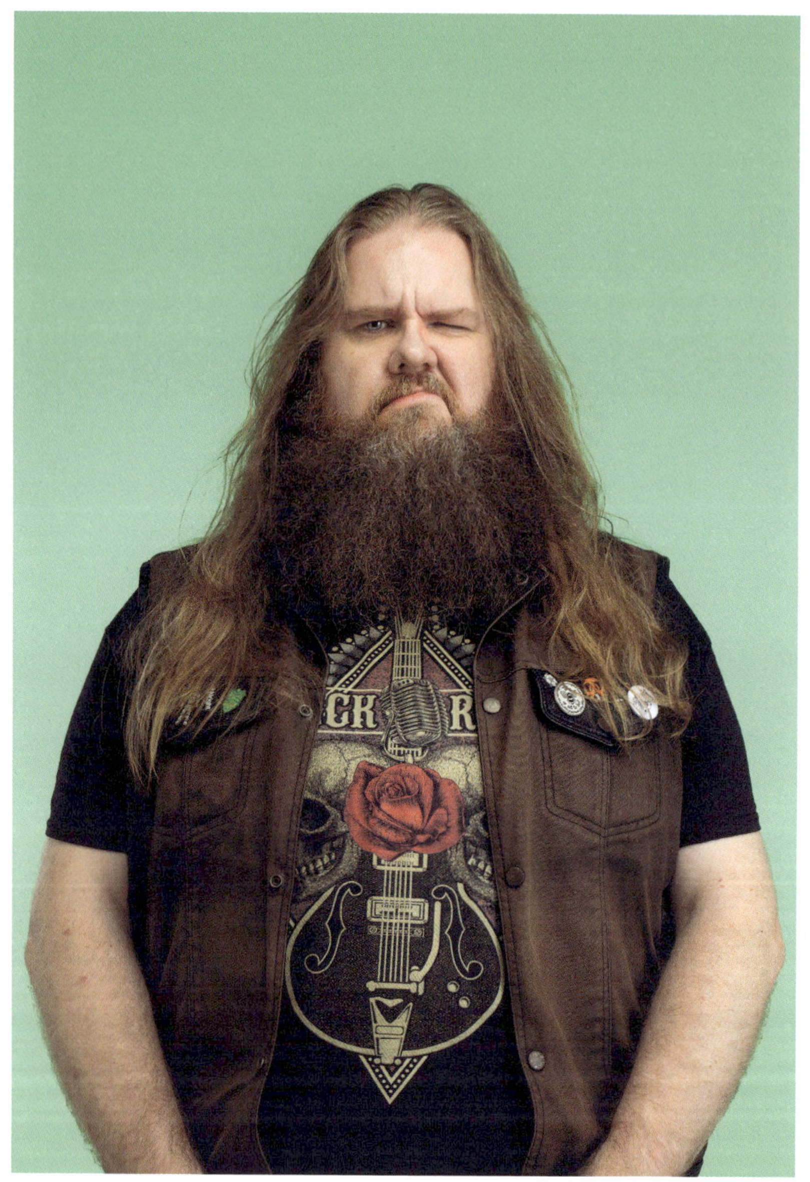

Gunther, 2019

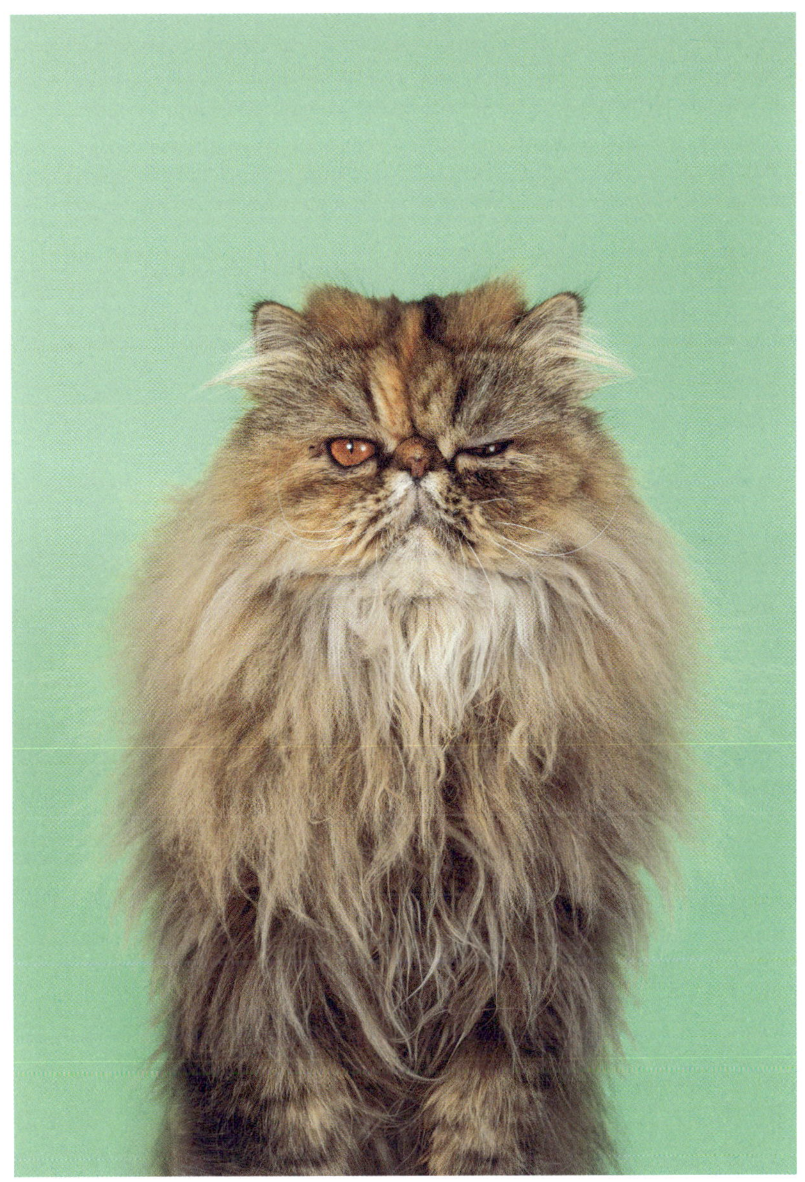

Albert (Exotic Longhair), 2019

UNDER-CATS
Andrius Burba

Under-Cats (a riff on 'underdog') sprang to life when Lithuanian fashion photographer Andrius Burba stumbled across a 'ridiculous-looking' picture online of a cat on a glass table, taken from underneath. Smitten with the view, and the detail in the cat's paws, he bought tickets to the International Cat Show in Vilnius to make professional, high-res versions of willing contestants.

Capturing the cats' quizzical reaction to their predicament and the quirks of each subject's personality, the results were so heartwarming and so immediately popular that Burba soon branched into dogs, horses, rabbits and mice, forming a whole new brand of photography called *Underlook*.

He used to secure his subjects with open calls offering a free photoshoot in his signature style. That ended when he advertised at a vet surgery in Cologne, Germany, and before two weeks were out, 600 people had come forward to volunteer their pets.

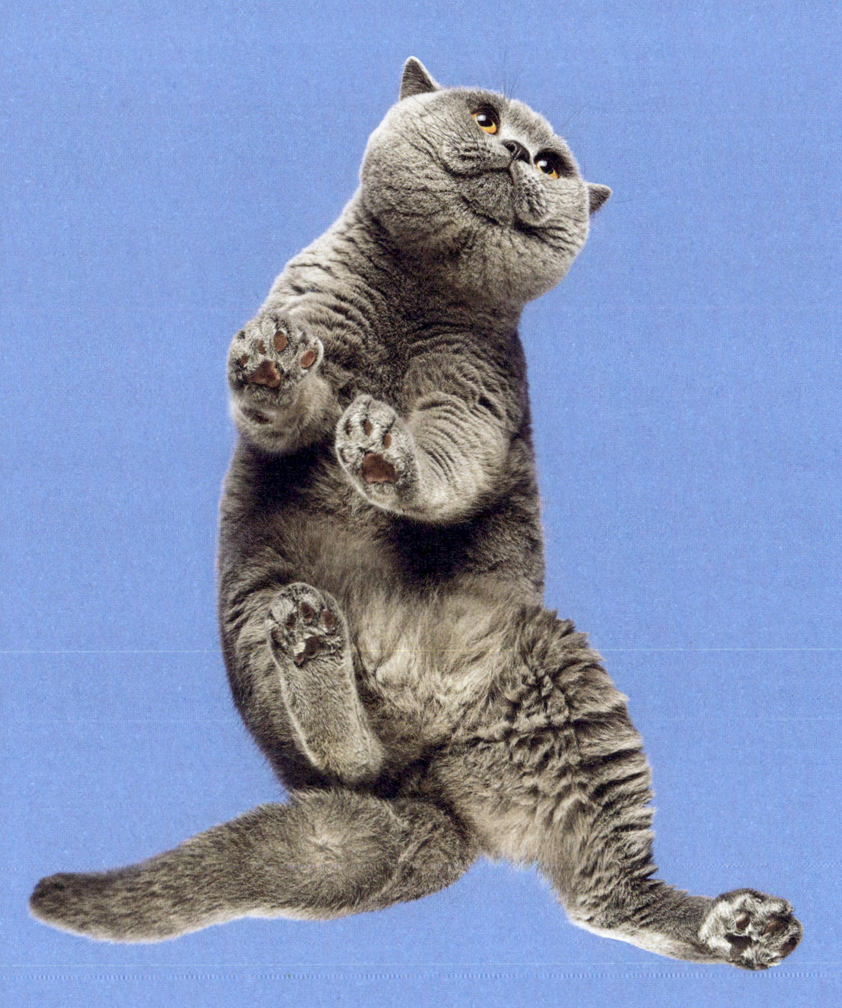

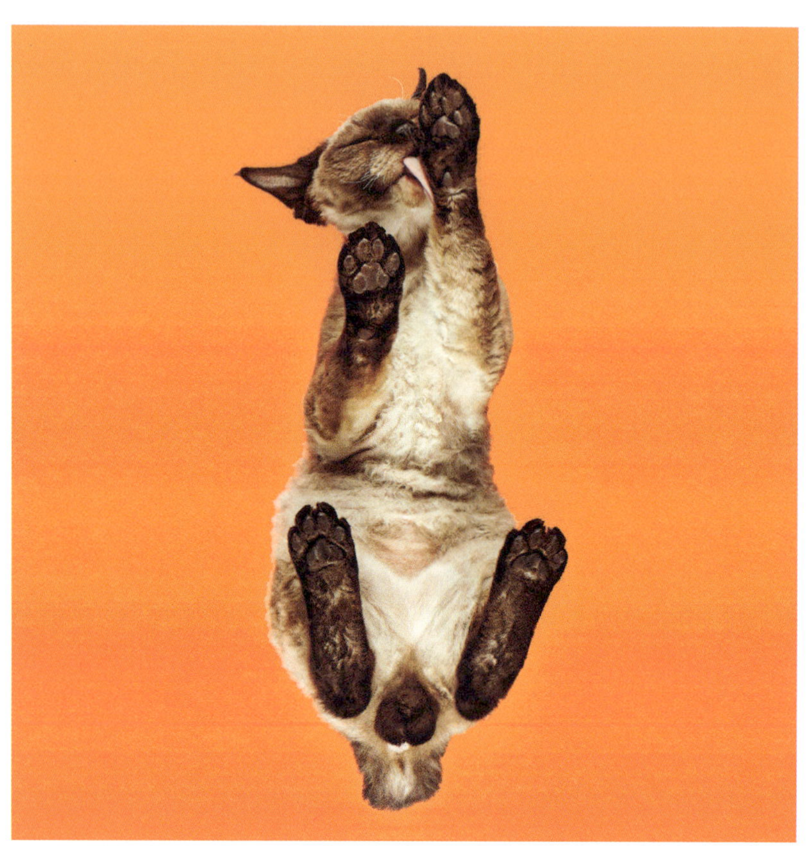

Devon Rex, 2017

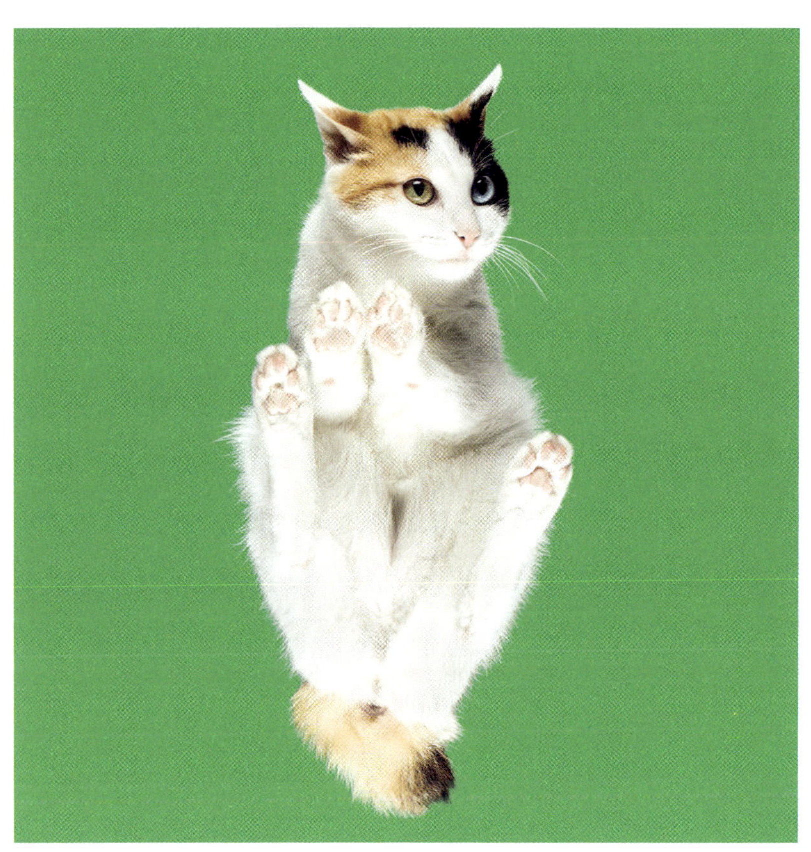

Japanese Bobtail, 2017

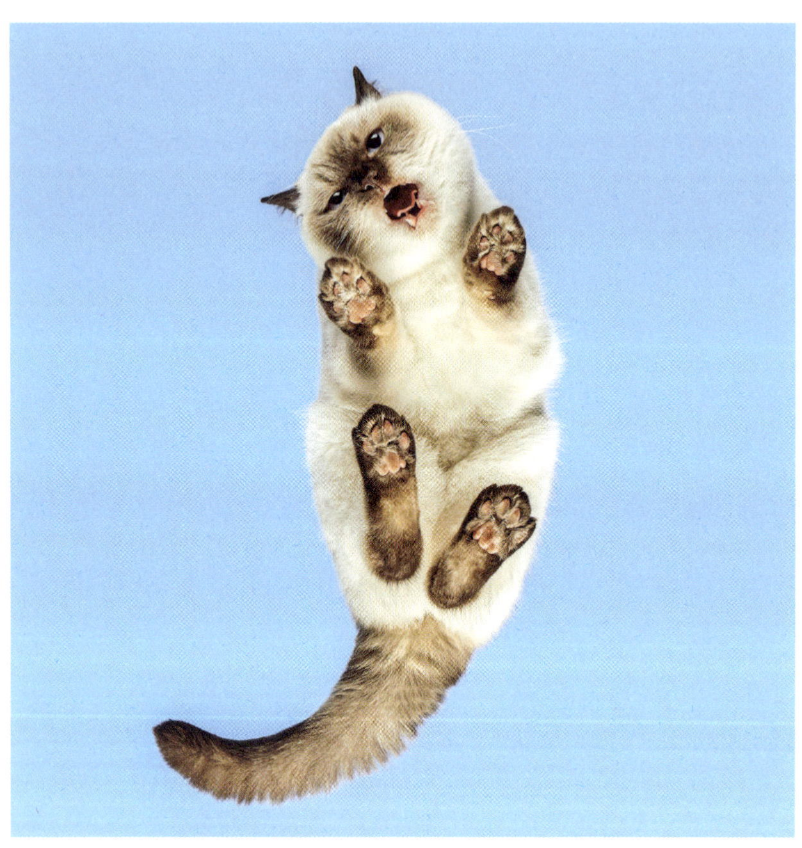

British Shorthair, 2017

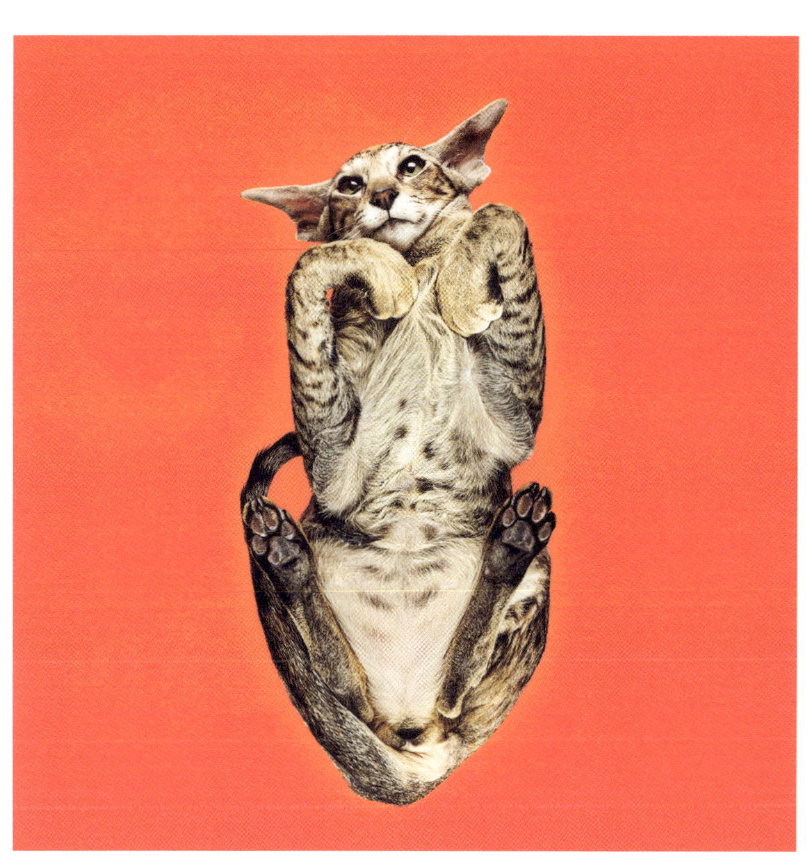

Above: *Oriental Shorthair*, 2017
Overleaf: *Devon Rex*, 2017

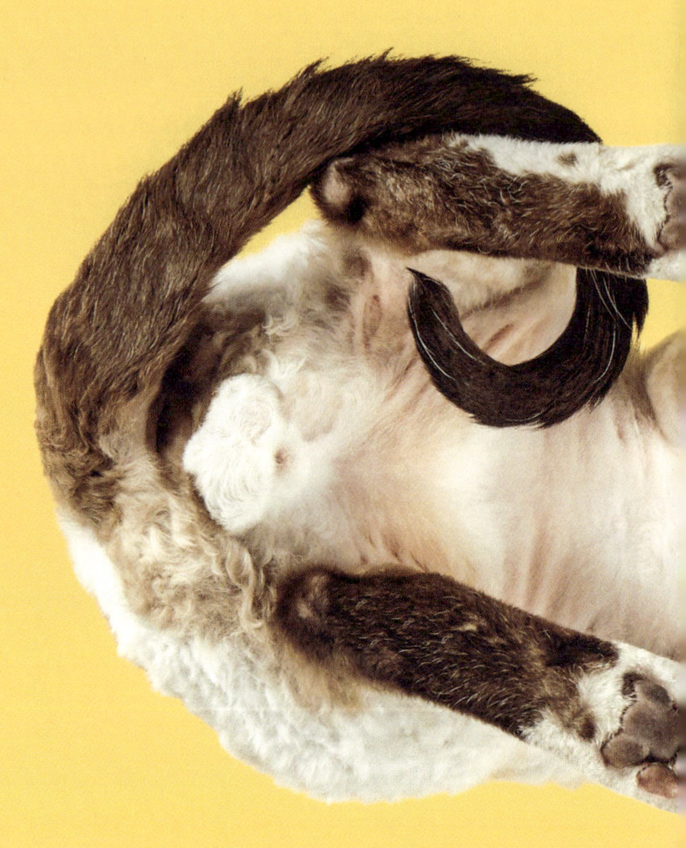

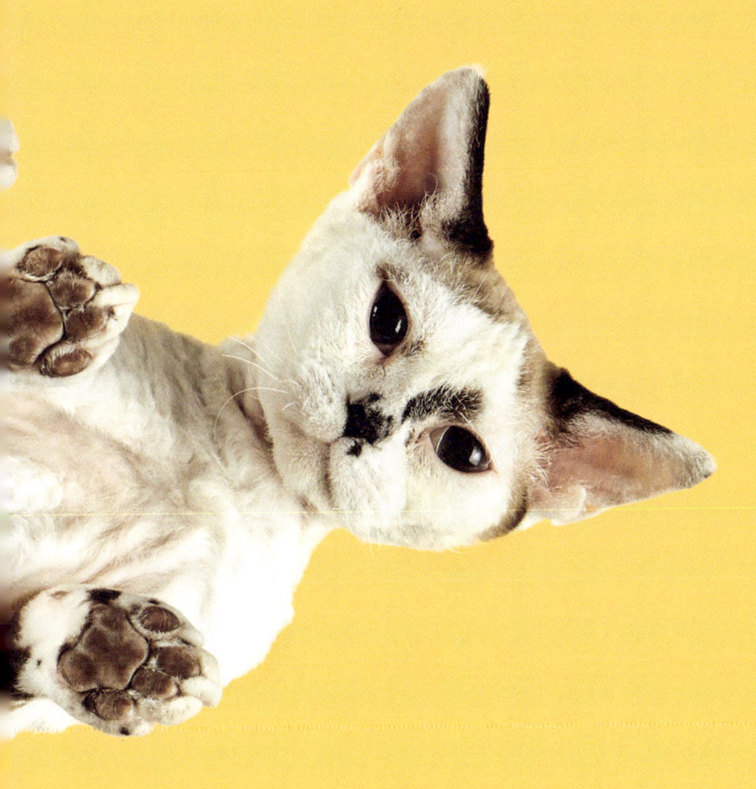

GIRLS AND THEIR CATS
BriAnne Wills

Pop culture and superstition have historically cast 'cat ladies' as crazy, dishevelled spinsters. But BriAnne Wills, a New York-based fashion and beauty photographer who grew up in a 'cat positive' household and has two cats of her own – Tuck and Liza – decided she'd had enough of this insidious, lazy stereotype and set out to debunk it.

Girls and Their Cats began life in 2015 as an Instagram account featuring her portraits and mini profiles of hundreds of stylish, spirited women with their furry companions. The project has since evolved into a book and a YouTube channel that presents tours of cat owners' homes and 'love stories' saluting the special feline–human relationship.

Michelle & Sue, 2021

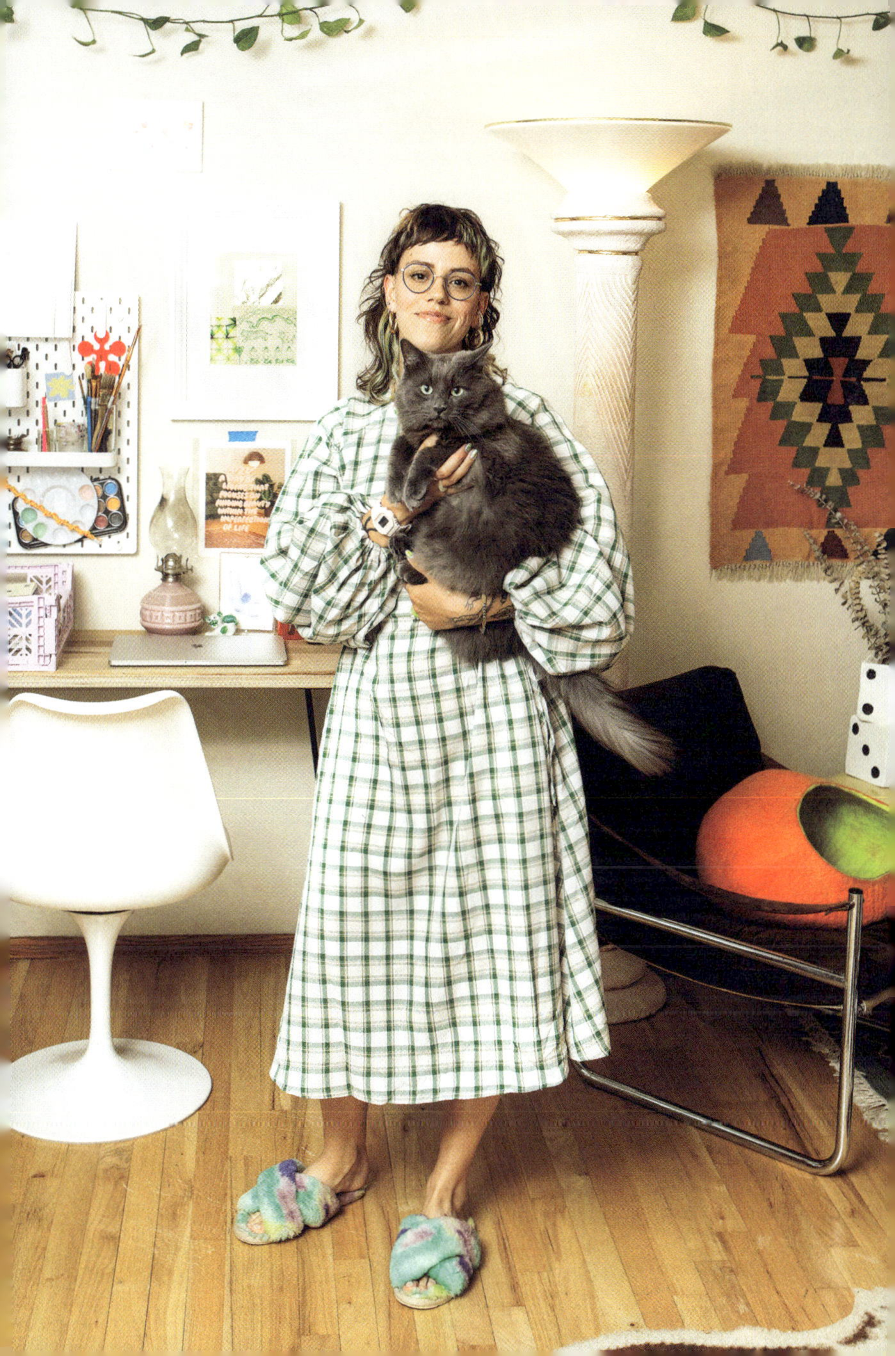

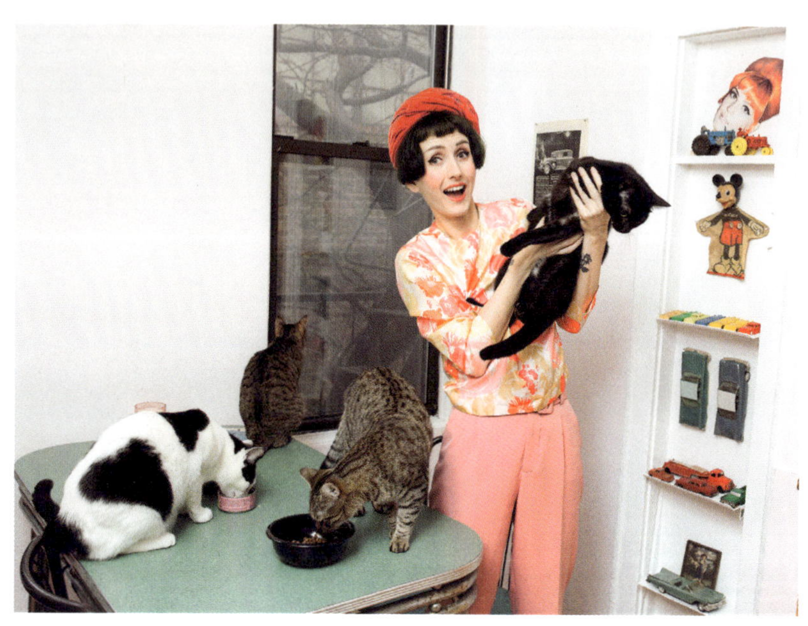

Stella, Filbert, Beeboo, Teddy, Joey & George, 2020

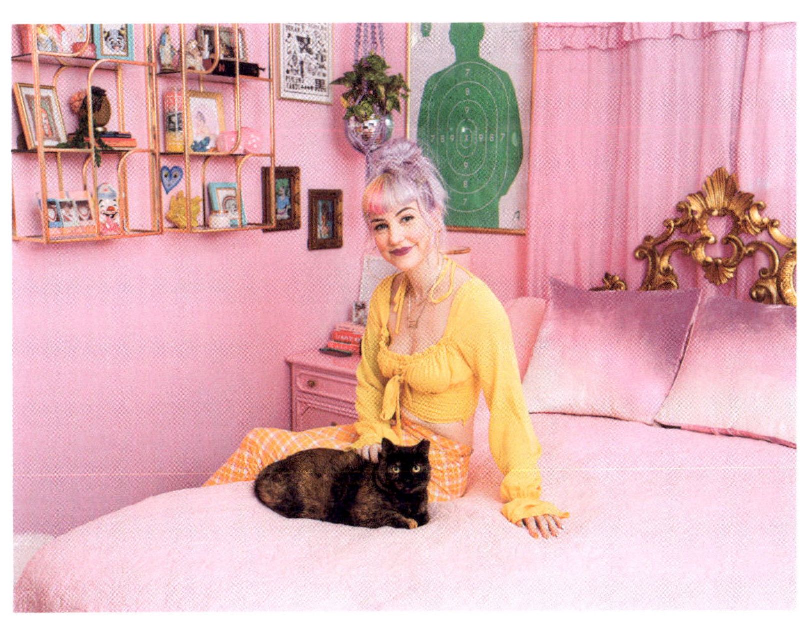

Sarah & Princess, 2019

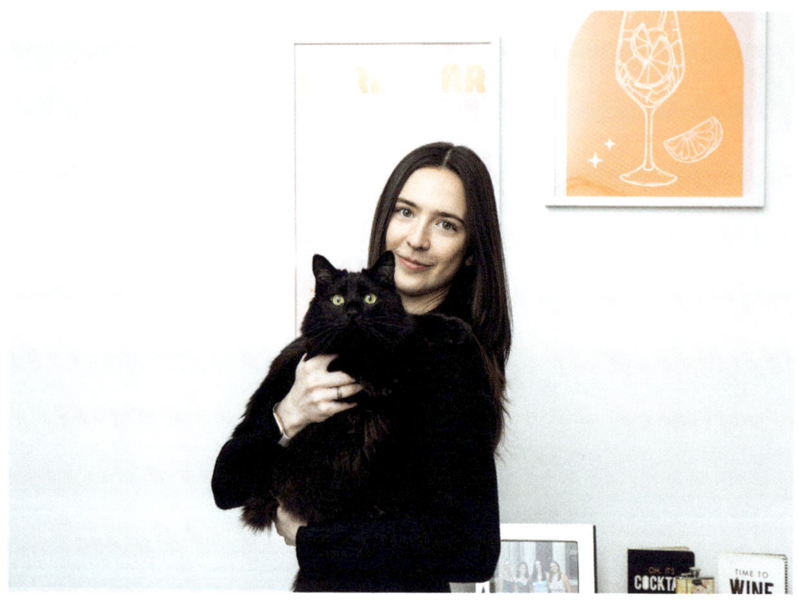

Gillian & Sage, 2024

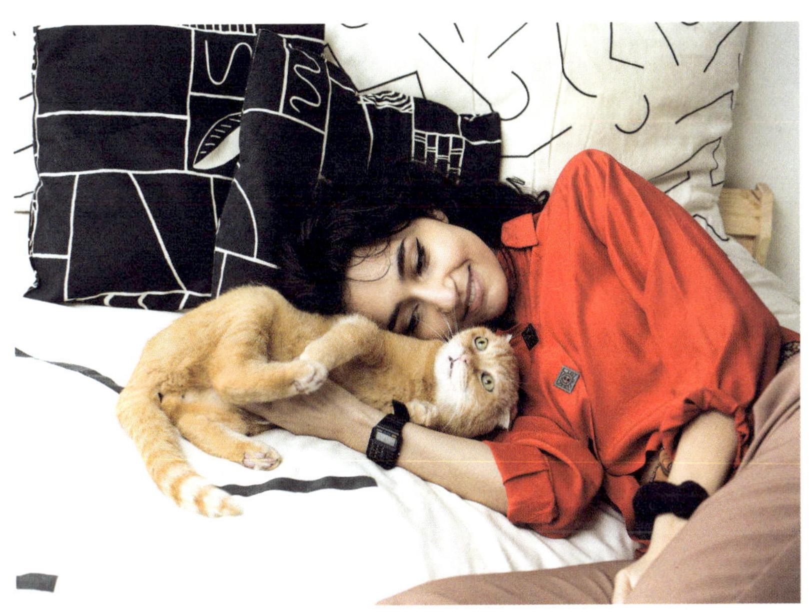

Sammy & Rasmus, 2020

WRITERS' CATS
Jouk Oosterhof

For a cat-themed special of its magazine, the Dutch newspaper *Volkskrant* commissioned Jouk Oosterhof to photograph five of the country's best-known writers who own cats.

The cats were the story here, however, and so Oosterhof relegated their celebrity owners to a peripheral, merely structural role. Camouflaged with patterned sheets and drapes, they became human furniture. The images echo Victorian 'hidden mother' portraits, in which mothers impersonated chairs or backdrops to be able to hold their babies in place for the camera's long exposure.

Oosterhof's subjects were Bosie (with novelist and children's author Mensje van Keulen), Emma (with former biologist turned broadcaster and author Midas Dekkers), Fons (with journalist Thomas Verbogt), Pootjes (with columnist Renske de Greef) and Whoopi (with novelist Susan Smit).

Bosie with Mensje van Keulen, 2015

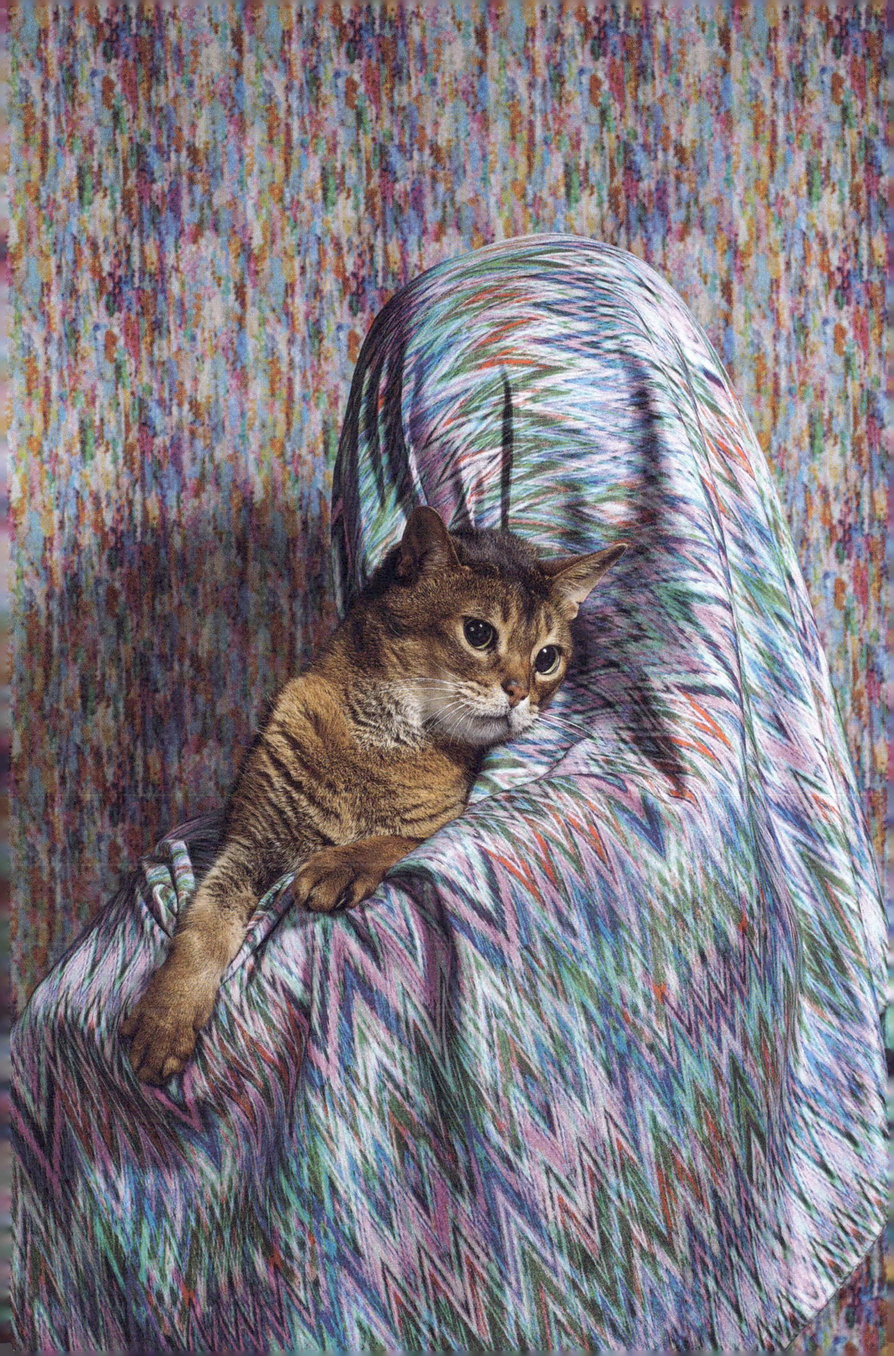

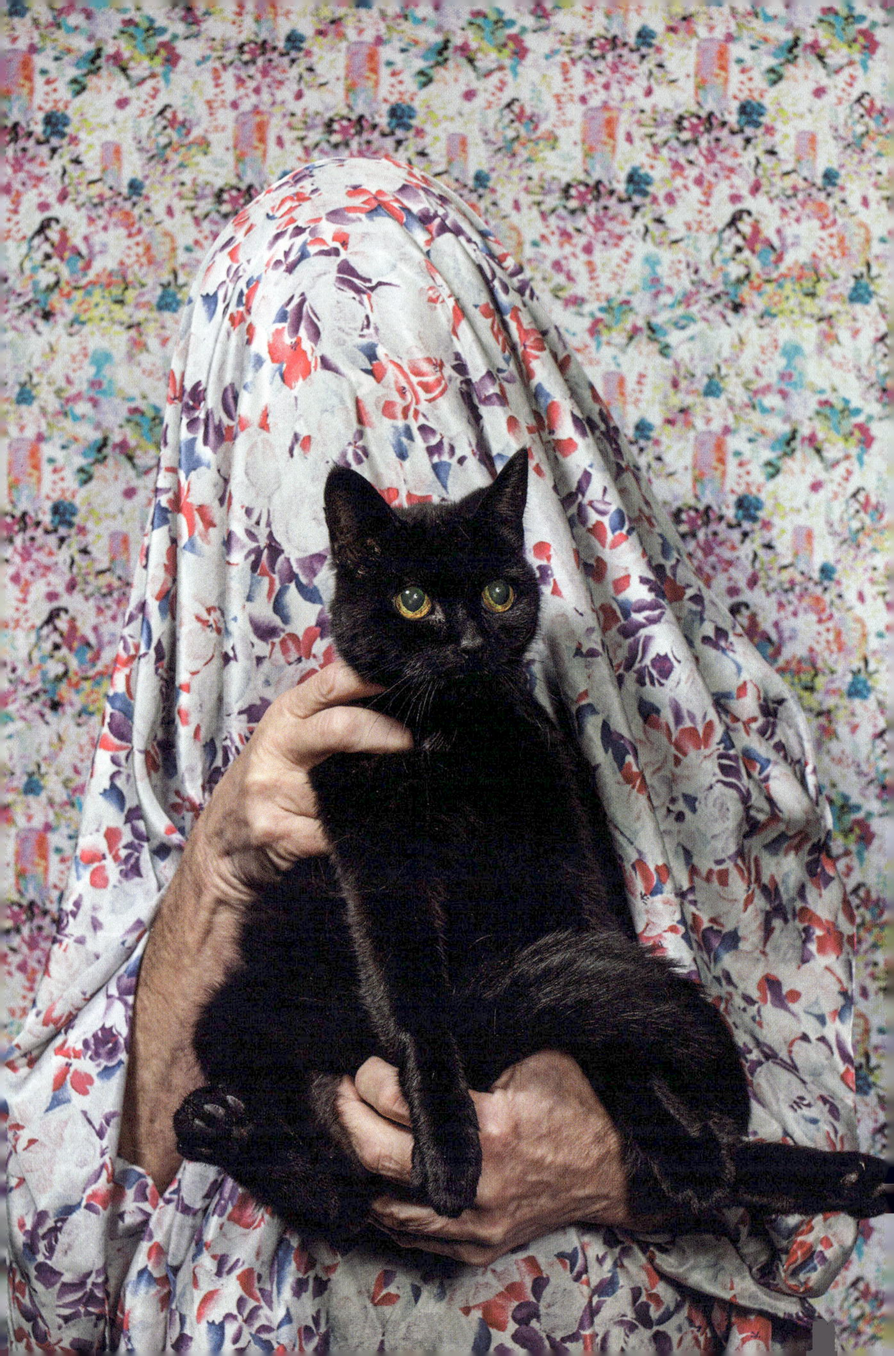

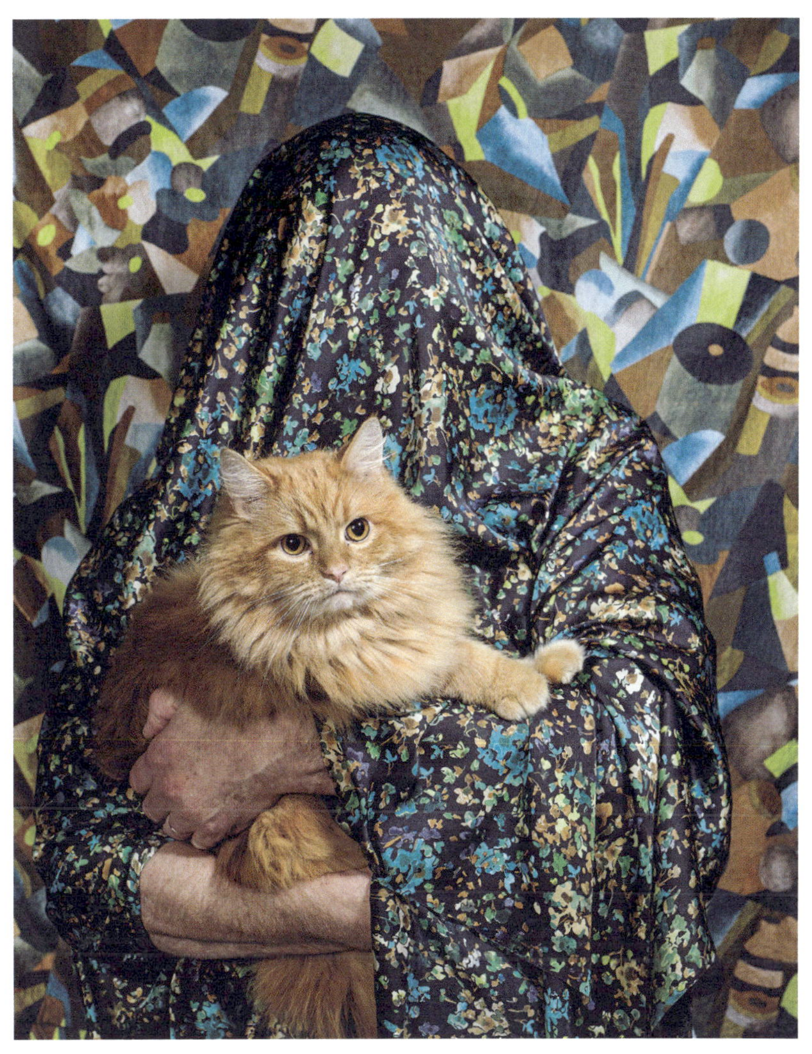

Above: *Fons with Thomas Verbogt*, 2015
Opposite: *Emma with Midas Dekkers*, 2015

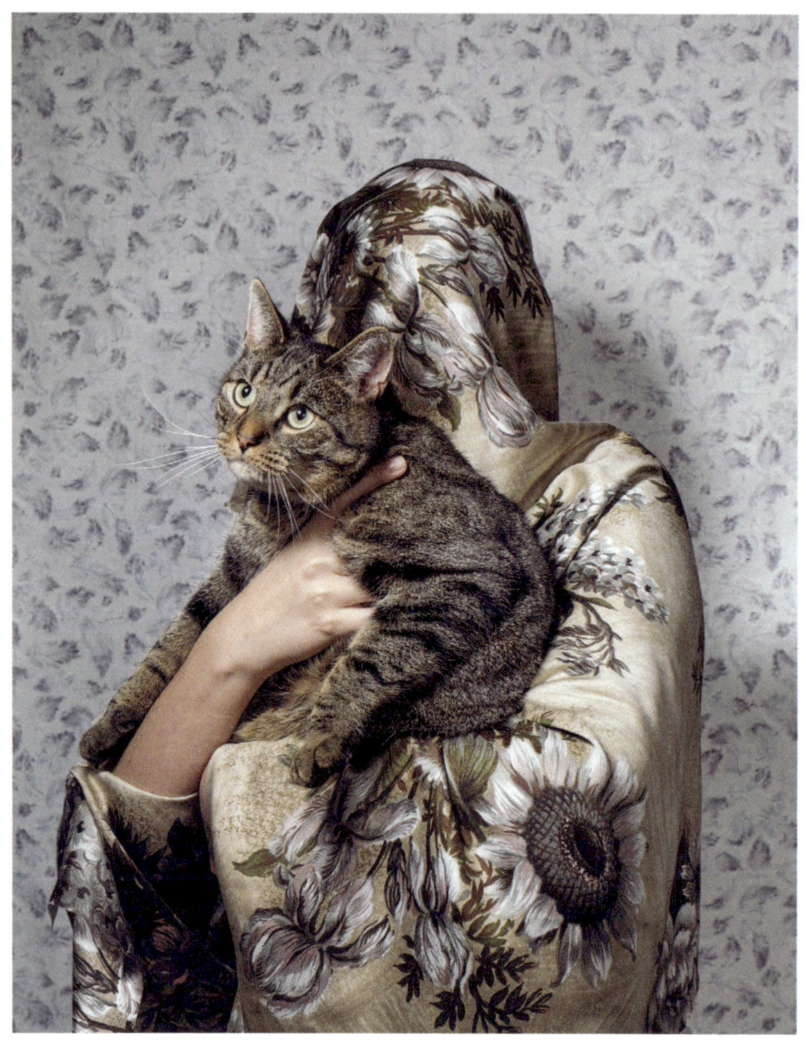

Above: *Pootjes with Renske de Greek*, 2015
Opposite: *Whoopi with Susan Smit*, 2015

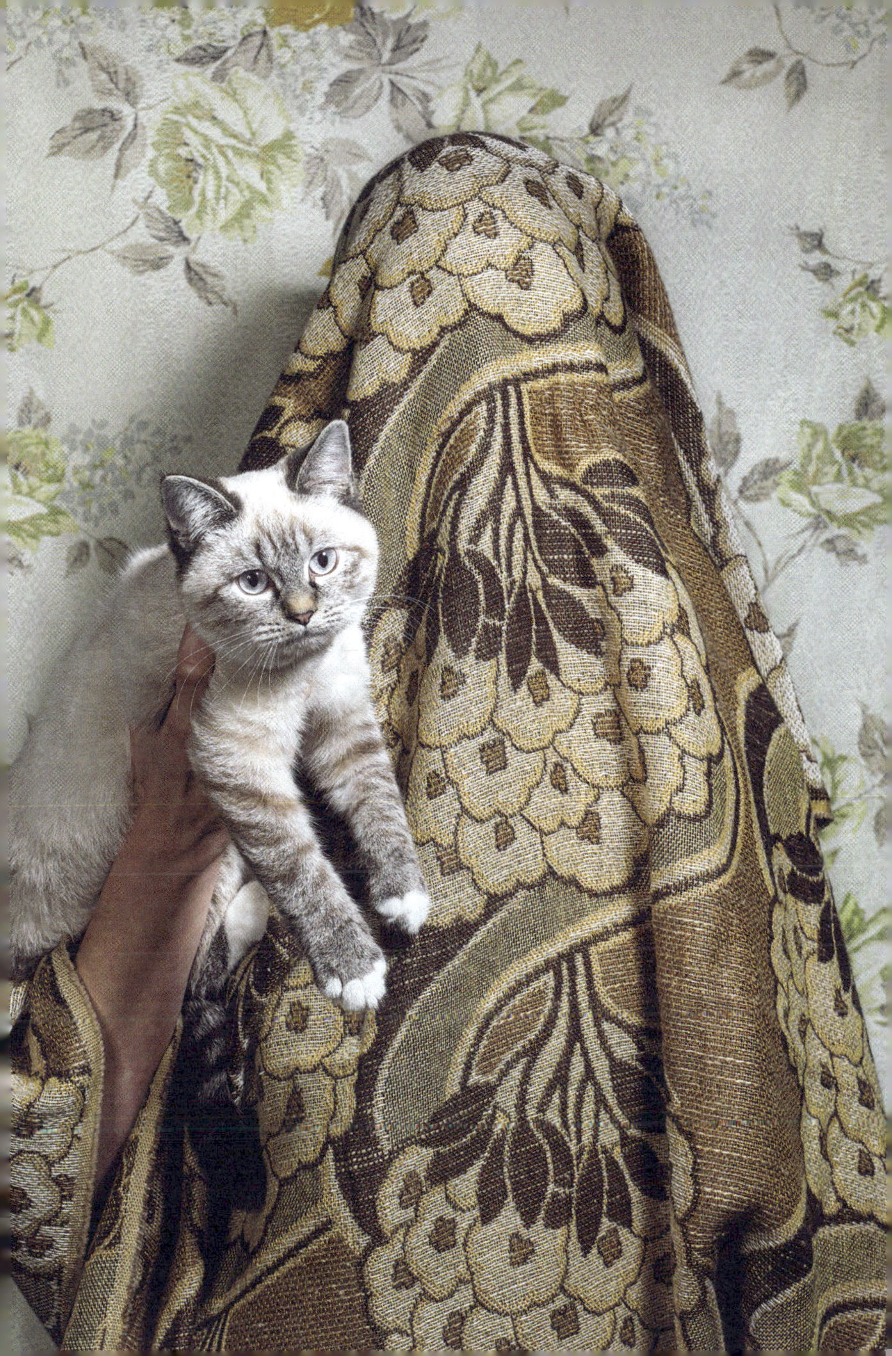

COMMUNITY CATS
Nguan

Until recently, it was illegal for residents of Singapore's public housing estates (in which 80 per cent of the city's population live) to own a cat. Instead, Singaporeans took to keeping 'community cats' – felines that roamed the common areas, responded to any number of names and purred amiably (when they felt like it) for all.

Singaporean photographer Nguan dedicated 12 years to photographing the cats with his old-fashioned film camera. Wandering through the estates' walkways and 'void decks' – open areas at ground level used for social gatherings, exercising and board games – he came to understand these liminal architectural spaces as a reflection of the 'state of betweenness' in which the cats existed: 'domesticated but homeless, neither truly stray nor fully fostered, belonging to everyone and no one,' he says.

To achieve the pastel-toned, tender and dreamlike quality for which his images have gained a cult following online – a style he describes as 'magical documentary' – he restricts himself to photographing in the final two hours of daylight, 'when the sun is low and everything is aglow'.

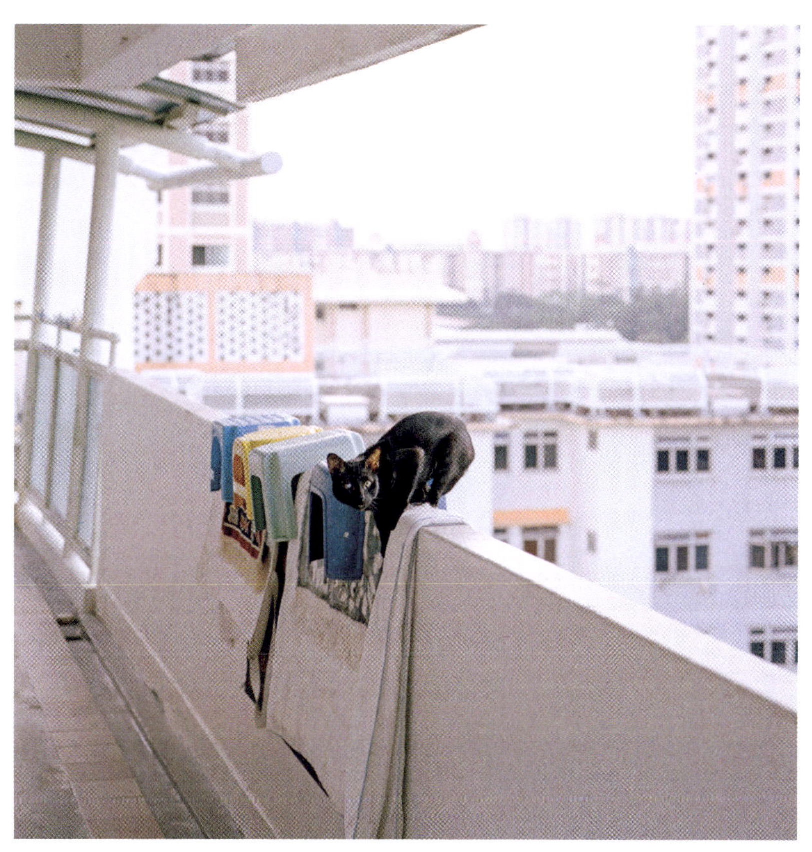

Bedok South Avenue 2, 2018

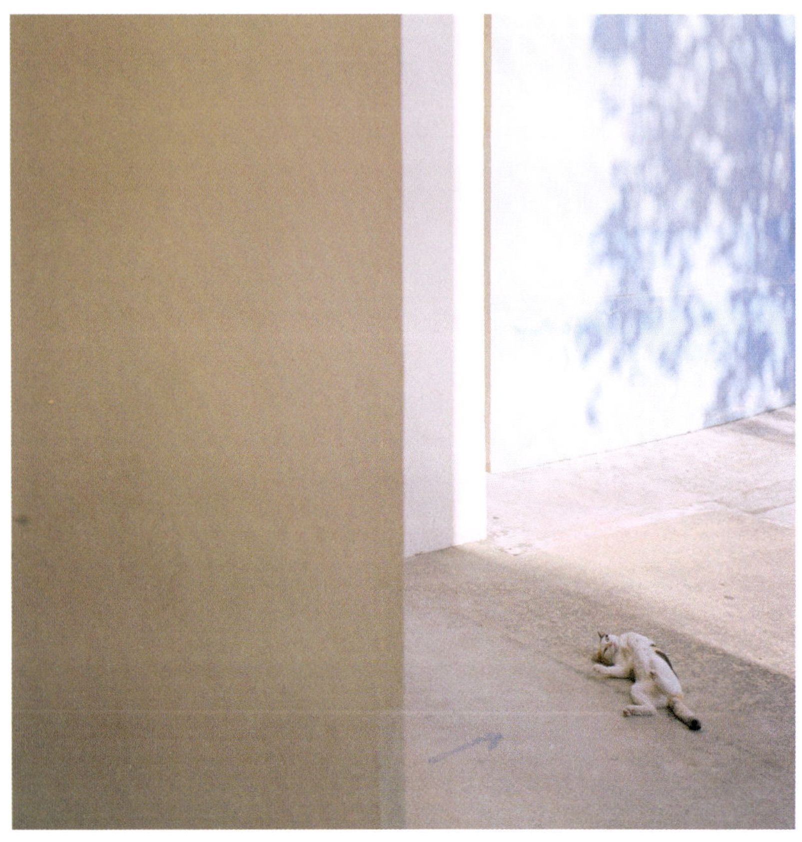

Tampines Street 42, 2022

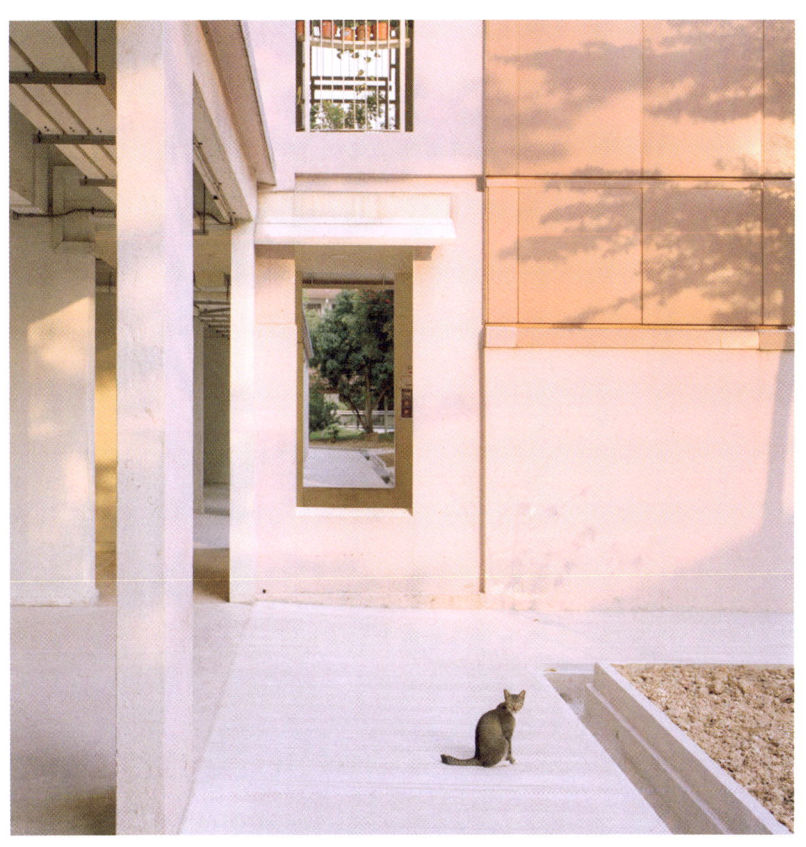

Jurong West Street 42, 2019

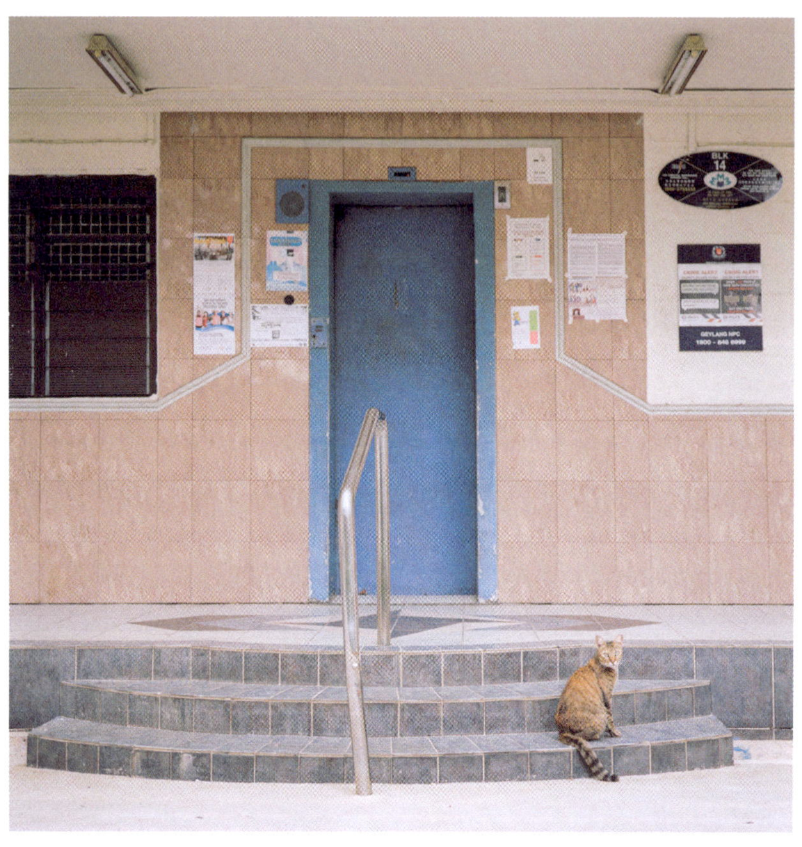

Dakota Crescent, 2016

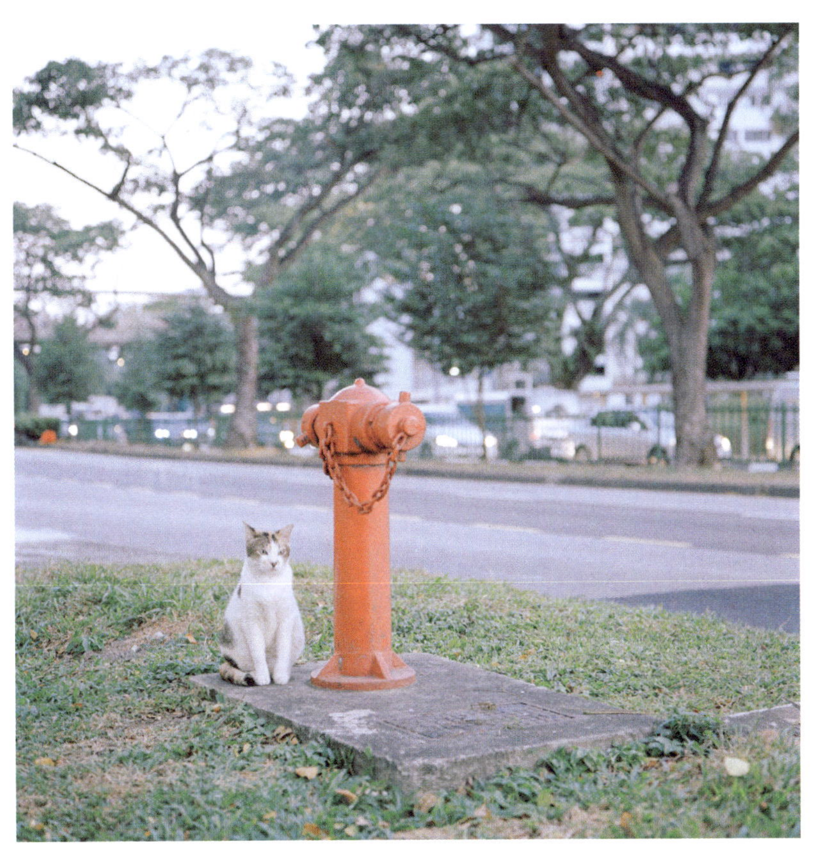

Hougang Avenue 3, 2017

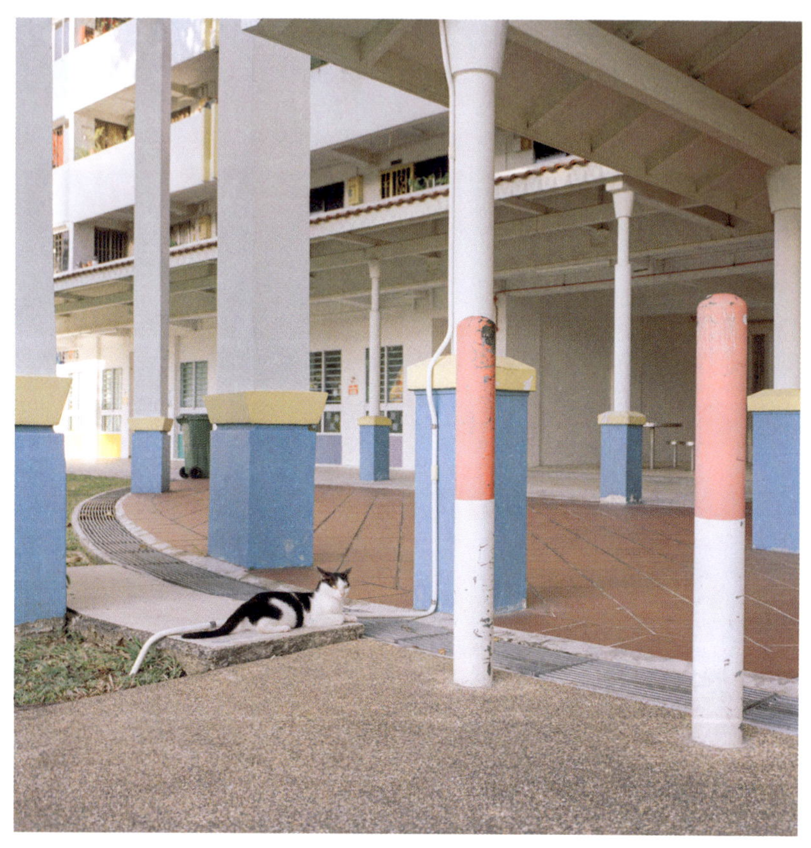

Upper Boon Keng Road, 2021

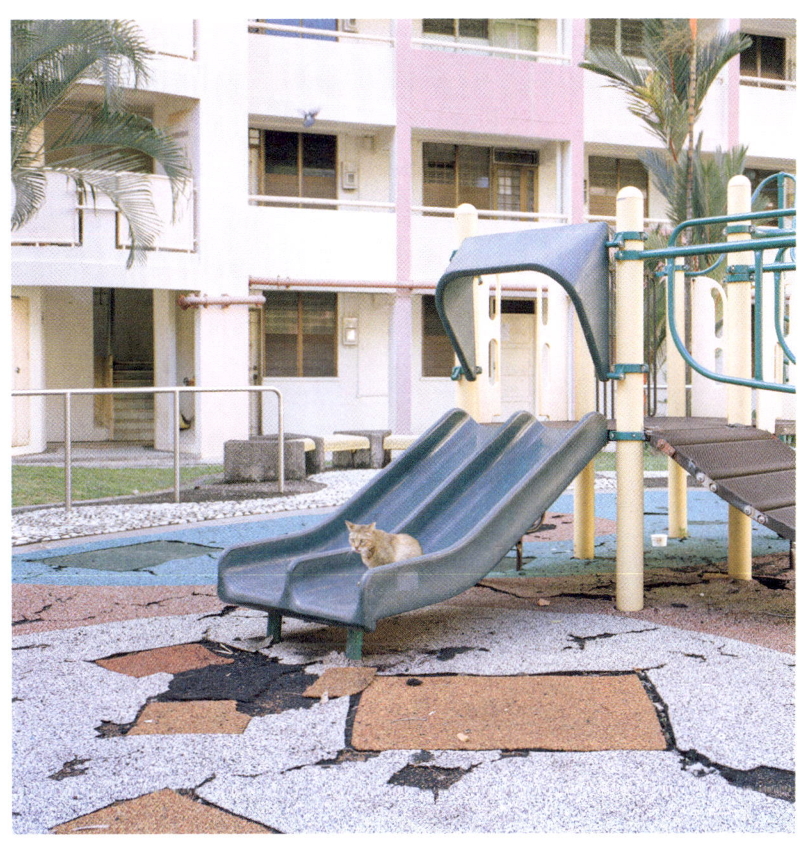

Tanglin Halt, 2022

CAT FEVER
Ekin Küçük

There are thought to be more than 120,000 stray cats roaming Istanbul's streets. Ekin Küçük began feeding the ones in her neighbourhood after her dogs passed away. The sight of the cats gathering hungrily in her garden gave her comfort. 'Friendship and healing were my priority,' she says, 'taking pictures of them came after.'

Growing up in the late 1990s, she remembered vividly the mass municipal culls of homeless pets by poisoning; an experience she describes as traumatising. Today, Istanbul's stray animals receive shelter, food, sterilisation and medical checks by veterinarians, though their lives remain challenging.

Struck by how clever, silly and rambunctious the cats in her garden seemed, Küçük sought to capture their 'happy times' in her photographs, and to honour the creatures' resilience and wit. She has adopted a stray of her own, too, rescued by the fire department from the inside of her car's engine.

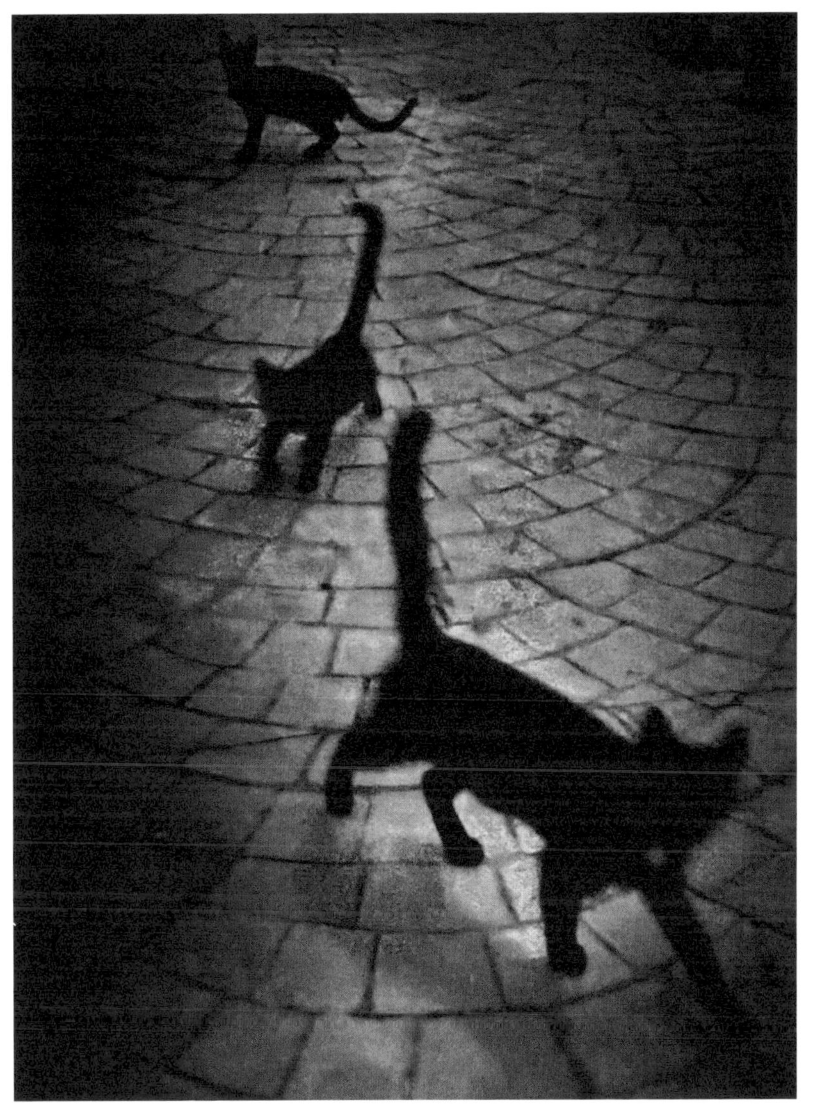

Istanbul, 2017

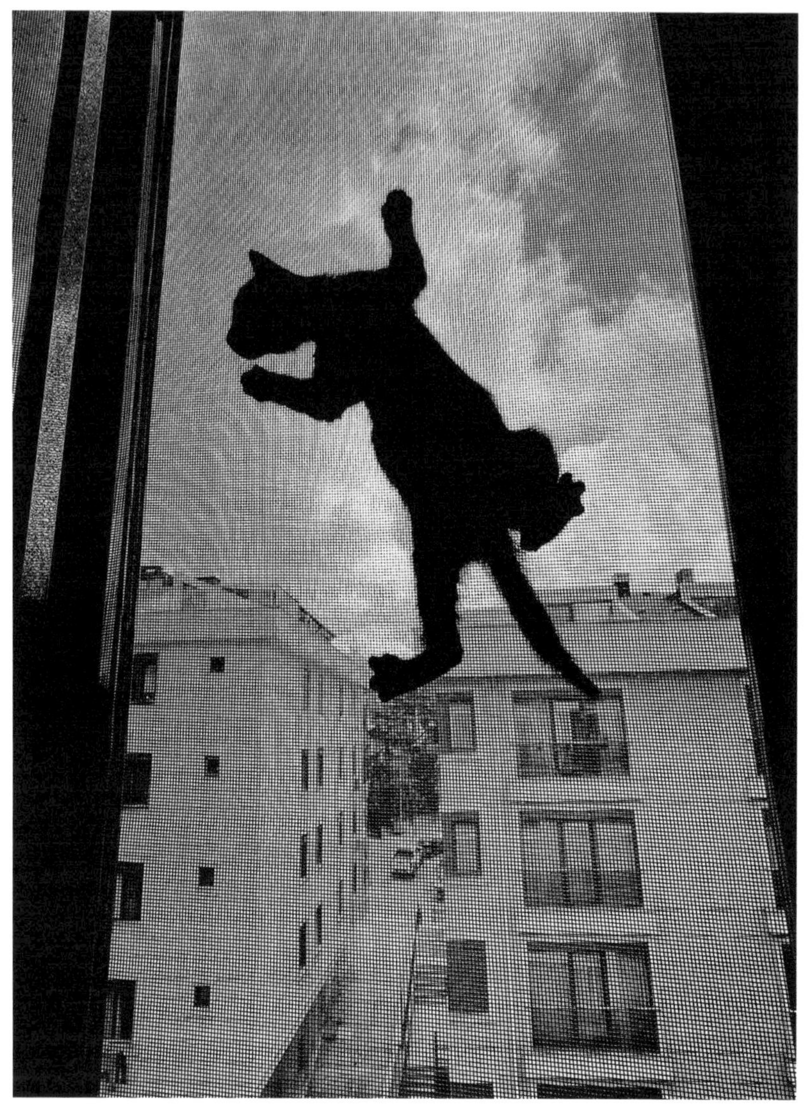

Istanbul, 2017

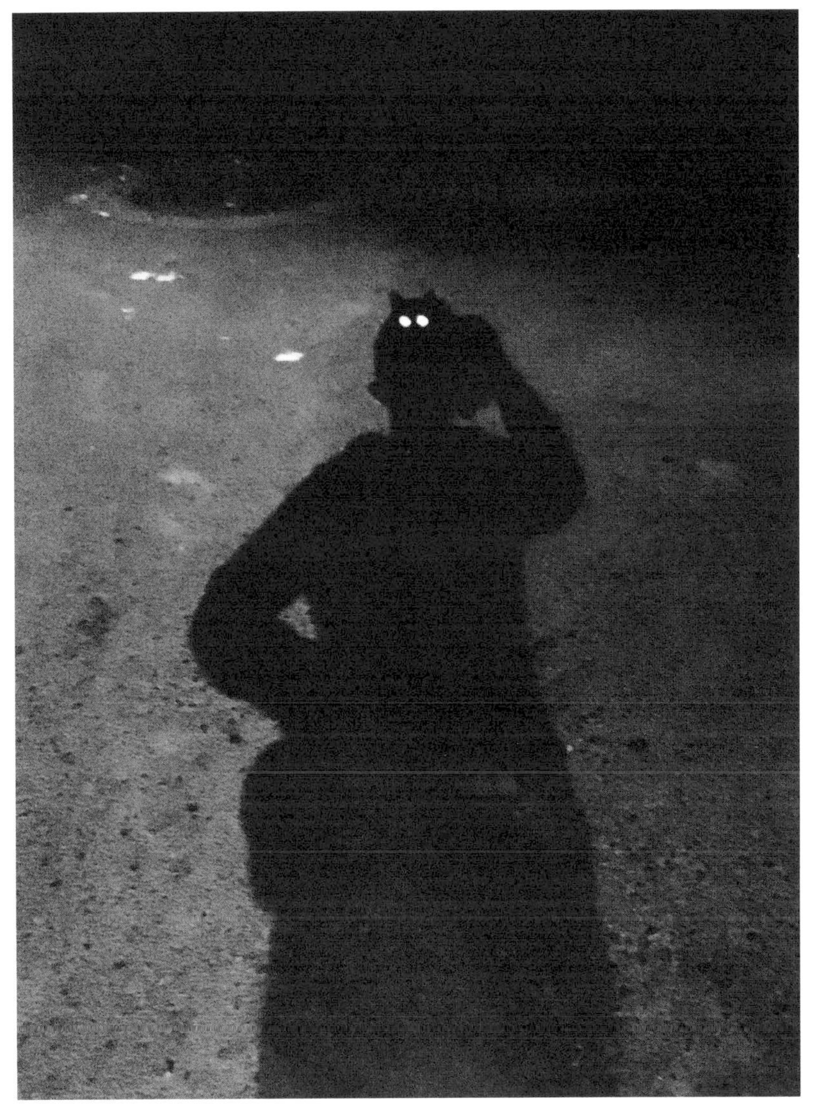

Istanbul, 2017

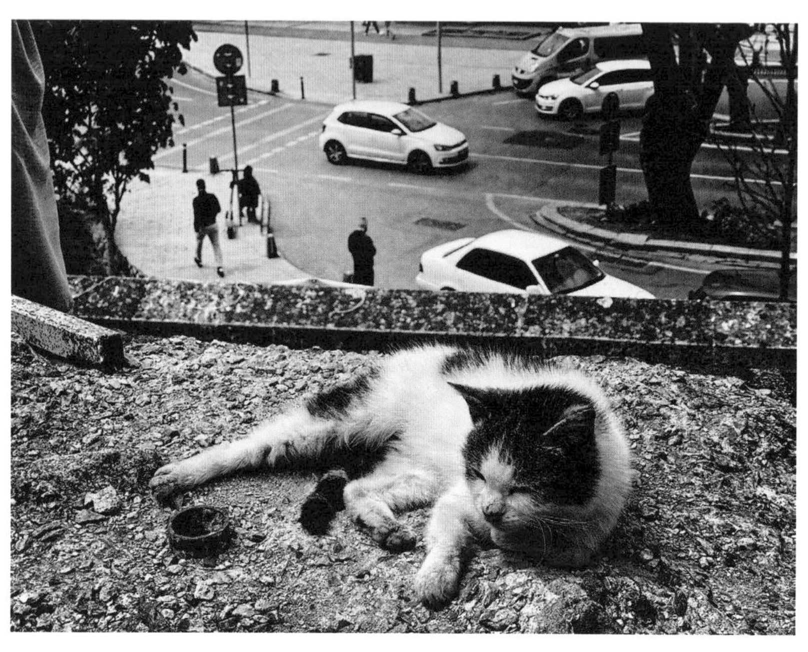

Istanbul, 2017

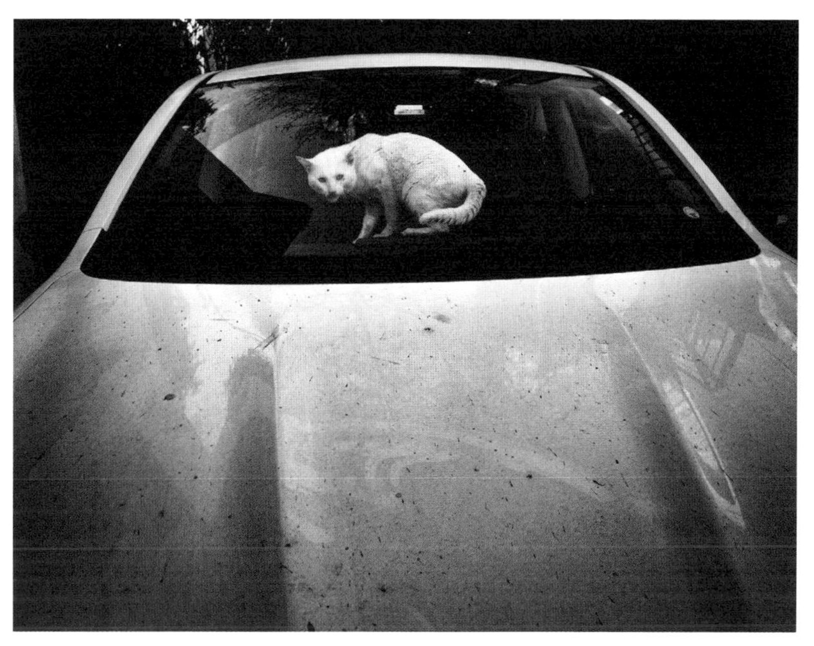

Istanbul, 2017

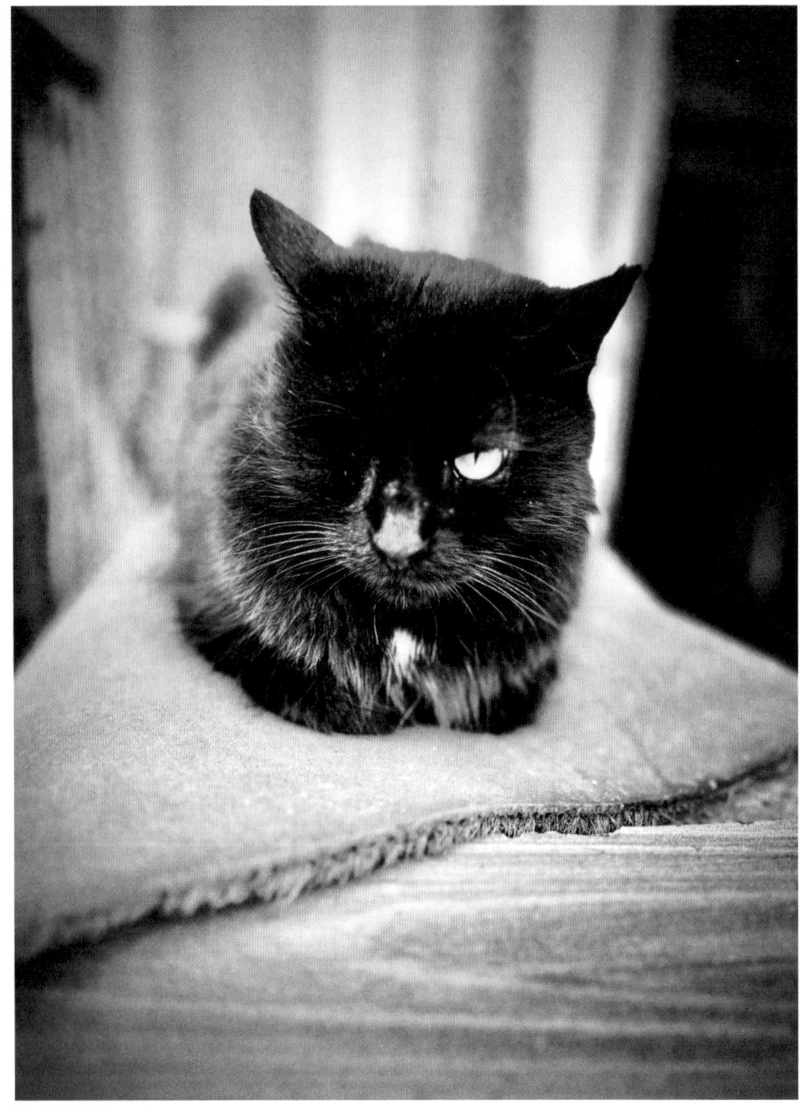

Istanbul, 2017

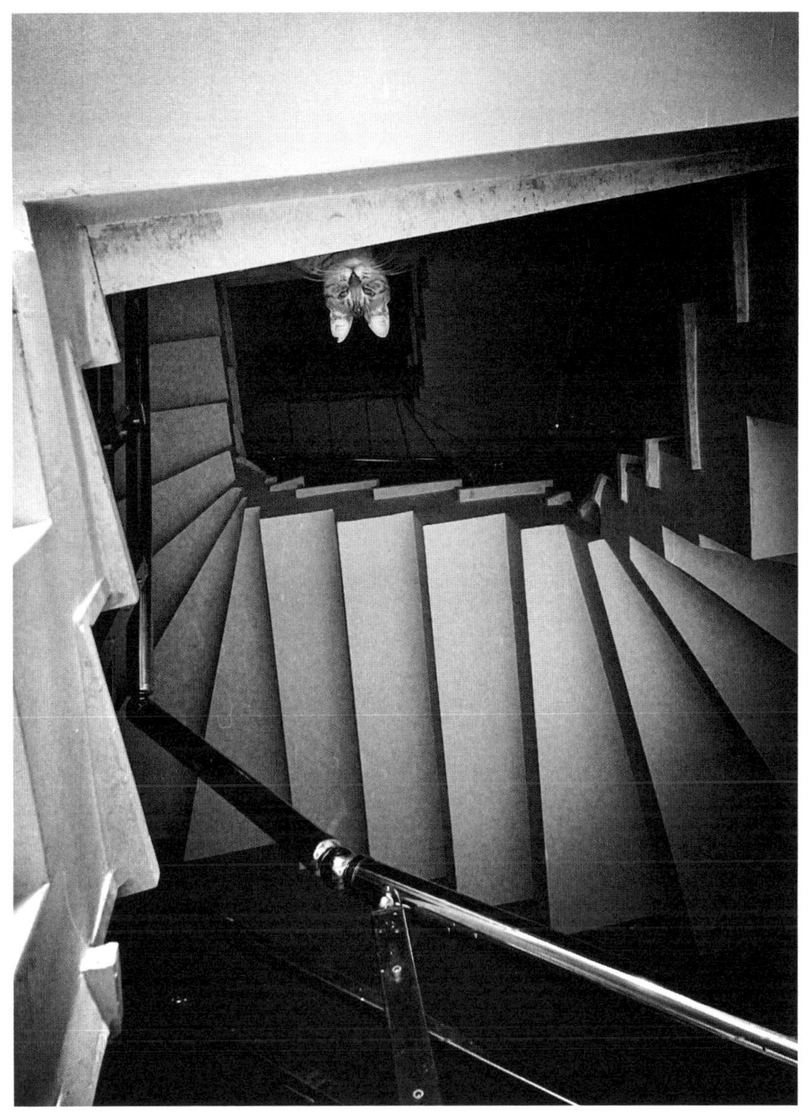

Istanbul, 2017

SHAKE CATS

Carli Davidson

Carli Davidson is a photographer and an animal rights activist from Oregon, whose feline subjects come from shelters or are adopted rescue cats. Her series *Shake Cats* captures them in freeze-frame form and mid head-waggle, after a spot of ear grooming, a splash of water or a gust of air.

Davidson made her first 'shake photograph' of her dog, Norbert, a French Mastiff whose whole-body manoeuvres and plentiful jowls would pepper the room with saliva: 'You spend enough time cleaning up drool and eventually you're going to want to know – how exactly does this happen?' For inspiration, Davidson turned to Victorian photographer, Eadweard Muybridge, who in 1878 used sequential cameras to prove that horses lift all four legs off the ground when they run. 'He captured an action that happens too quickly for our minds to grasp what it looks like,' she explains.

To take her pictures, Davidson uses strobe lights that pause motion at 1/13,000th of a second and a camera that shoots ten frames per second.

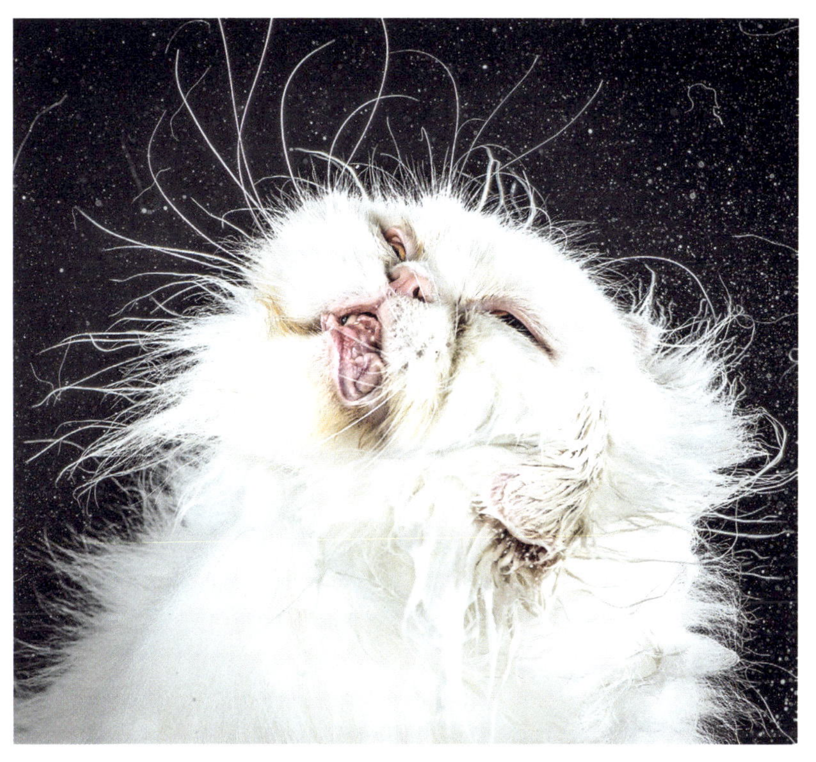

Lorax, 2014

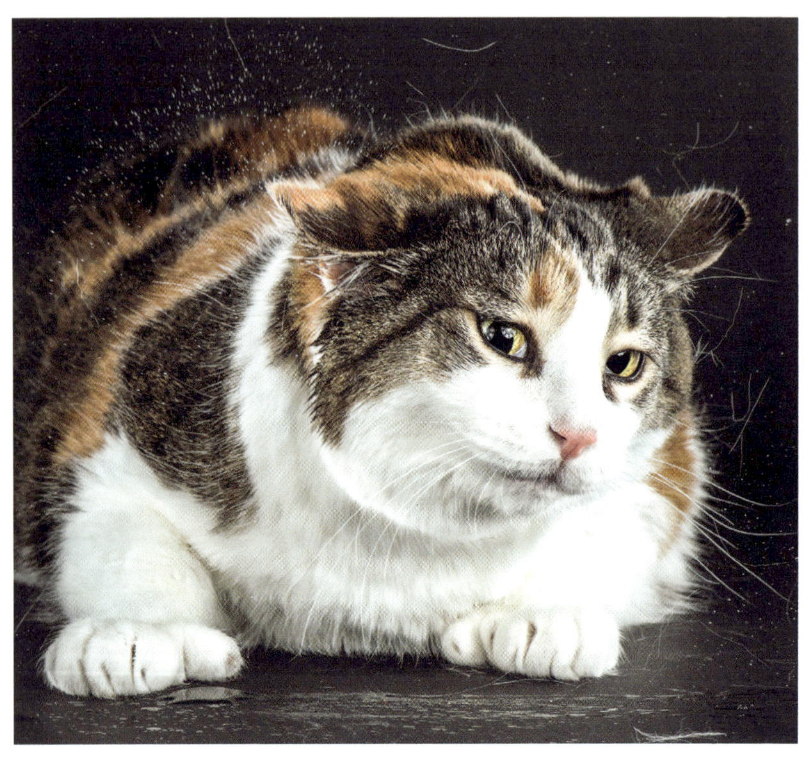

Katie, 2014

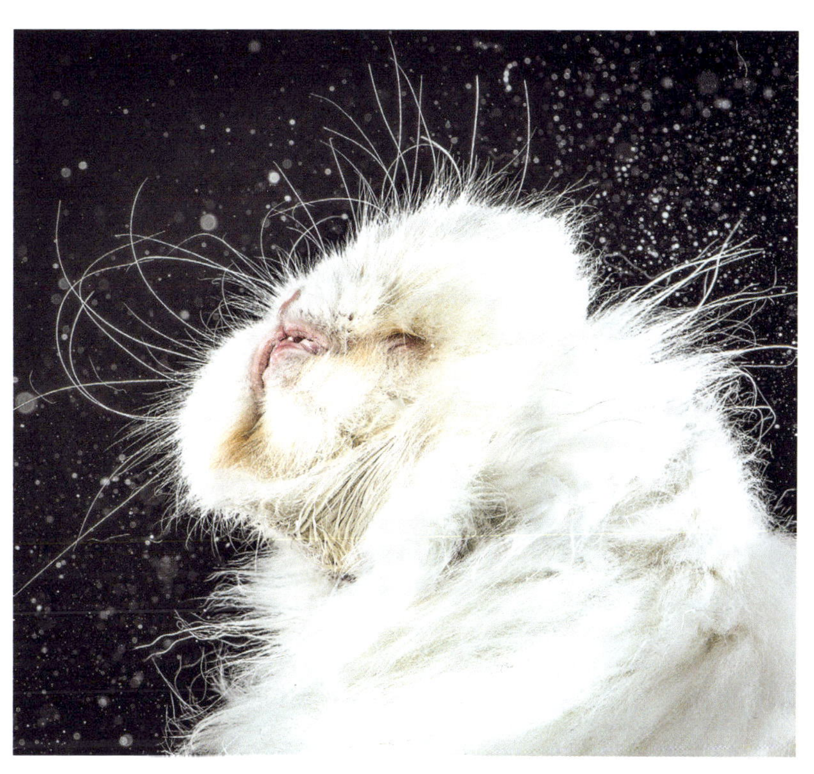

Above: *Lorax*, 2014
Overleaf: *Ewya*, 2014

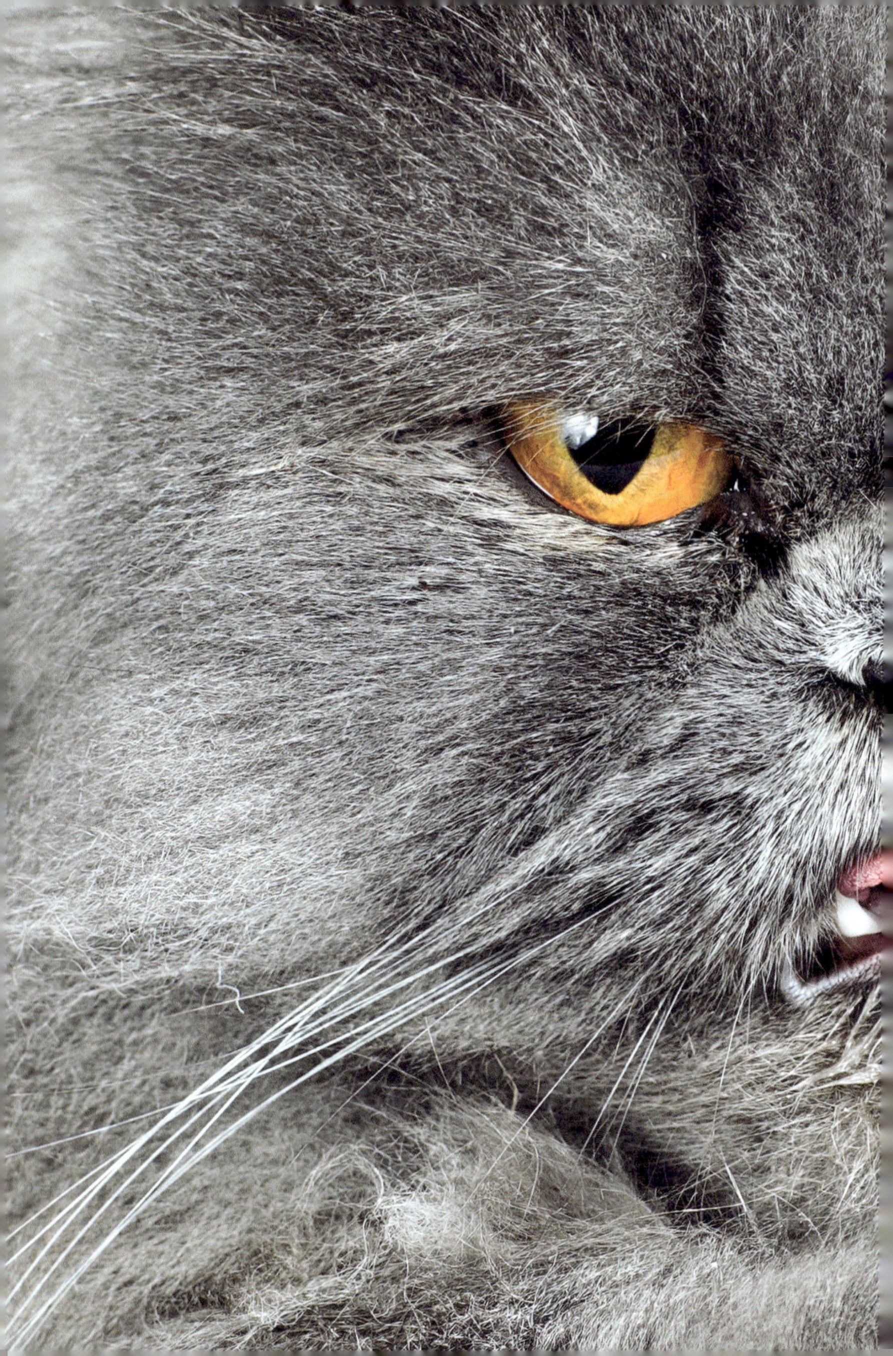

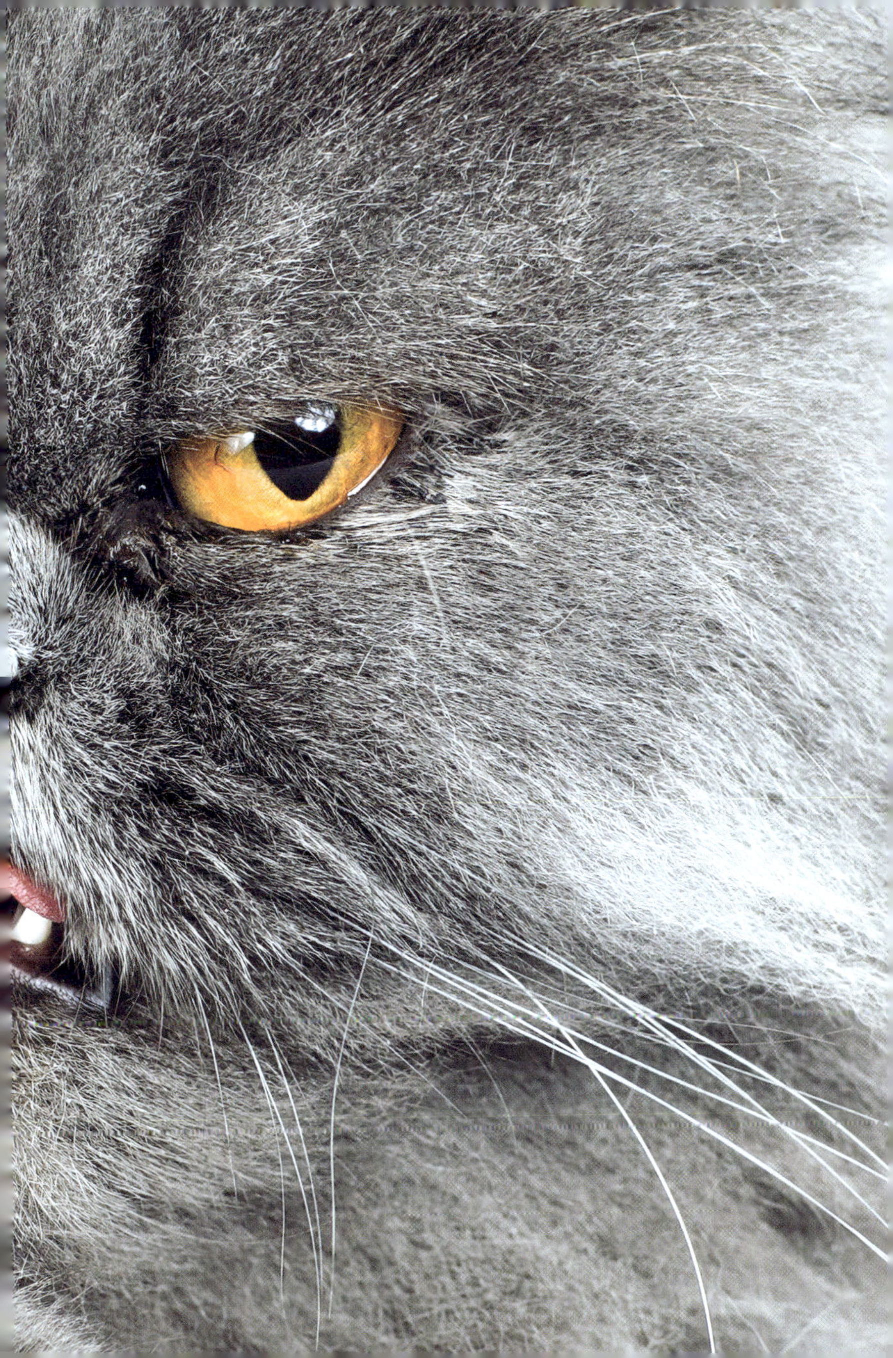

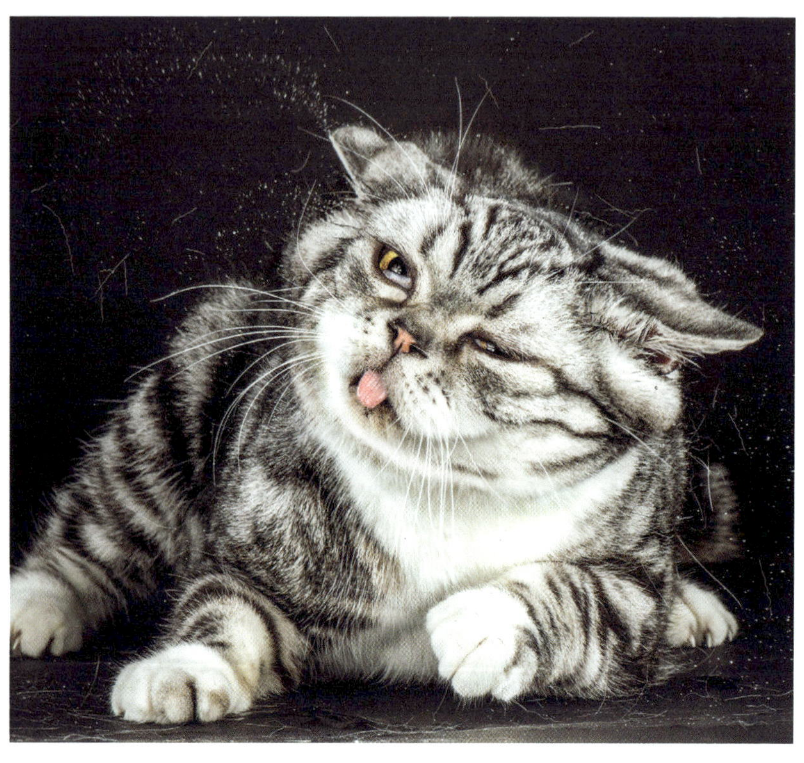

Jaz, 2014

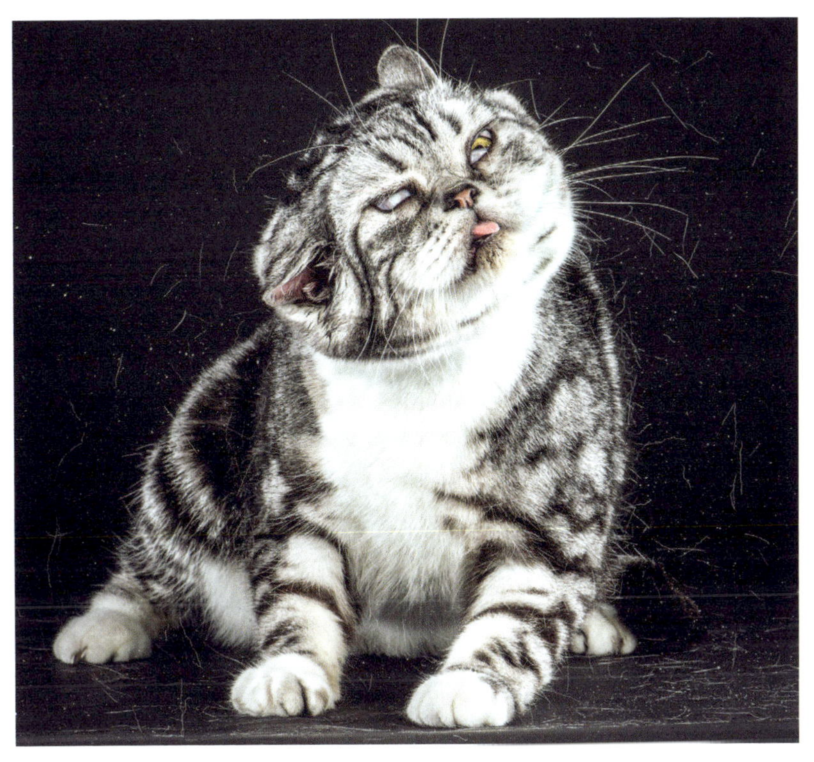

Jaz, 2014

SYMMETRICAT
Dag Knudsen

Nothing in nature is perfectly symmetrical – even snow-flakes and butterfly wings display natural variations that create miniscule asymmetries. Which is why, when we see something that *is* 100 per cent symmetrical, 'it has a sort of hypnotic effect on our perception,' says Dag Knudsen. The Norwegian photographer has been experimenting with the phenomenon since 2012, taking a fraction of something real and multiplying or repeating it to form impossible cityscapes – even a Statue of Liberty with both arms raised.

His *Symmetricat* series began in 2017, while shooting a fashion story for a New York magazine that featured a Sphynx cat as a co-model: 'He was very comfortable in front of the camera, literally posing for the pictures. I made a symmetrical version of him and immediately decided to make a series. Twelve Sphynxes later, his *Symmetricats* were hanging on gallery walls in Miami, New York and Knudsen's hometown of Oslo. He followed up with other cats, dogs, lizards, frogs, sheep, a silver fox, a fallow deer, a hedgehog and owls.'For me, symmetric animal portraits appear as creatures from another world,' he says, 'I suddenly understood how the ancient Egyptians worshipped cats.'

Buster, Maine Coon, 2019

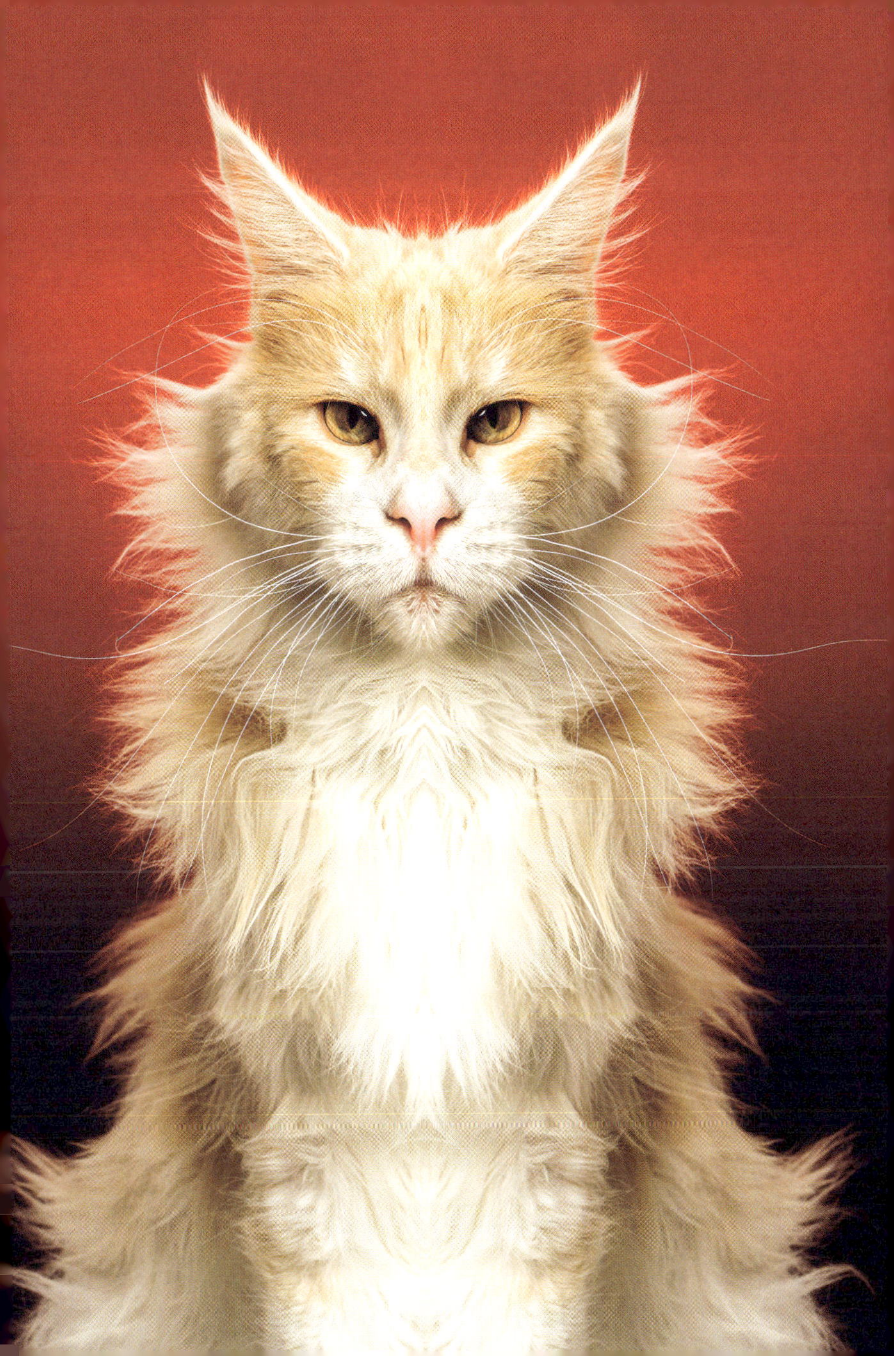

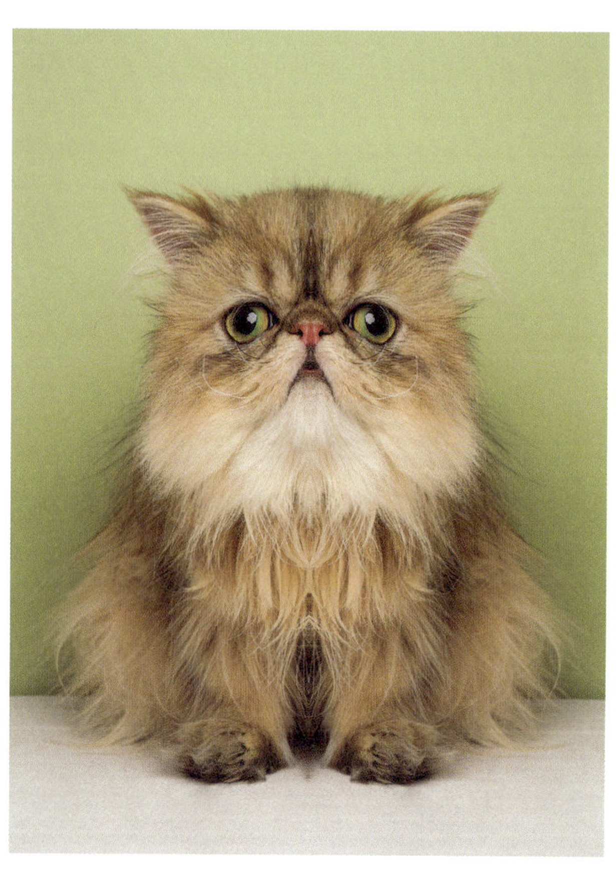

Above: *Oliver, Shaded Golden Persian*, 2019
Opposite: *Wafer, Elf*, 2018

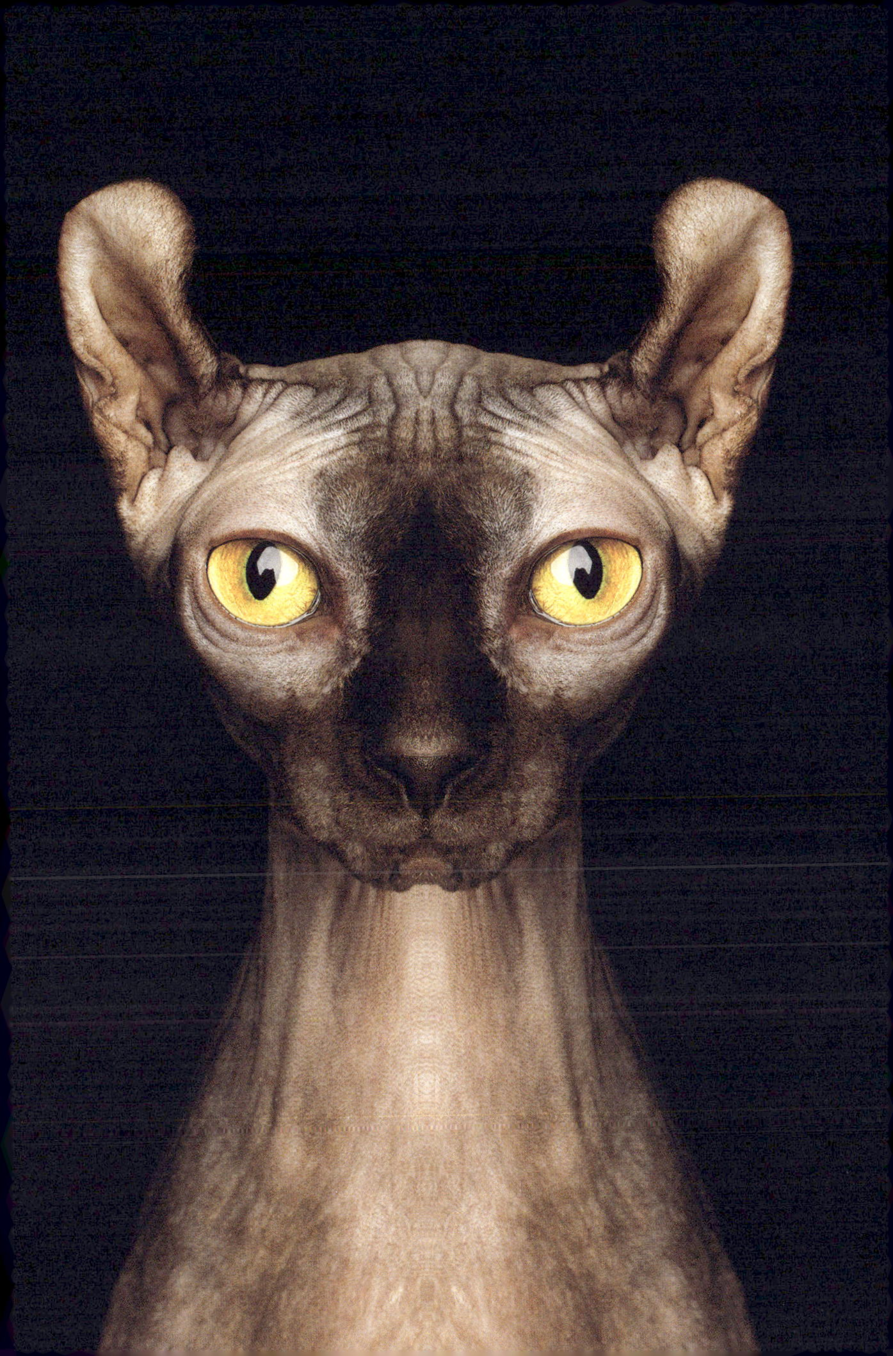

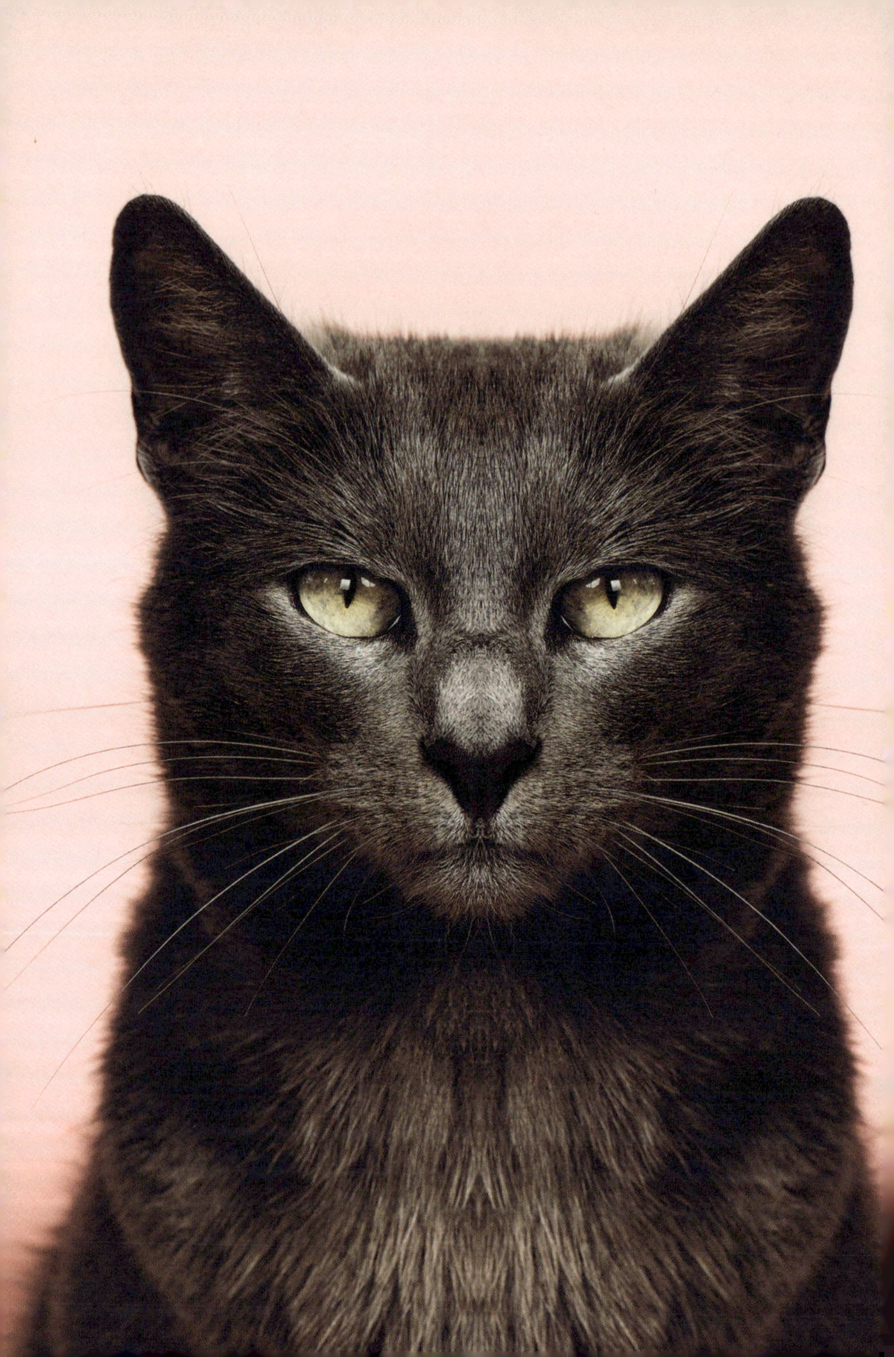

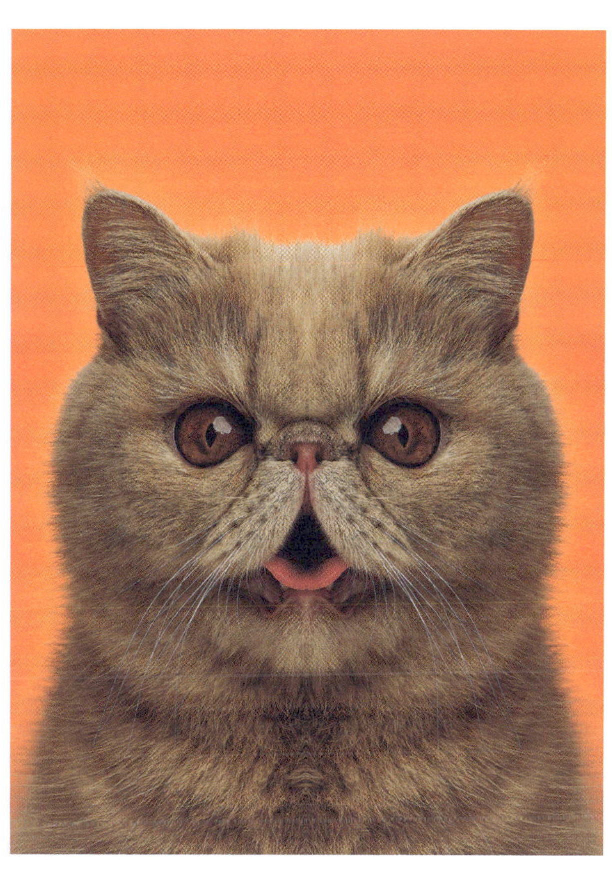

Above: *Frank, Exotic British Shorthair*, 2019
Opposite: *Aurora, Russian Blue & Oriental Mix*, 2020

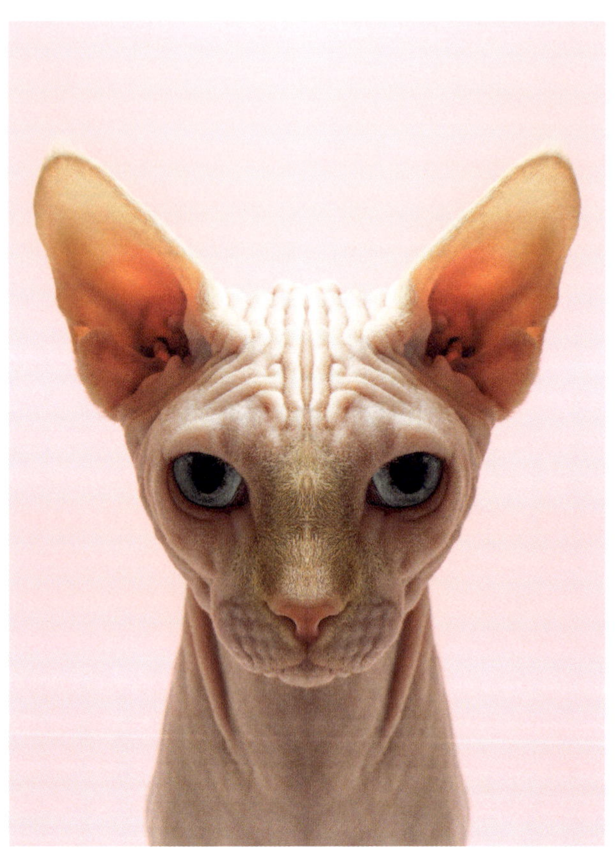

Above: *Safran, Sphynx*, 2016
Opposite: *Esaias, Holy Birman*, 2018

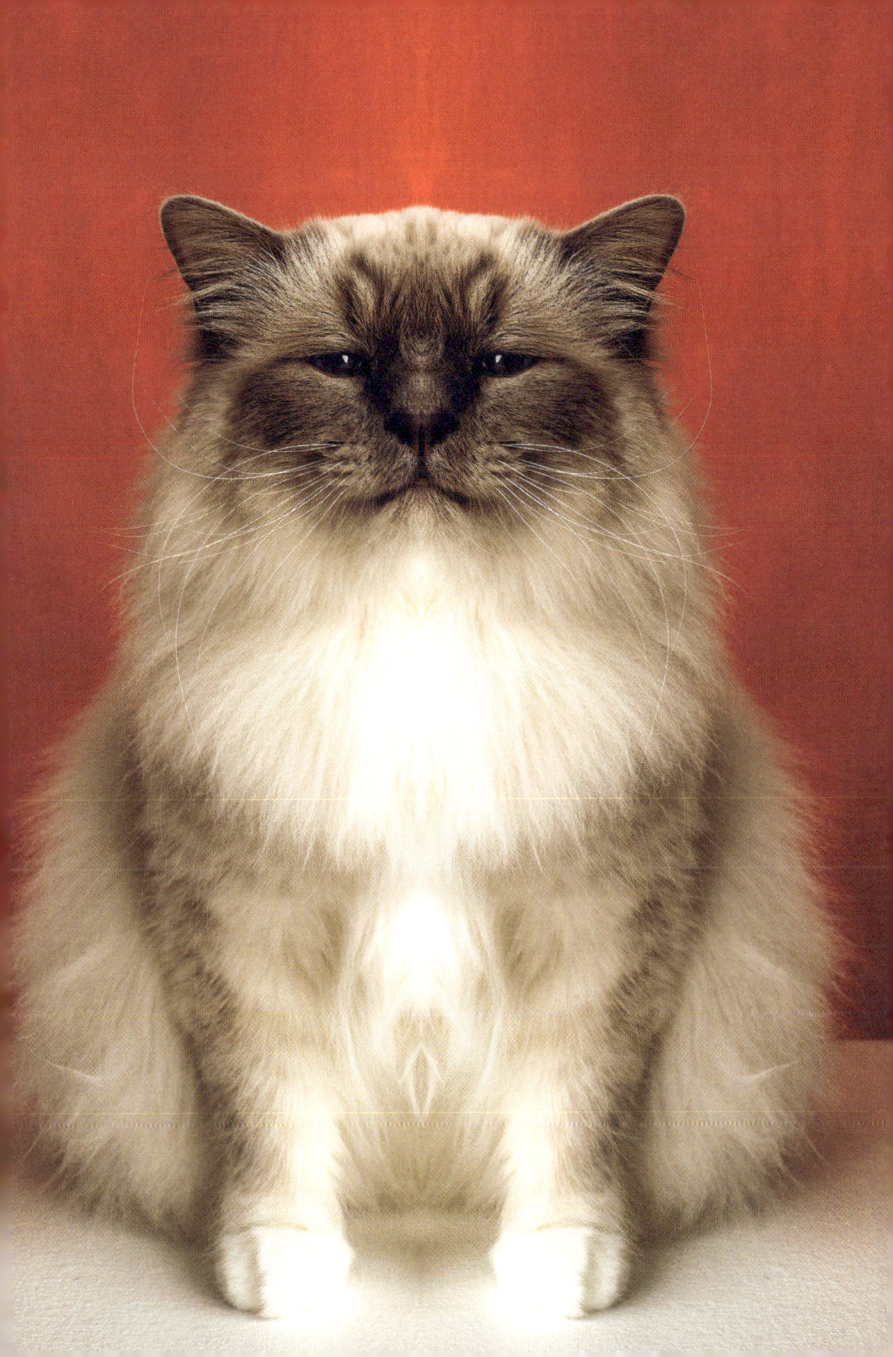

CAT WORSHIP
Jack Kenyon

The Supreme Cat Show is one of the largest cat competitions in Europe and always a big cross on any cat-lover's calendar. The event, which began in 1976 and is now held in Warwickshire, is organised by the world's oldest cat registry, the eminent Governing Council of the Cat Fancy (founded in 1910).

Judging is open to the public and categories range from 'Semi-Longhair' and 'British', to 'Best Decorated Pen' and the magnificent-sounding 'Imperial Grand Champion' or 'Supreme Kitten'. The winner of the latter gets to use the honorific before their name – as in 'Supreme Kitten Fluffy'.

Jack Kenyon is drawn to photographing cat shows all over the country, capturing some of 'life's delightful peculiarities'. He first visited the Supreme Show in 2019, and again in 2023: 'Amid a sea of ribbons, trophies and fur primped to perfection, I captured the unique bond between these pets and their people,' he says.

Coventry Cat Show. A young owner cradles her Seal Point Ragdoll moments after judging, 2020

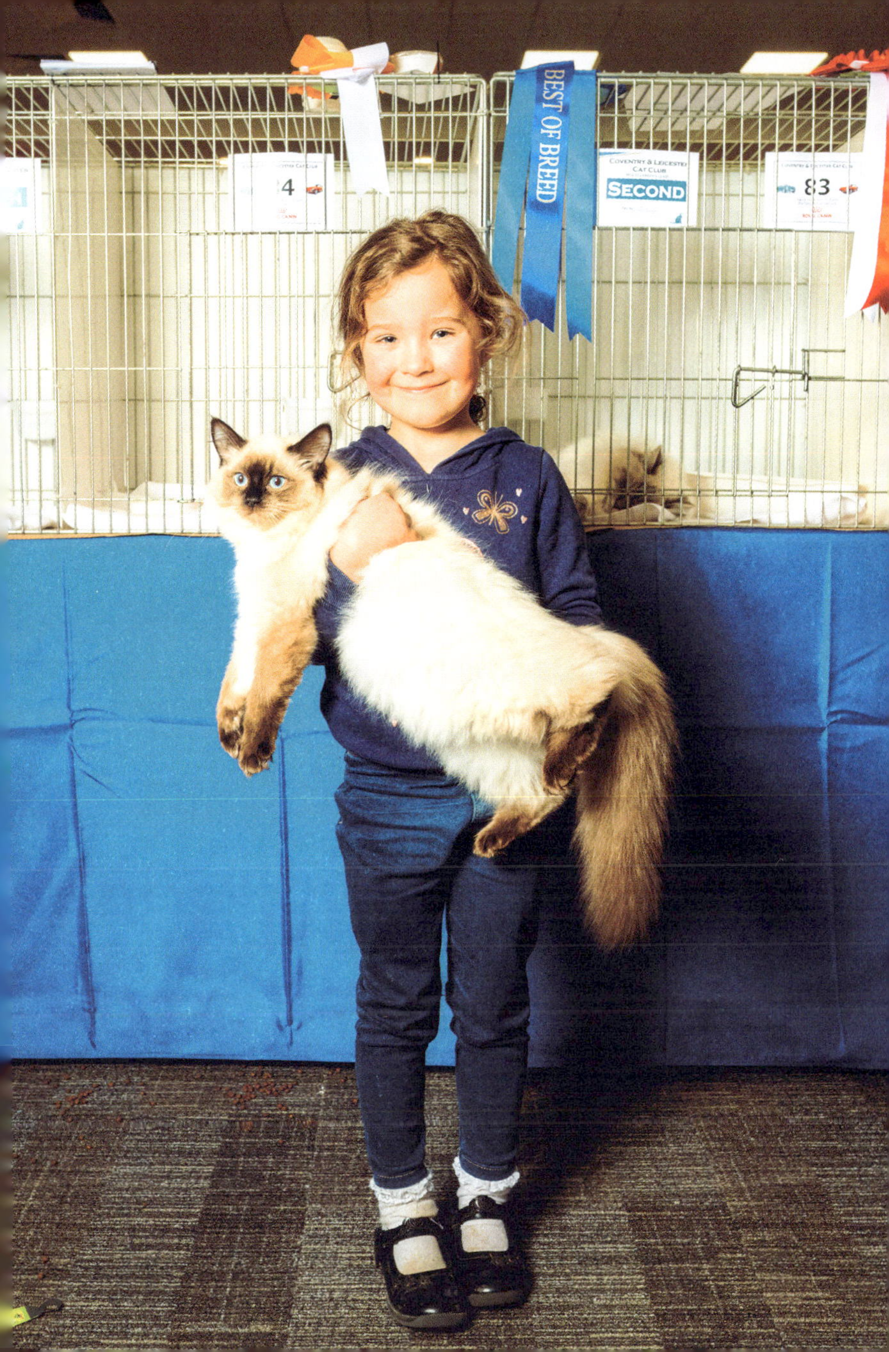
BEST OF BREED
COVENTRY & LEICESTER CAT CLUB
SECOND
83

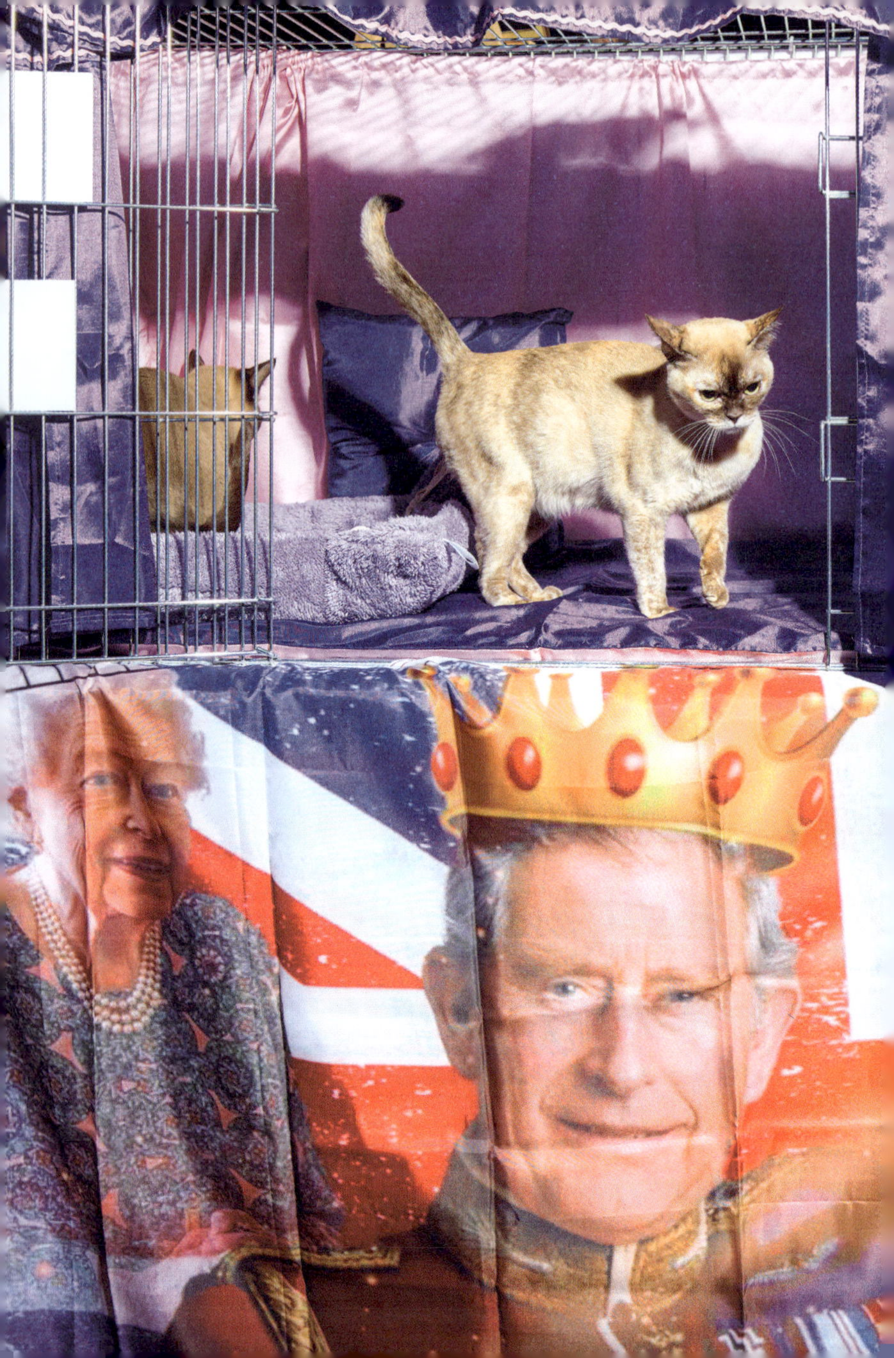

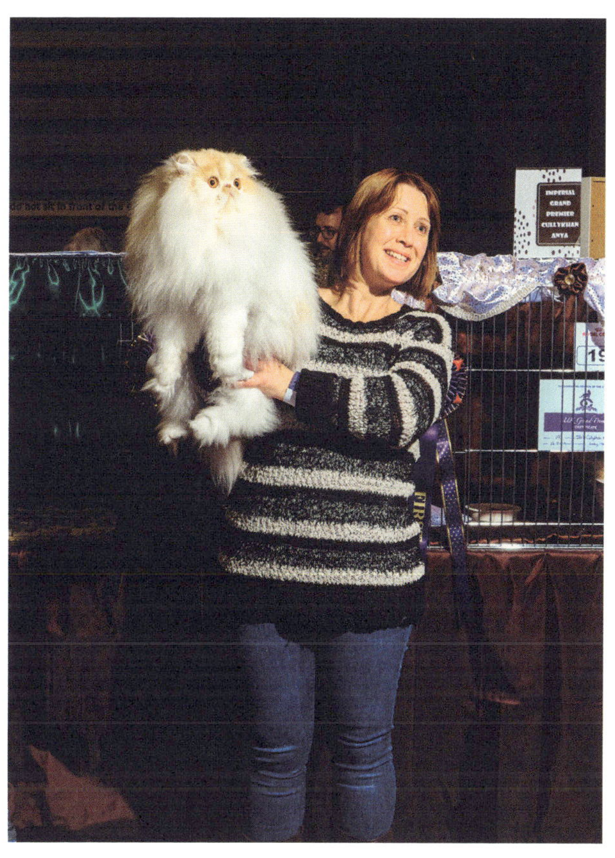

Above: *Supreme Cat Show. A freshly groomed Persian and its proud owner pose beneath the show lights,* 2020
Opposite: *Supreme Cat Show. A Burmilla tips her head to the new king,* 2023

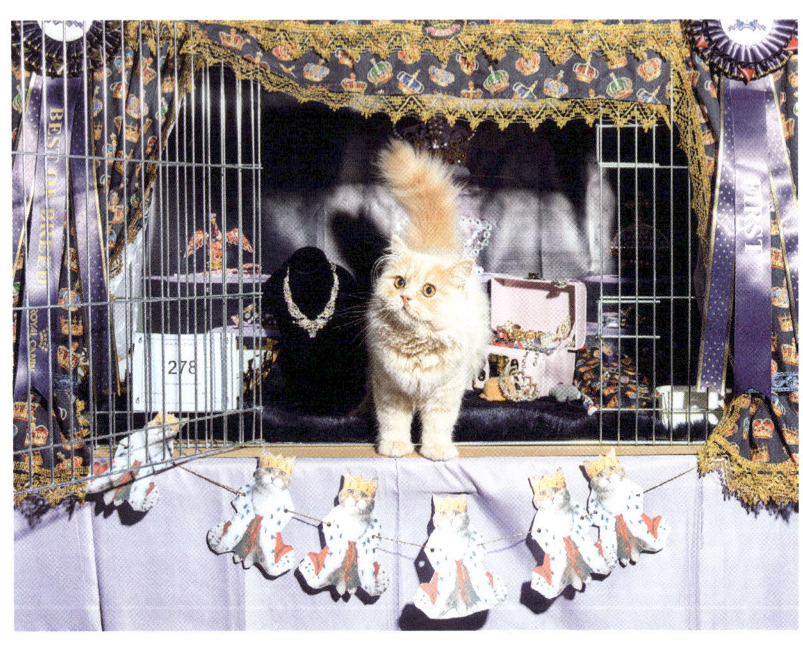

Supreme Cat Show. Fluffy cream Longhair emerges from its royal shrine, 2023

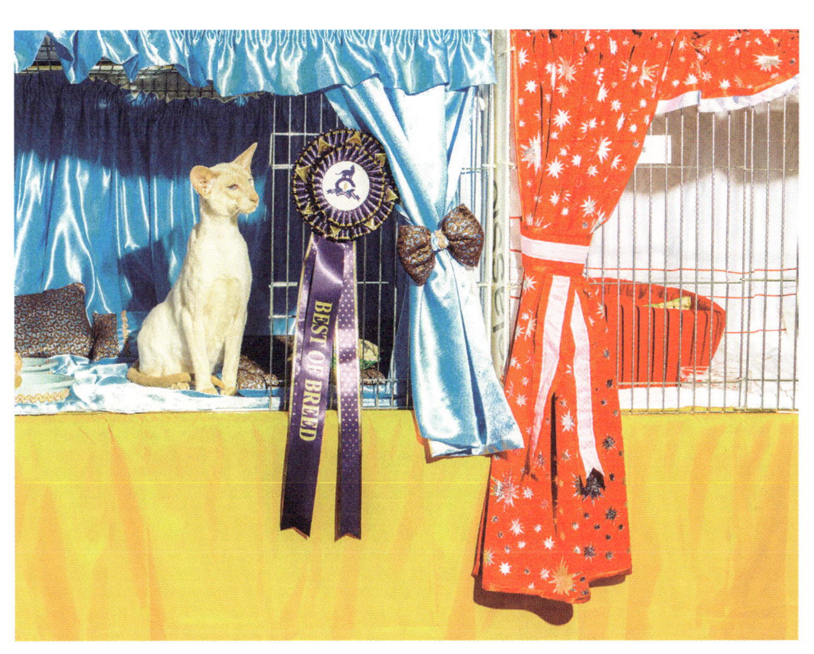

Above: *Supreme Cat Show. Best of Breed winner sits resolutely beside its ribbon*, 2019
Overleaf: *Supreme Cat Show. A long cat nap after a hard day's work*, 2019

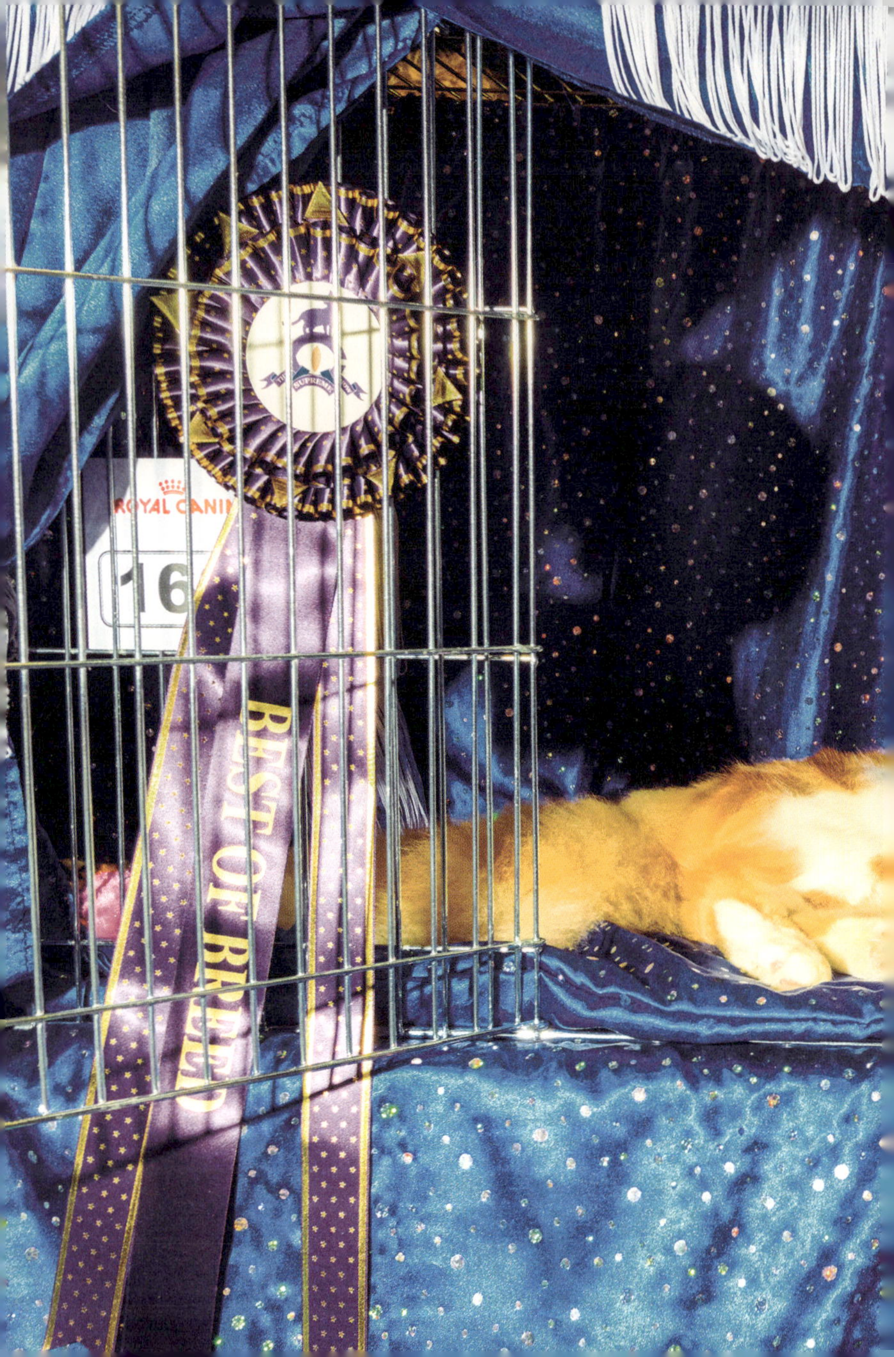

ROYAL CANIN
16
SUPREME
BEST OF BREED

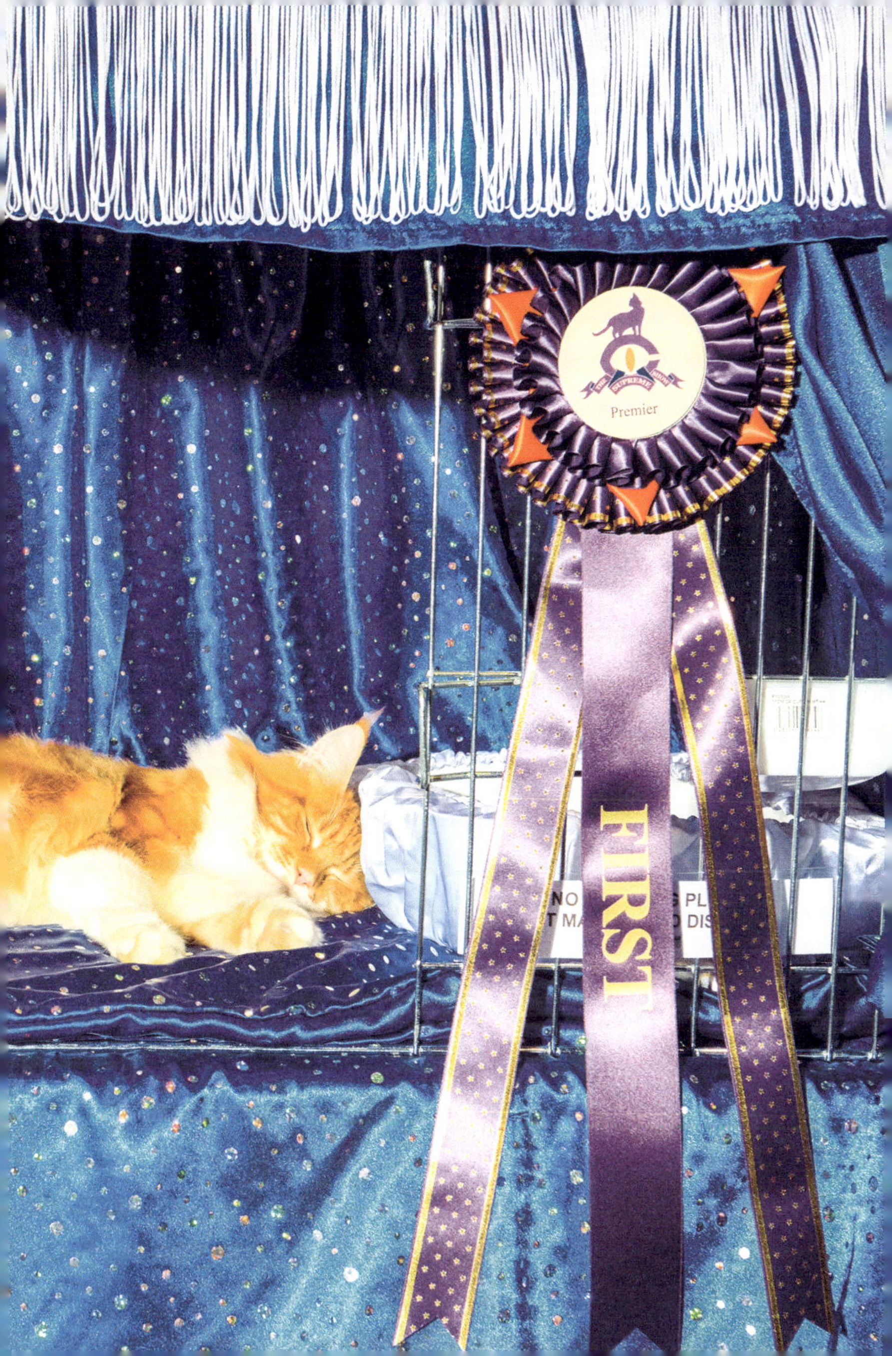
THE SUPREME SHOW
Premier
FIRST

BACKYARD DIARIES
Nikita Teryoshin

While attending a defence trade fair in St. Petersburg for a series of photographs documenting the 'back office' of war, Nikita Teryoshin noticed a group of alley cats sleeping on a car in his friend's backyard. A welcome distraction from 'guys in grey suits selling weapons', the cats offered an 'immediate warm connection' and so he set about photographing their hidden world.

Since then, he has sought out street cats in Atlantic City, Istanbul, New Delhi and Bangkok. Teryoshin likes to crouch down and capture them at eye-level, applying the techniques he learned as a high-end fashion and advertising photographer (stark flash, saturated colours and so on) to isolate the cats from their gritty, grey environment, and to give their daily struggle a strong sense of the real. 'Their appearance often speaks of a tough life. They seem very human to me.'

Untitled, 2019

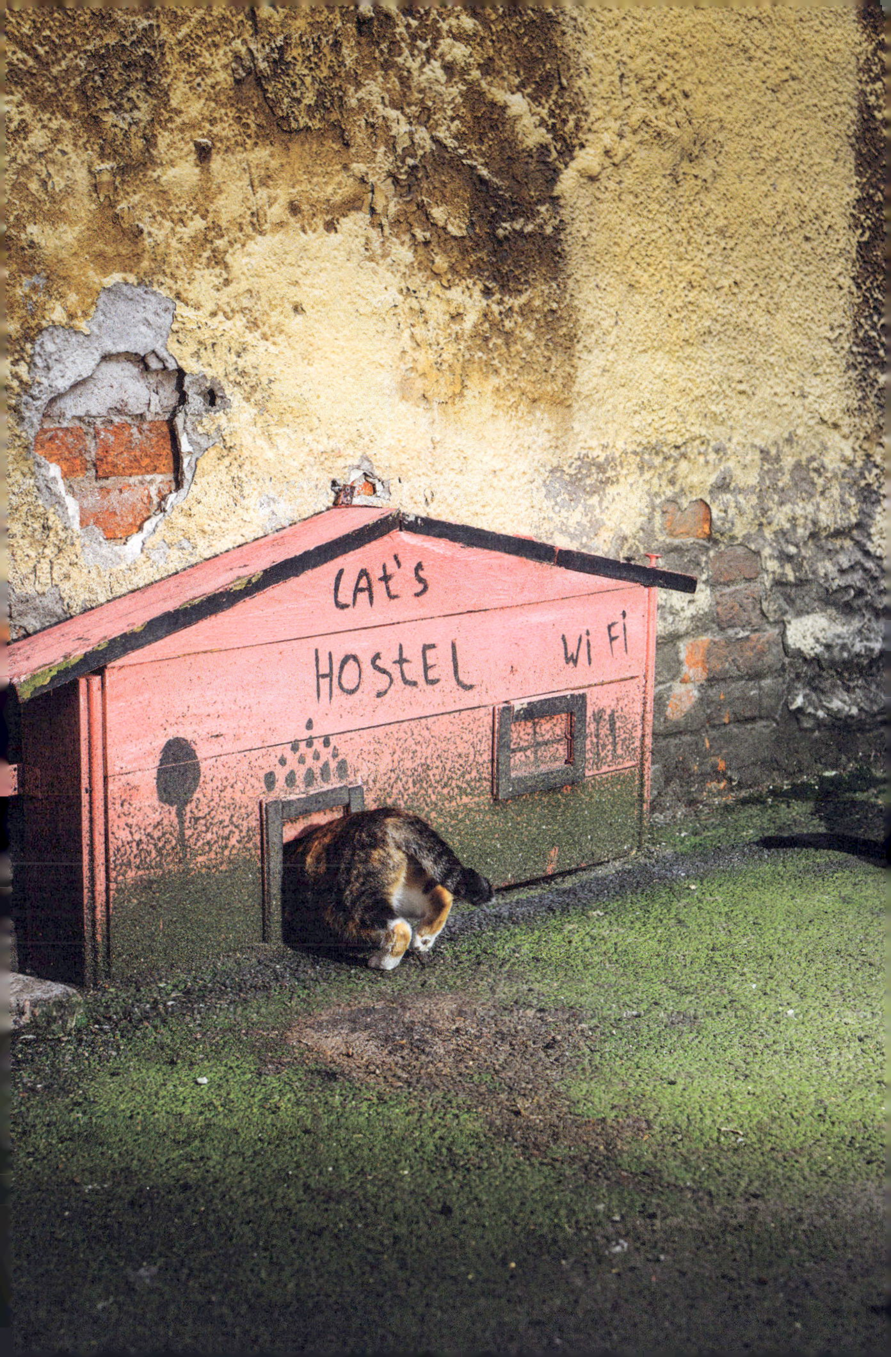
CAt's
HOStEL
wi Fi

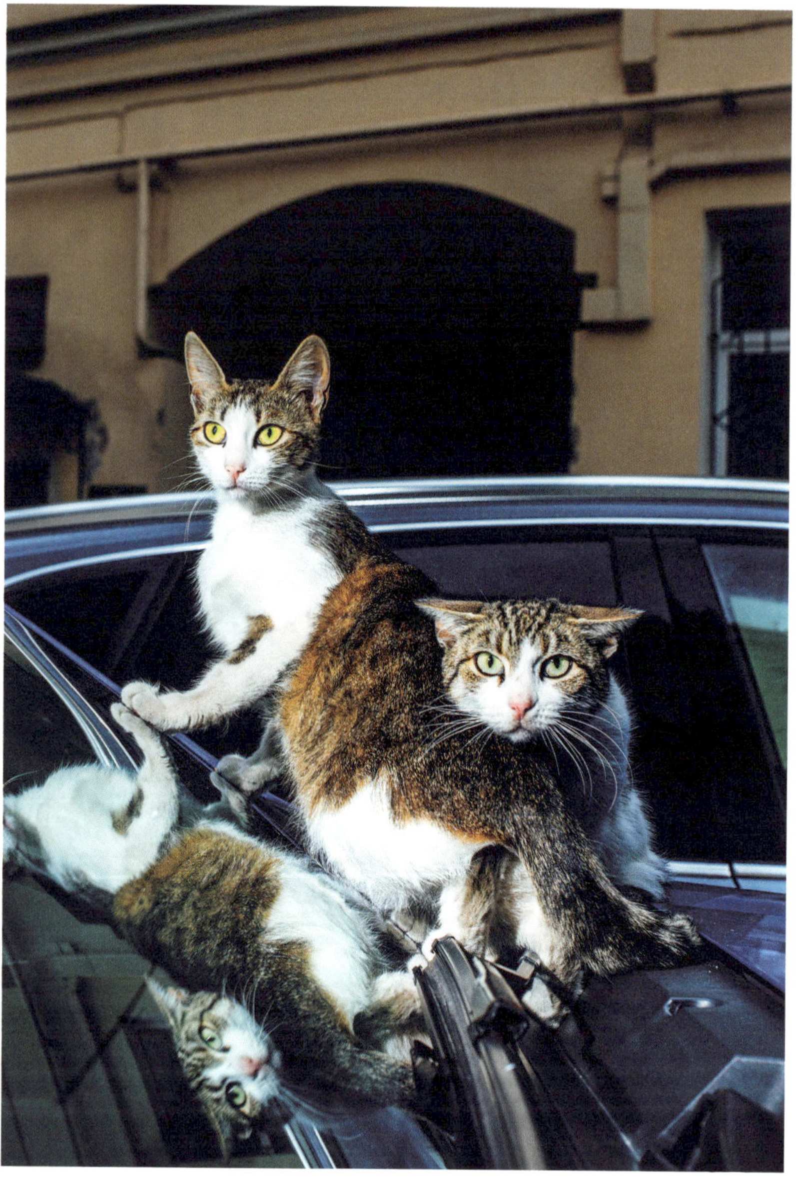

Untitled, 2019

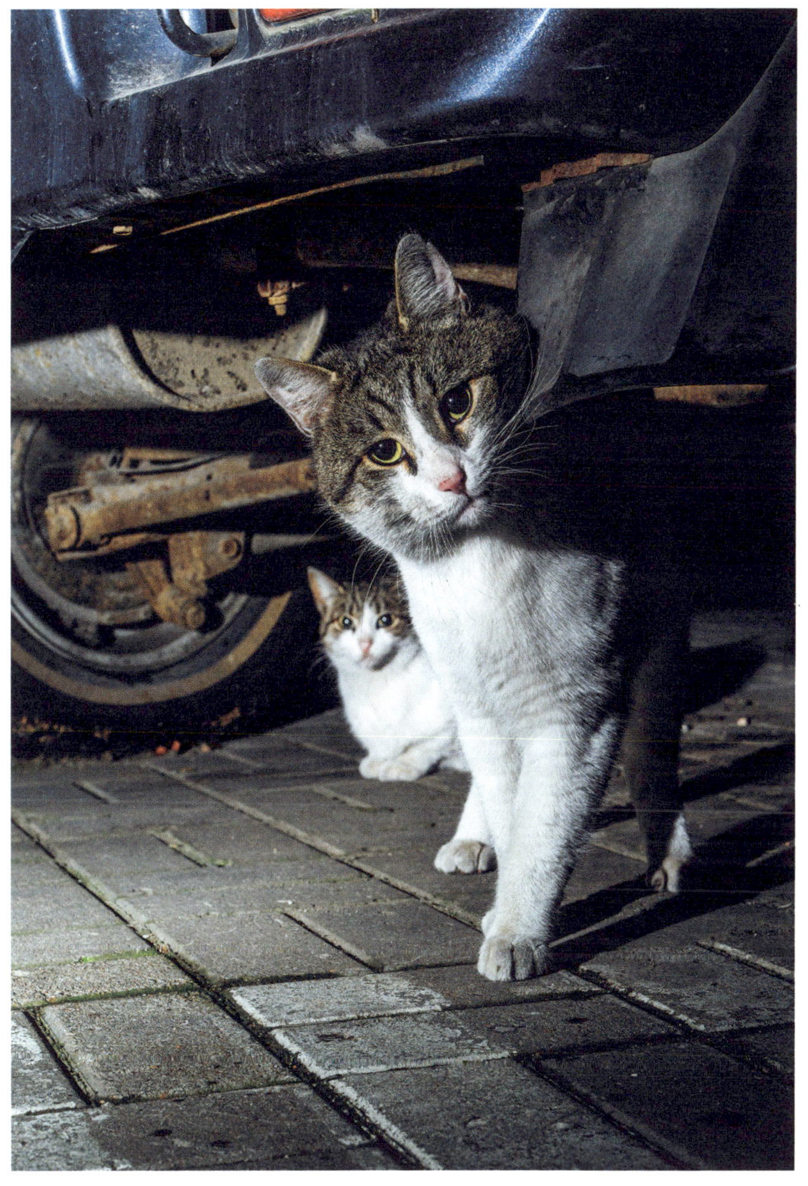

Untitled, 2019

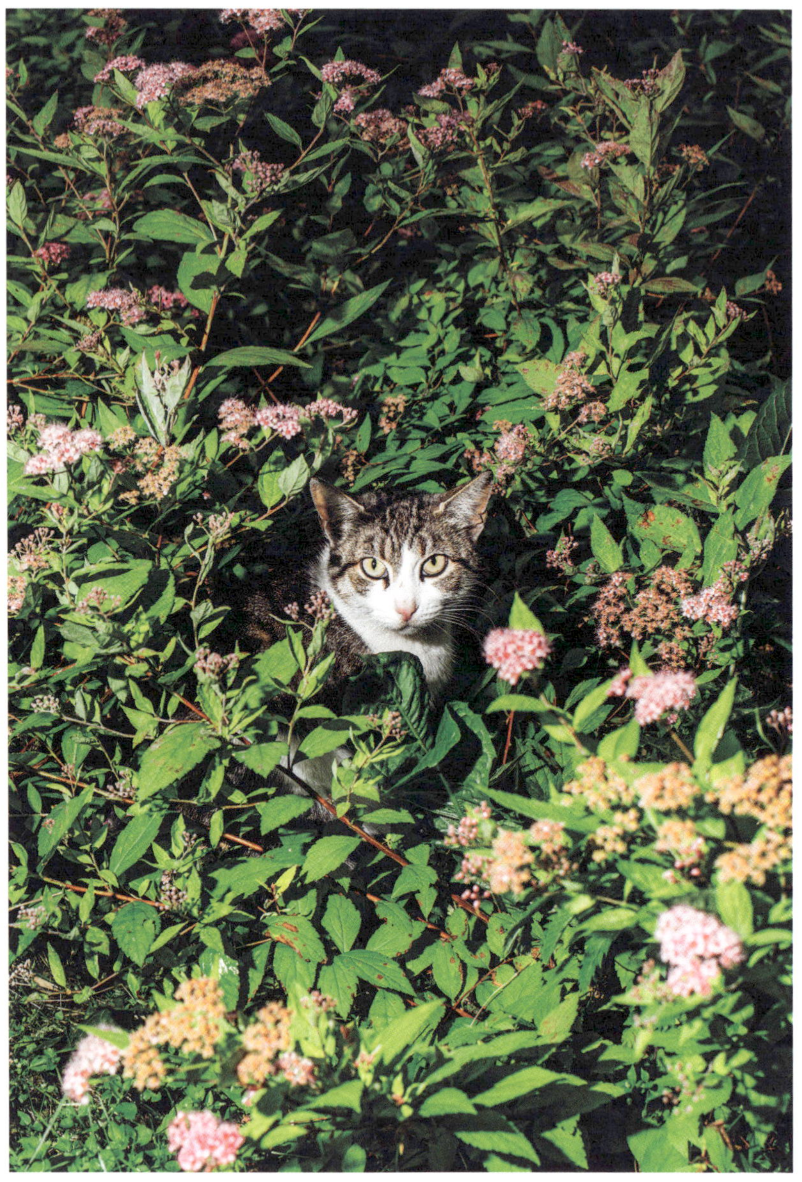

Untitled, 2019

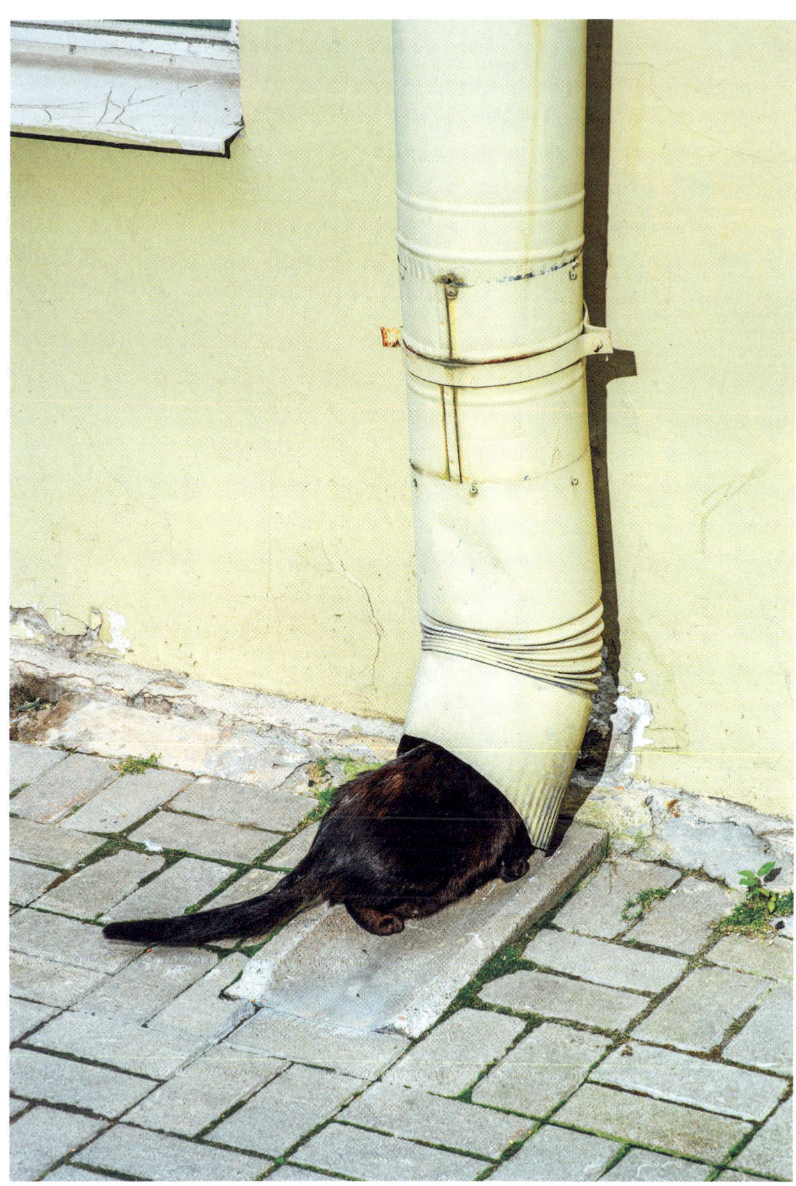

Above: *Untitled*, 2019
Overleaf: *Untitled*, 2019

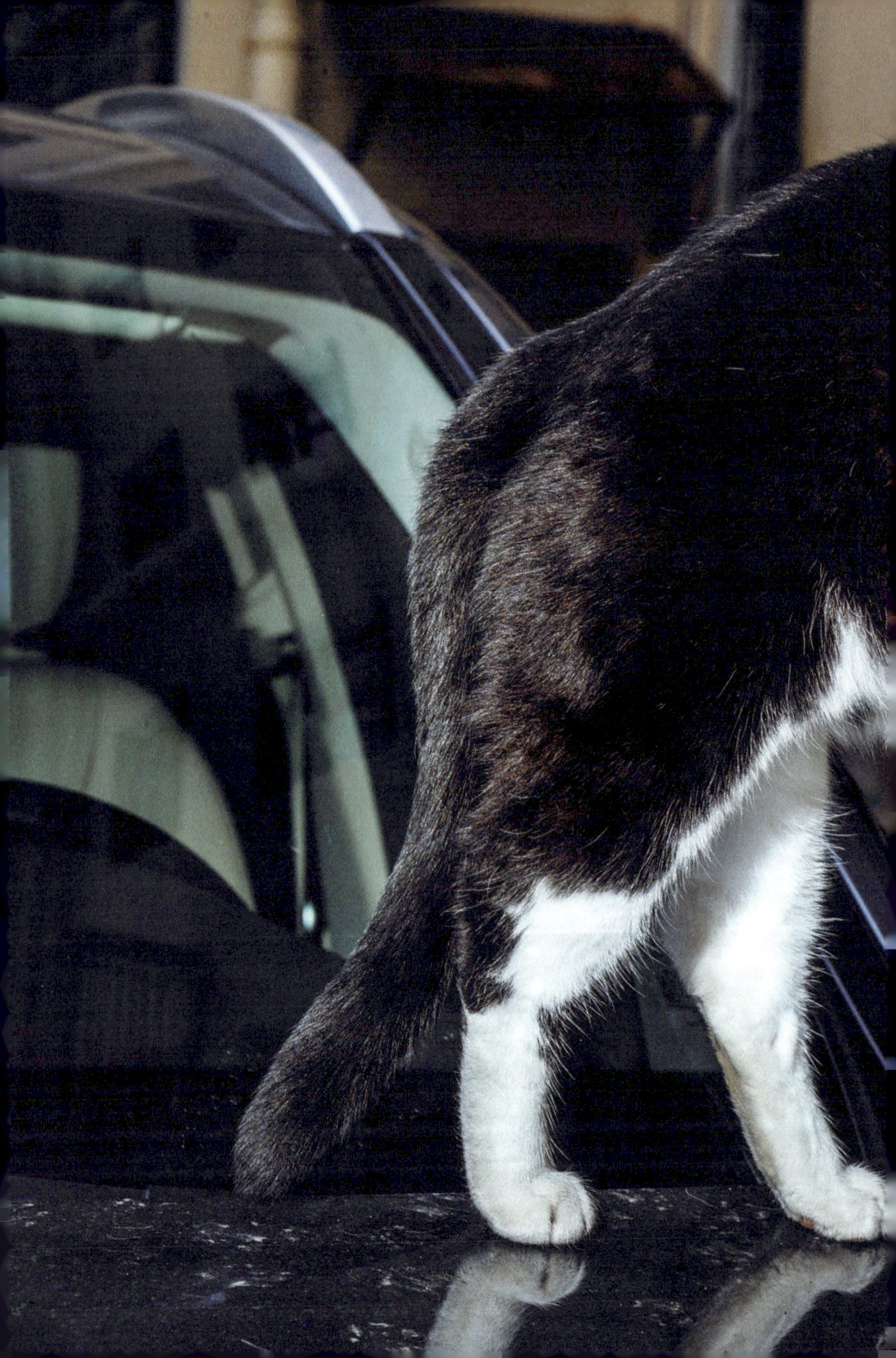

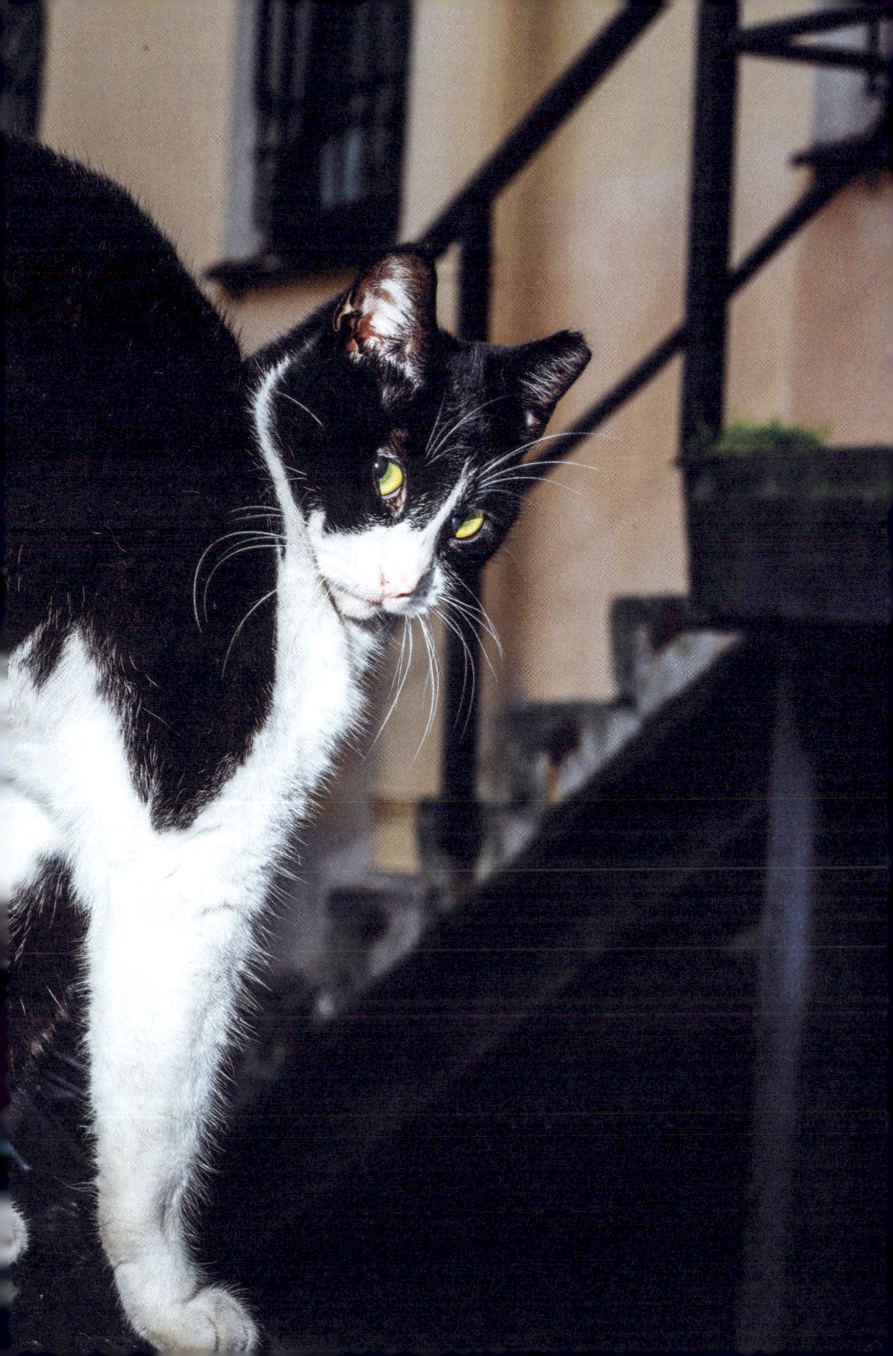

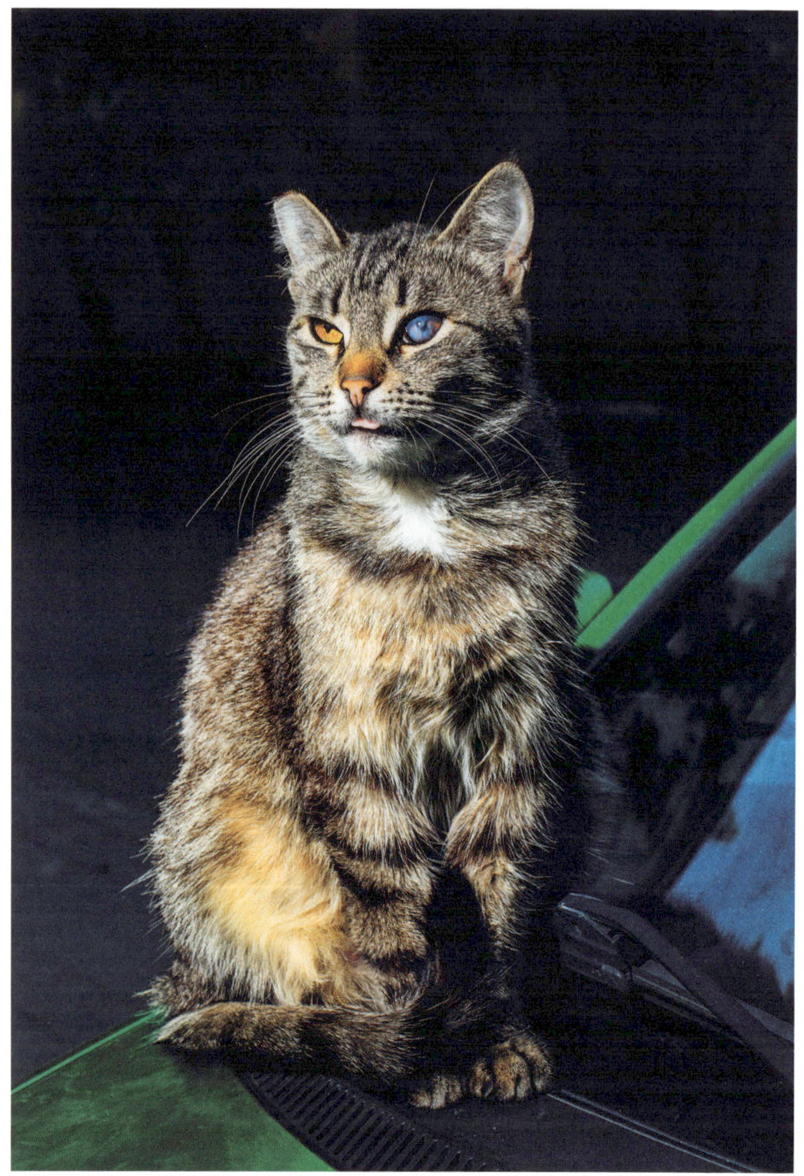

Untitled, 2019

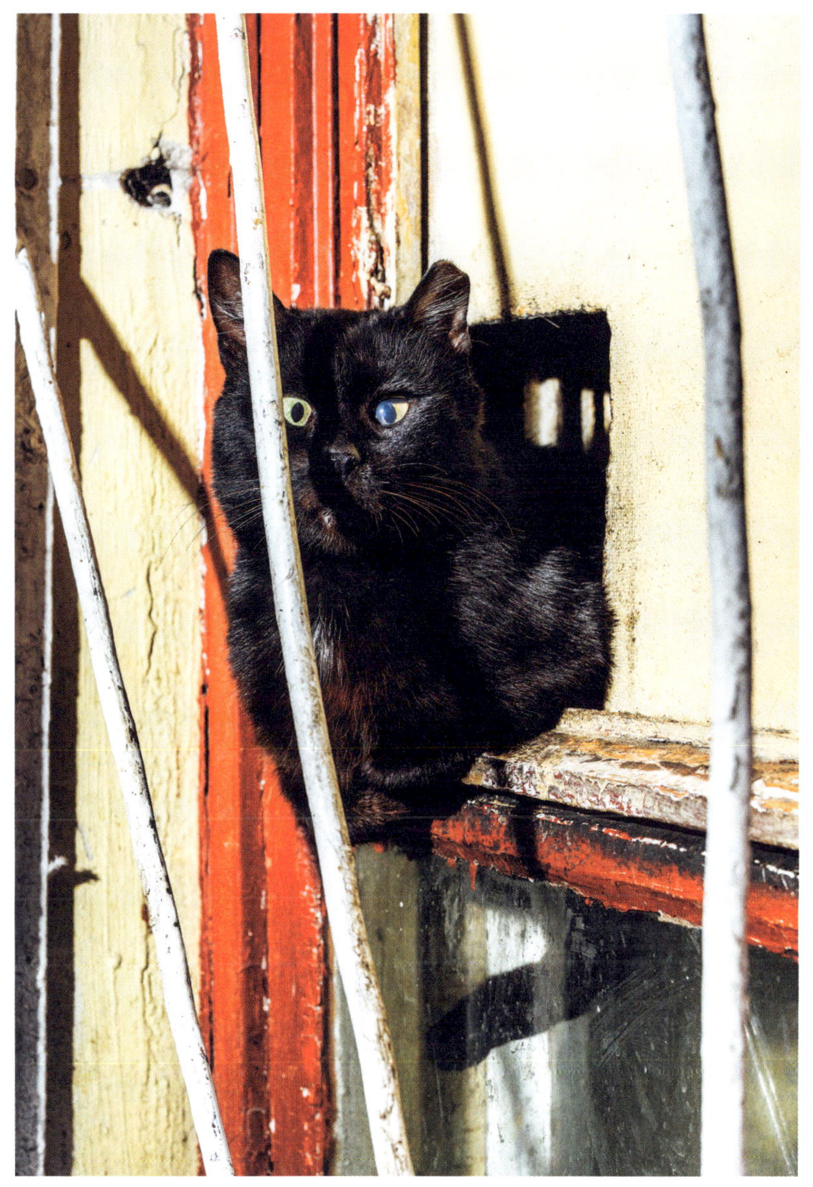

Untitled, 2019

CATS & PLANTS
Stephen Eichhorn

What do cats and houseplants have in common? What makes a Siamese and a succulent such a perfect pairing? According to collage artist Stephen Eichhorn, the odd way in which both are photographed.

He made the connection around 2008, while combing his bookshelves for new source material. In titles from the 1980s and 1990s, he found photos of cats that were set up like traditional still lifes, which reminded him of pictures he had previously cut from a stash of houseplant books. The moment he combined the two, he knew he had struck surreal gold. The unions are led by the expression or the pose of the cat. Eichhorn works the old-fashioned way, using a craft knife and glue. In scoring, slicing and recombining them, the images step outside their former humdrum roles and become something more witty and more vital.

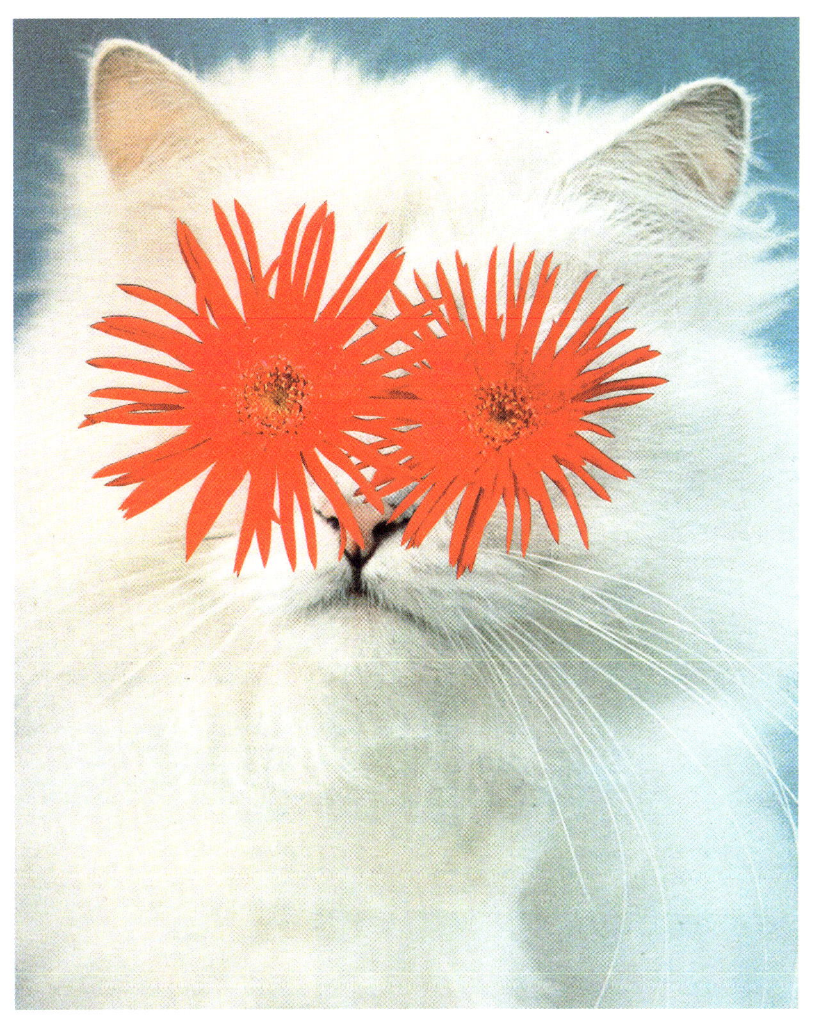

Red Eyes, 2010

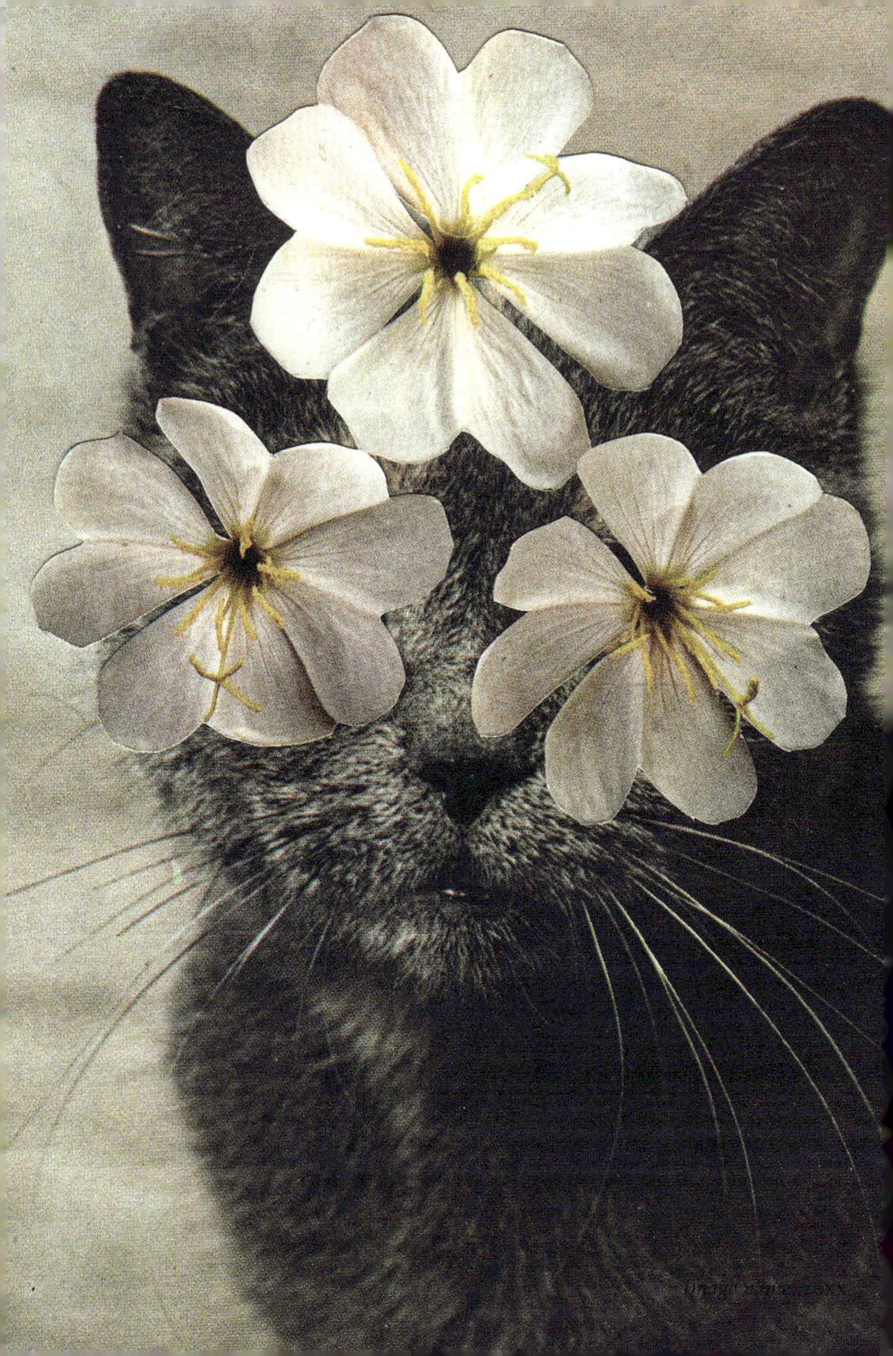

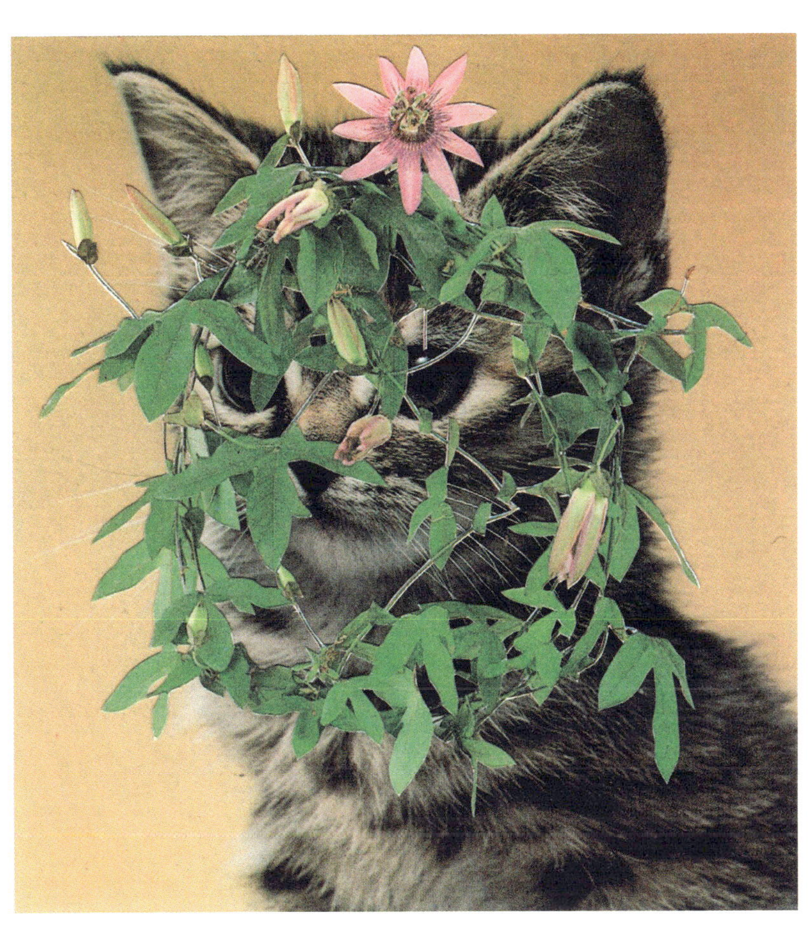

Above: *Purple Flower*, 2011
Opposite: *Three*, 2010

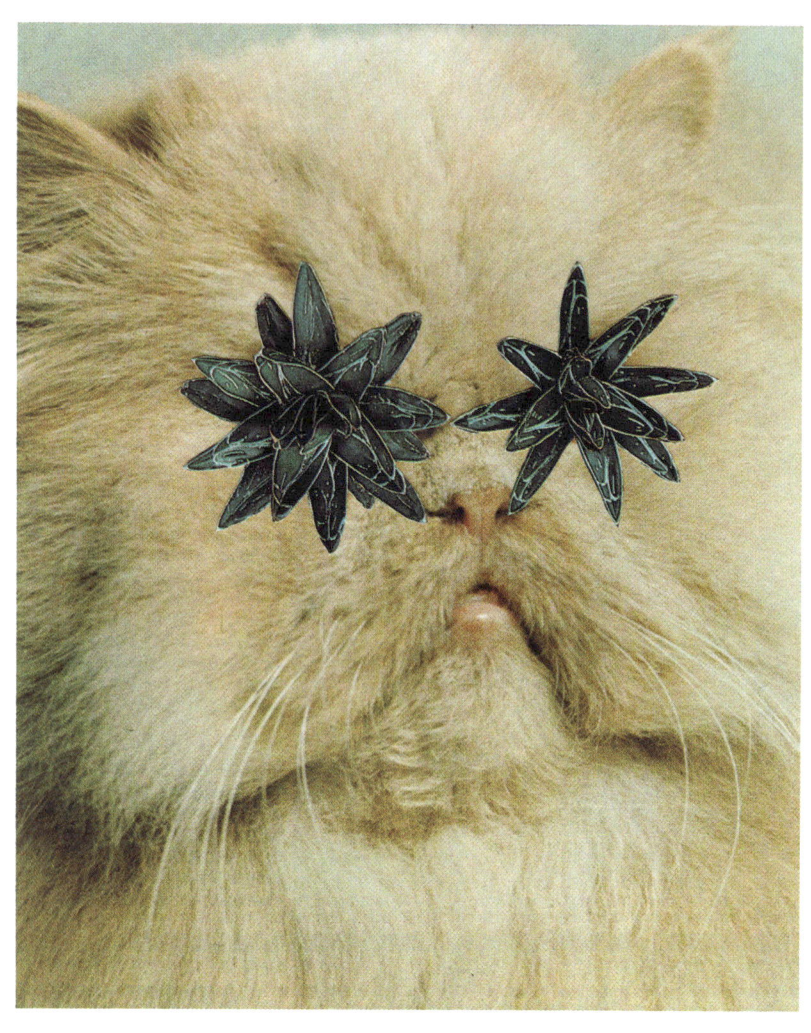

Above: *Green Eyes*, 2011
Opposite: *Horns*, 2011

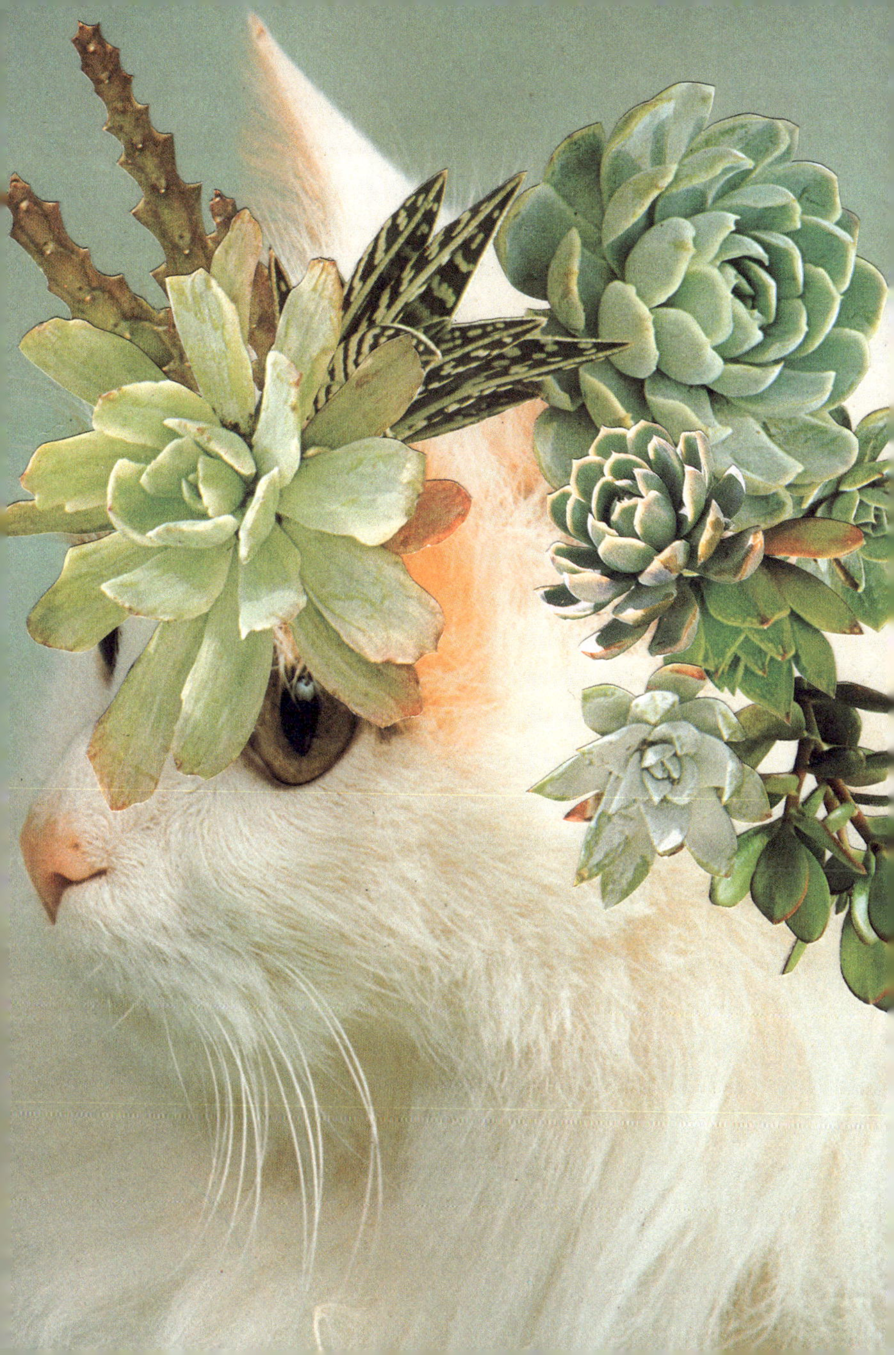

FOR CATS ONLY
Pascale Weber

They come in mid-century modern or minimalist, with caves or hammocks, made from sisal, natural wood or corrugated cardboard, in the style of a castle or an ice-cream van. This is the world of cat trees – one which, once entered, is not easily forgotten.

Pascale Weber travelled the length and breadth of her native Switzerland to find four-footed models willing to be photographed, *Cribs*-style, reclining in their opulent 'homes'. Some were territorial, others real show-offs and a few sweetly camera-shy.

To best present the structural qualities of each domicile, Weber – who earns her living as an advertising still-life photographer – carried a mobile studio in her car with a range of vividly coloured backdrops. Her scrupulous attention to presentation transforms each one into an object of extraordinary design. Look at them long enough, and you find yourself asking: which one would *you* live in?

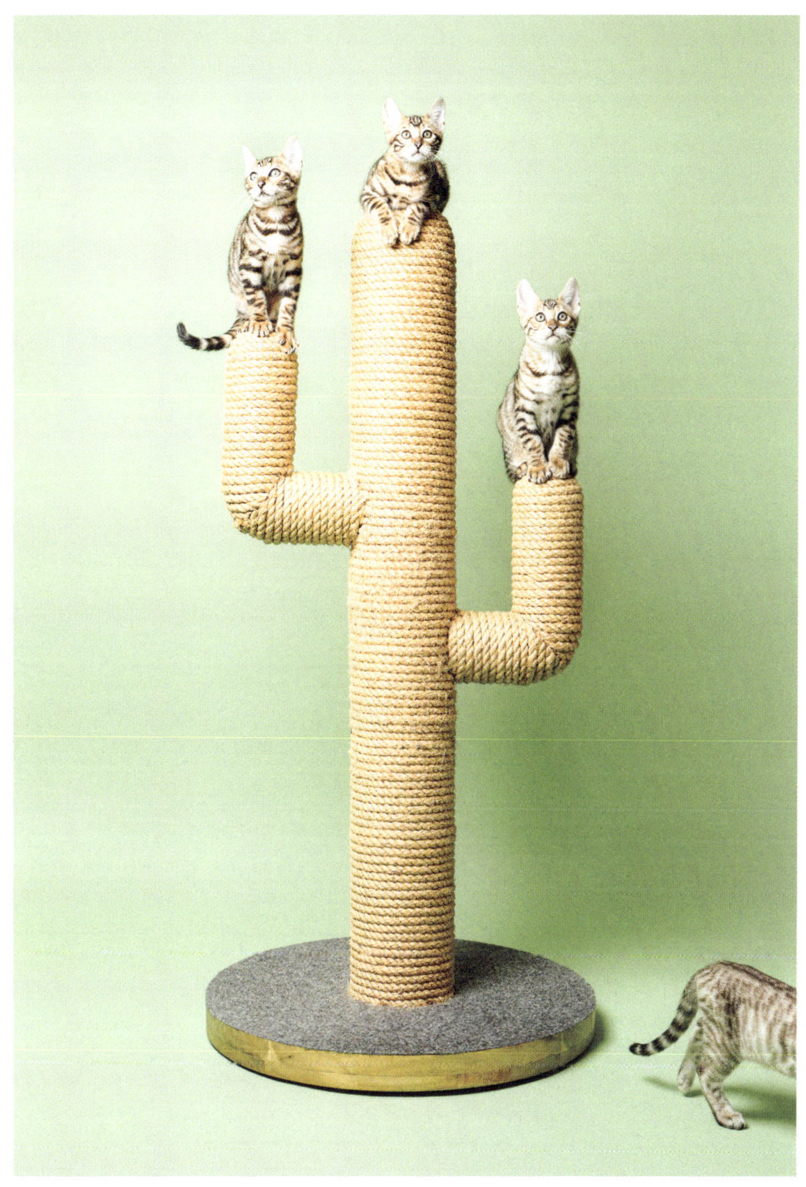

For Cats Only, 2021

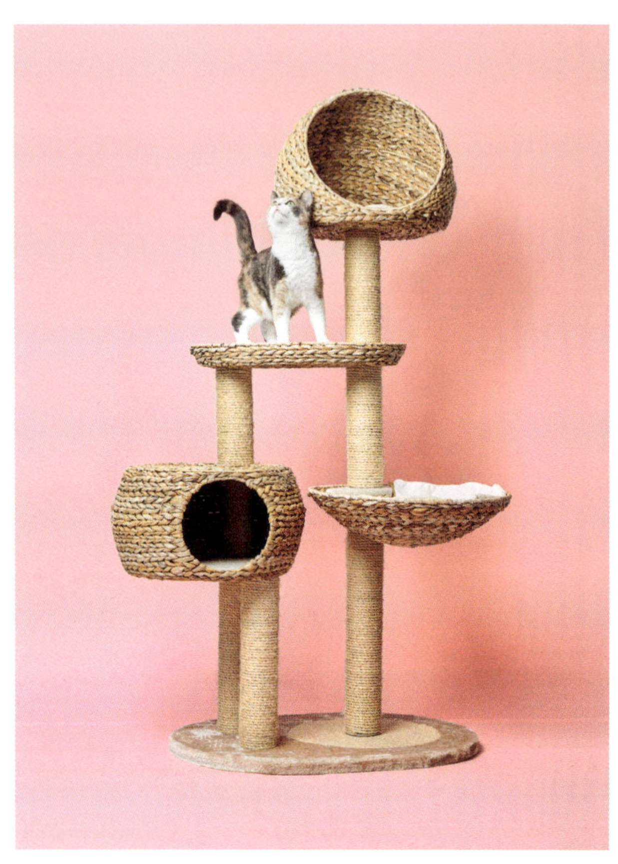

For Cats Only, 2021

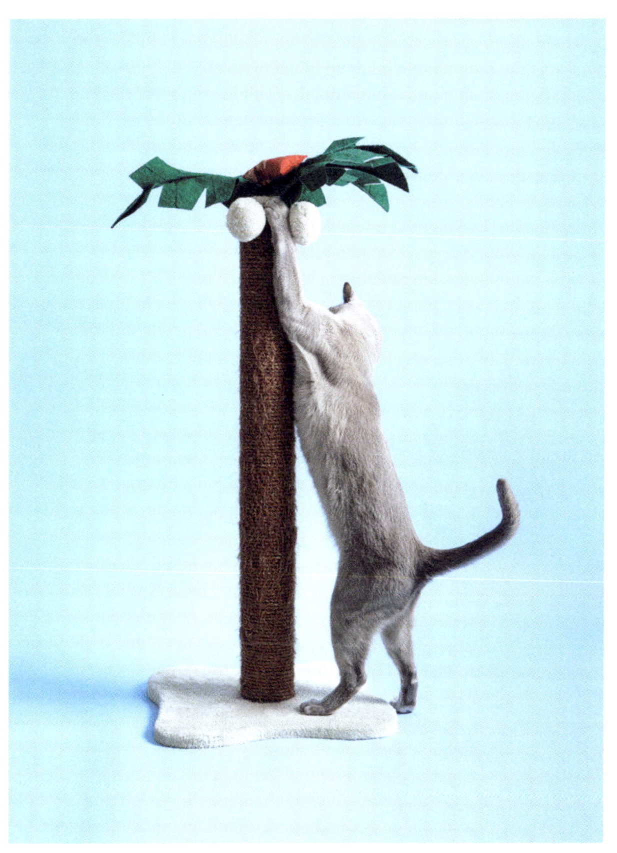

For Cats Only, 2021

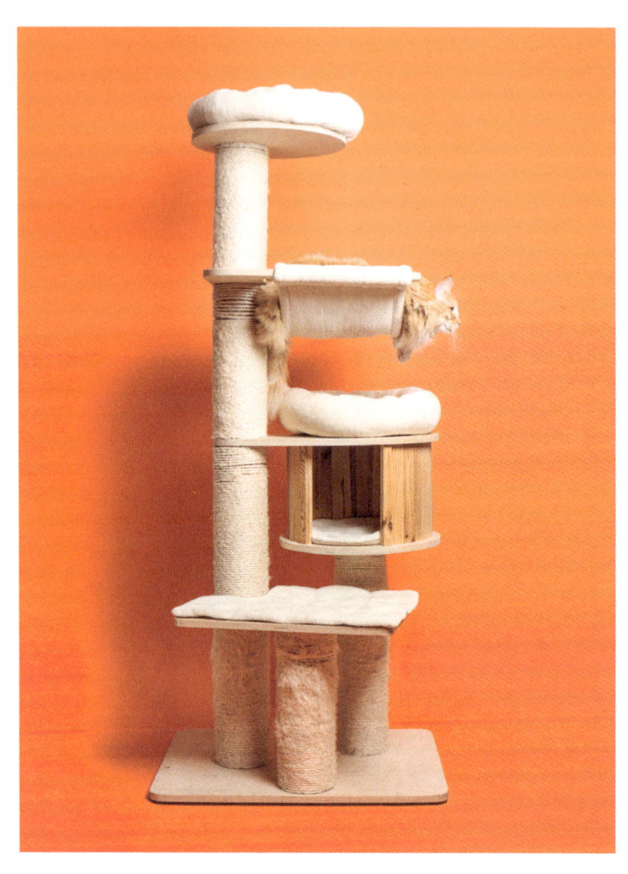

For Cats Only, 2021

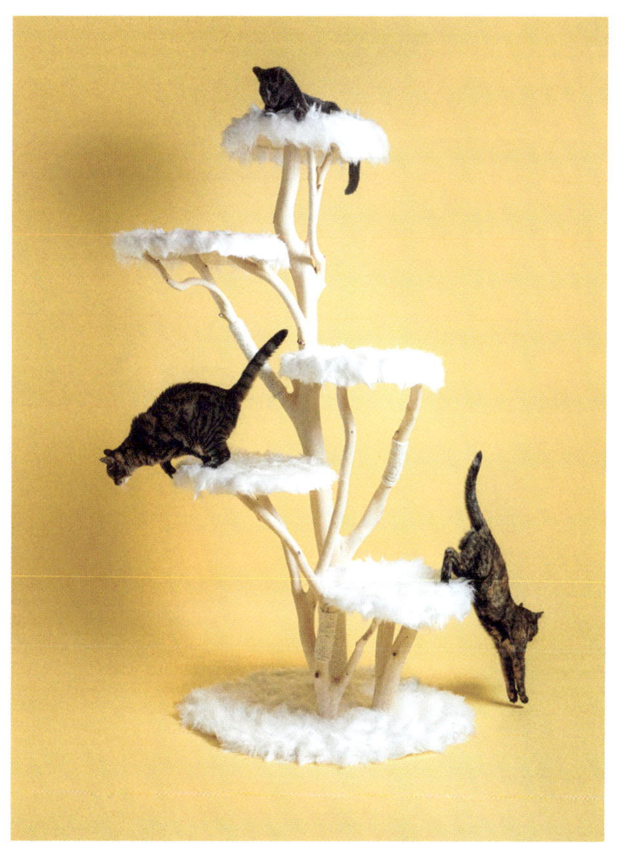

For Cats Only, 2021

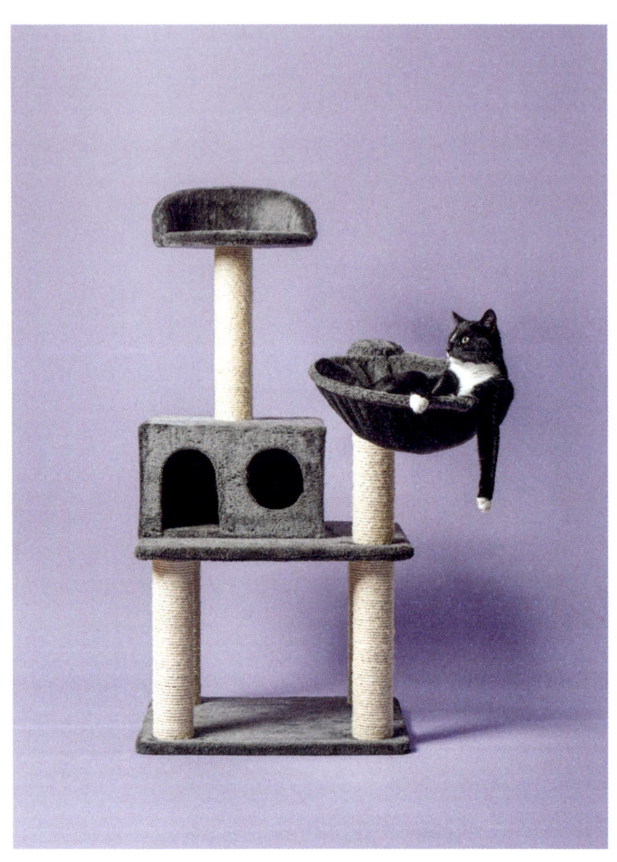

For Cats Only, 2021

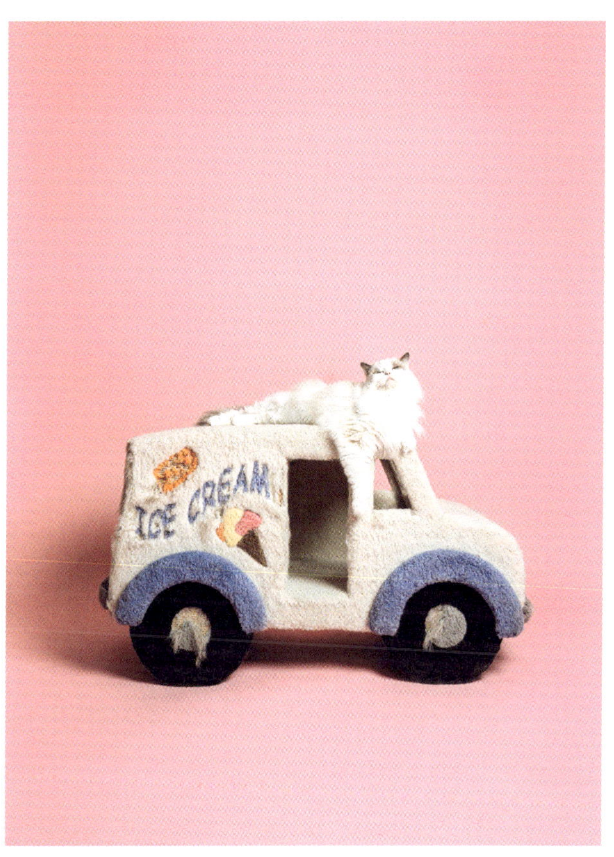
ICE CREAM

CATS IN HATS
Rojiman & Umatan Yamazaki

Fed up with removing shed cat fur from her furniture, Umatan Yamazaki one day placed a clump of fur – collected while brushing her Scottish Fold cat – back onto the animal's head, sculpting it into a quiff. Her husband Rojiman's photo was so popular when published online that the couple embarked on a fully-fledged feline fashion operation.

A decade on, they have hundreds of designs in their portfolio, from Princess Leia buns and wizard domes, to elaborate samurai helmets, bunny ears and deerstalkers. Each hat takes about a bowlful of fur to create, but since the amount of shed fur is limited, Umatan sometimes dismantles old hats and reuses the material to make way for new models.

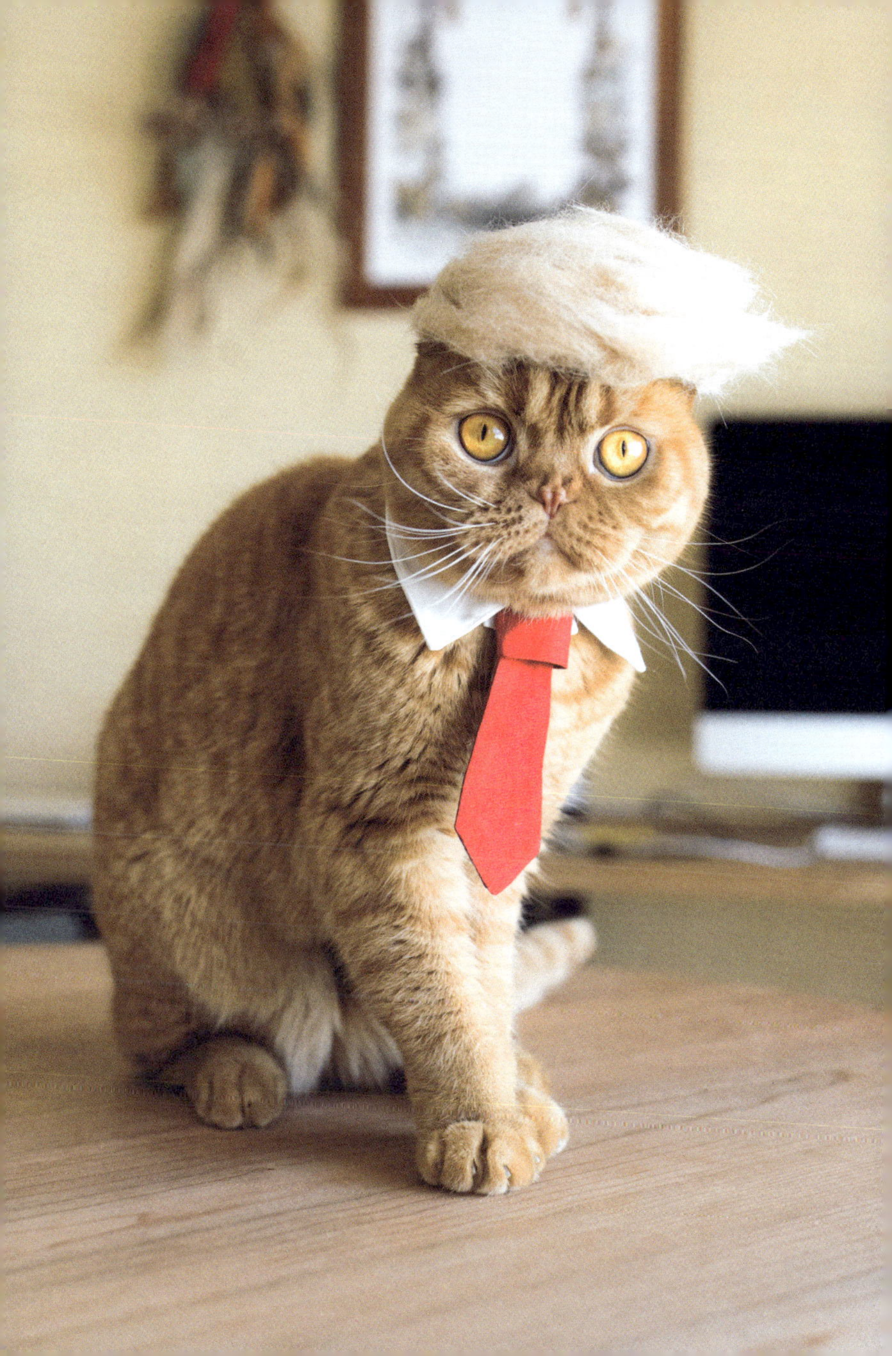

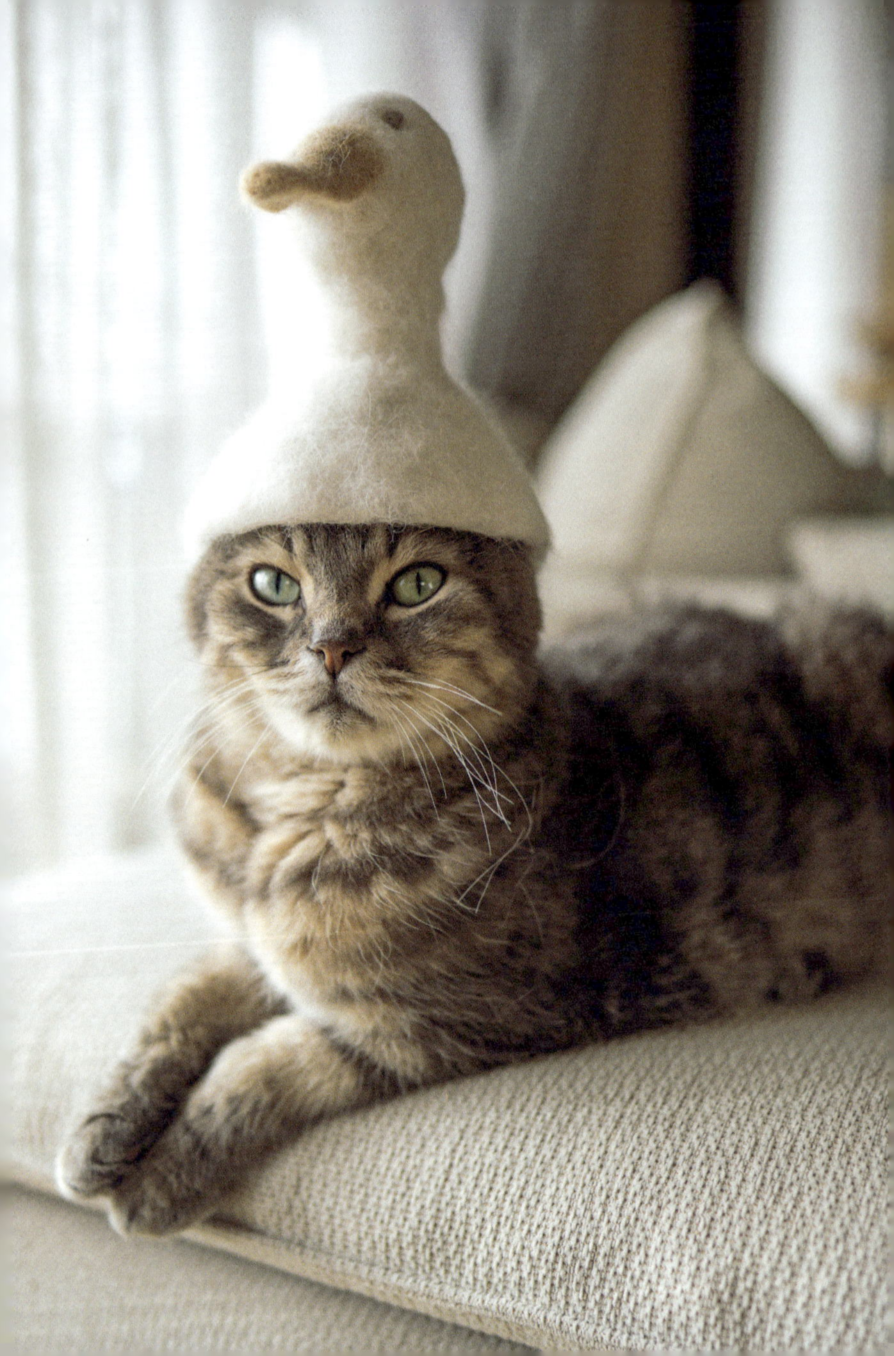

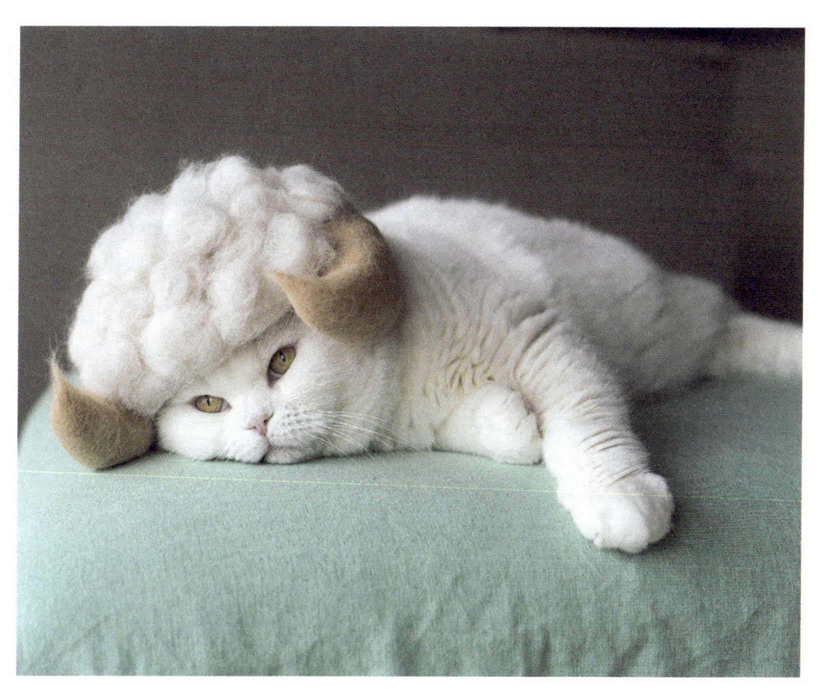

Above: *Sheep*, 2021
Opposite: *Duck*, 2019

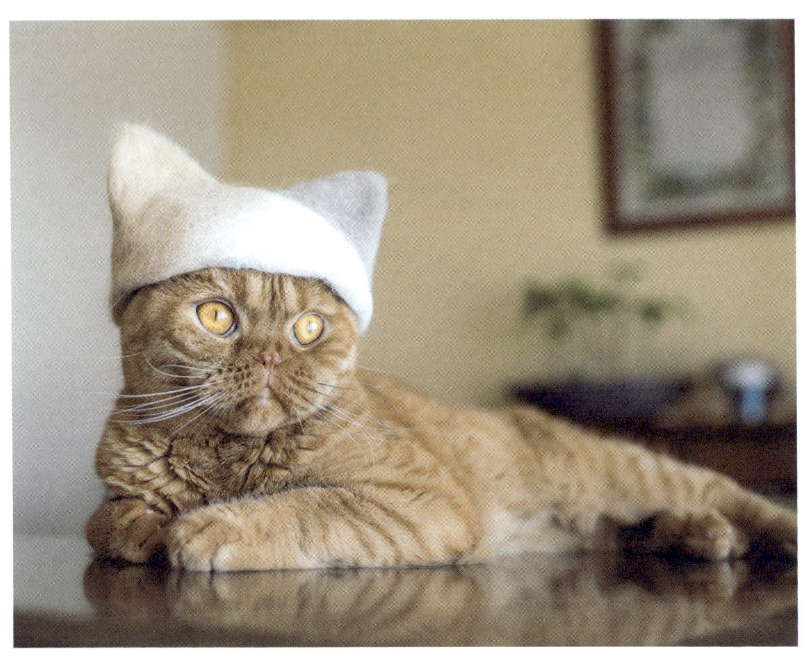

Above: *Calico Cat*, 2017
Opposite: *Amabie*, 2020

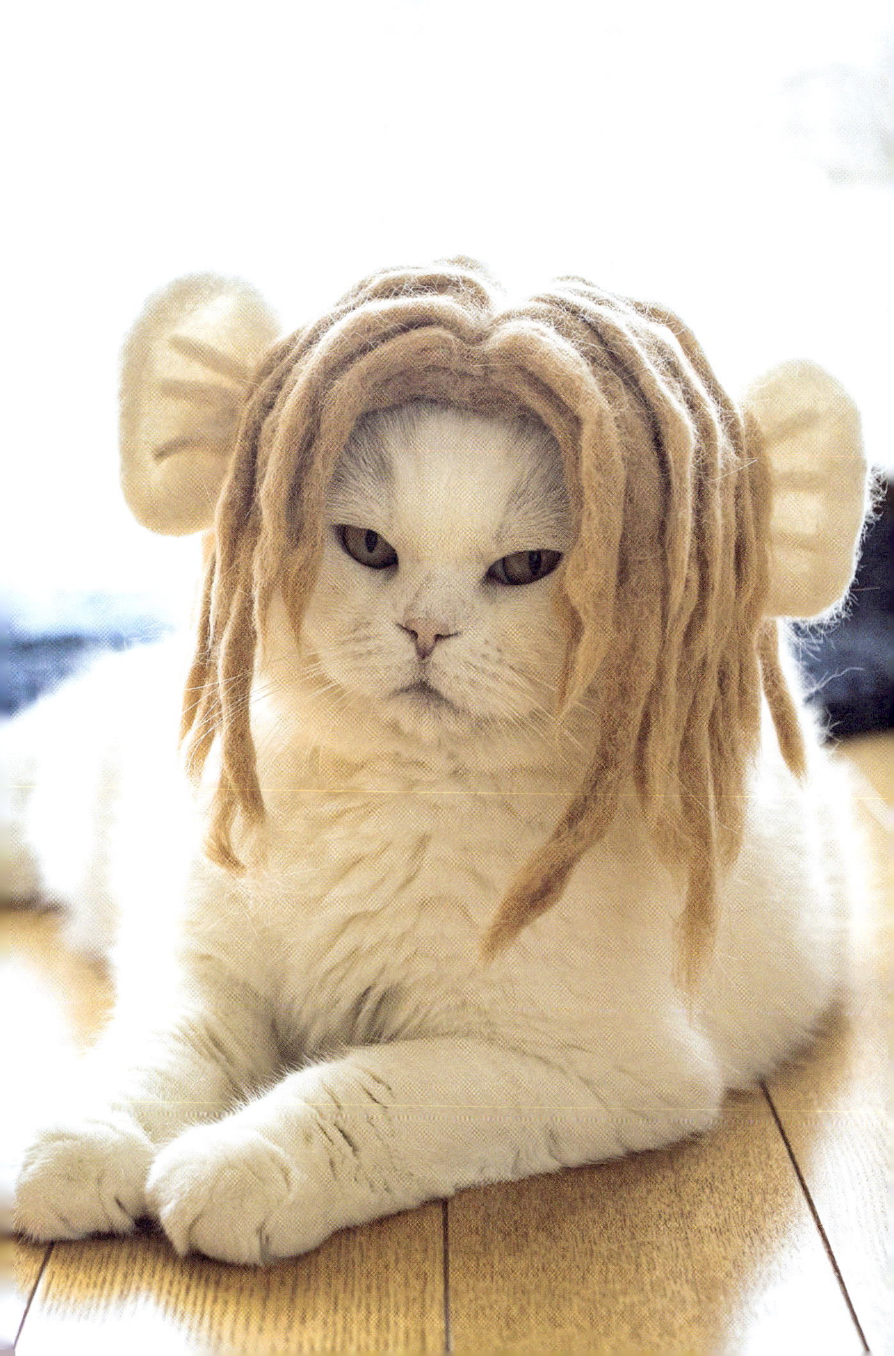

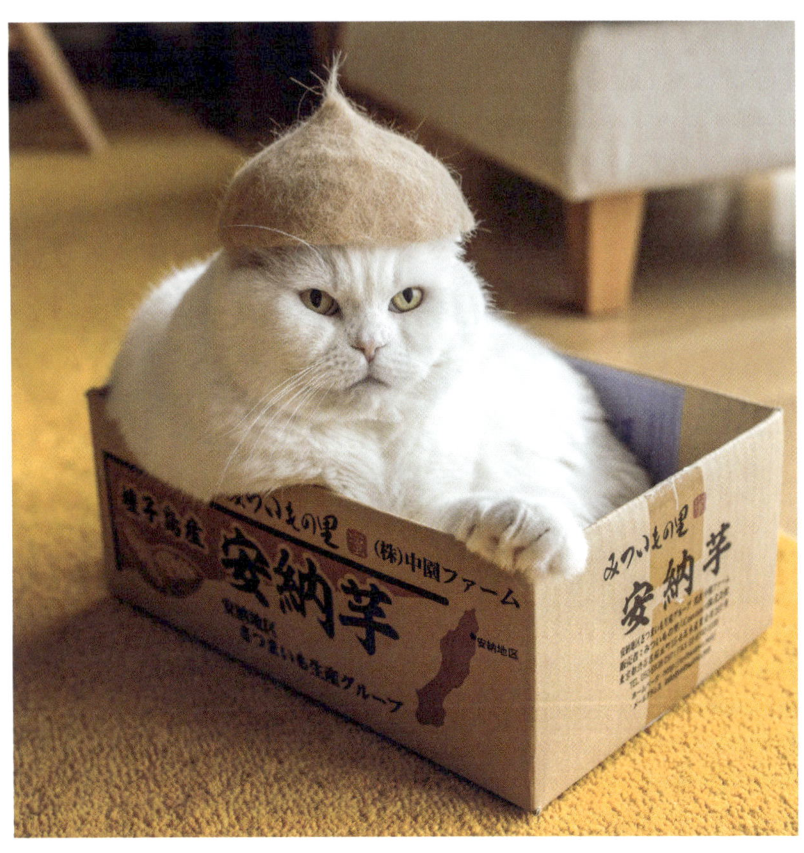

Acorn Hat, 2019

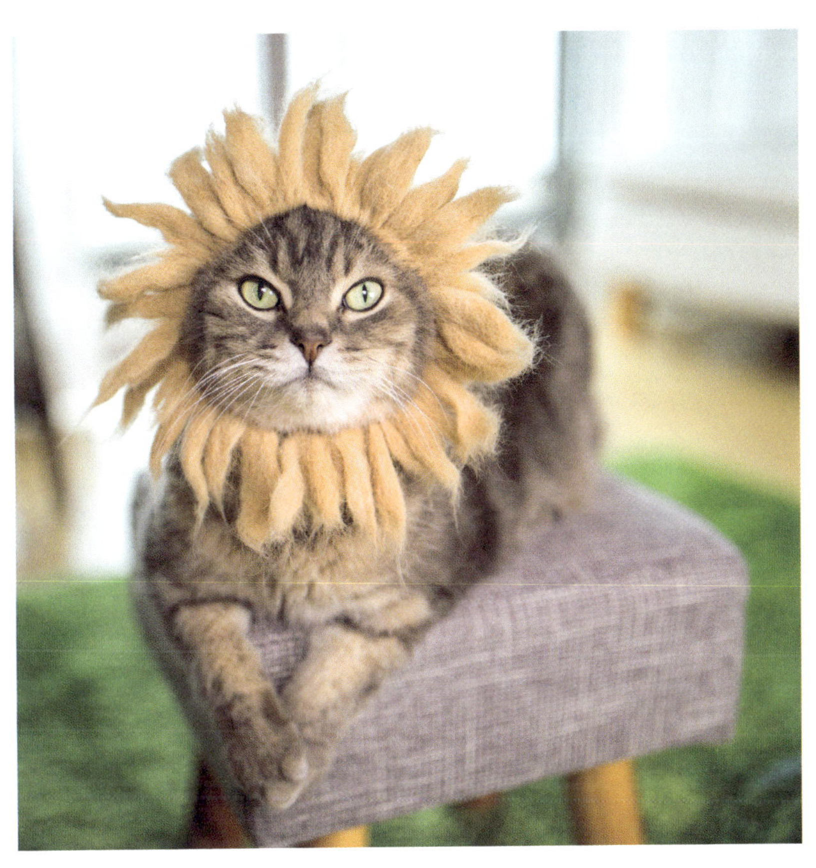

Above: *Lion*, 2019
Overleaf: *Lop-eared Bunny*, 2018

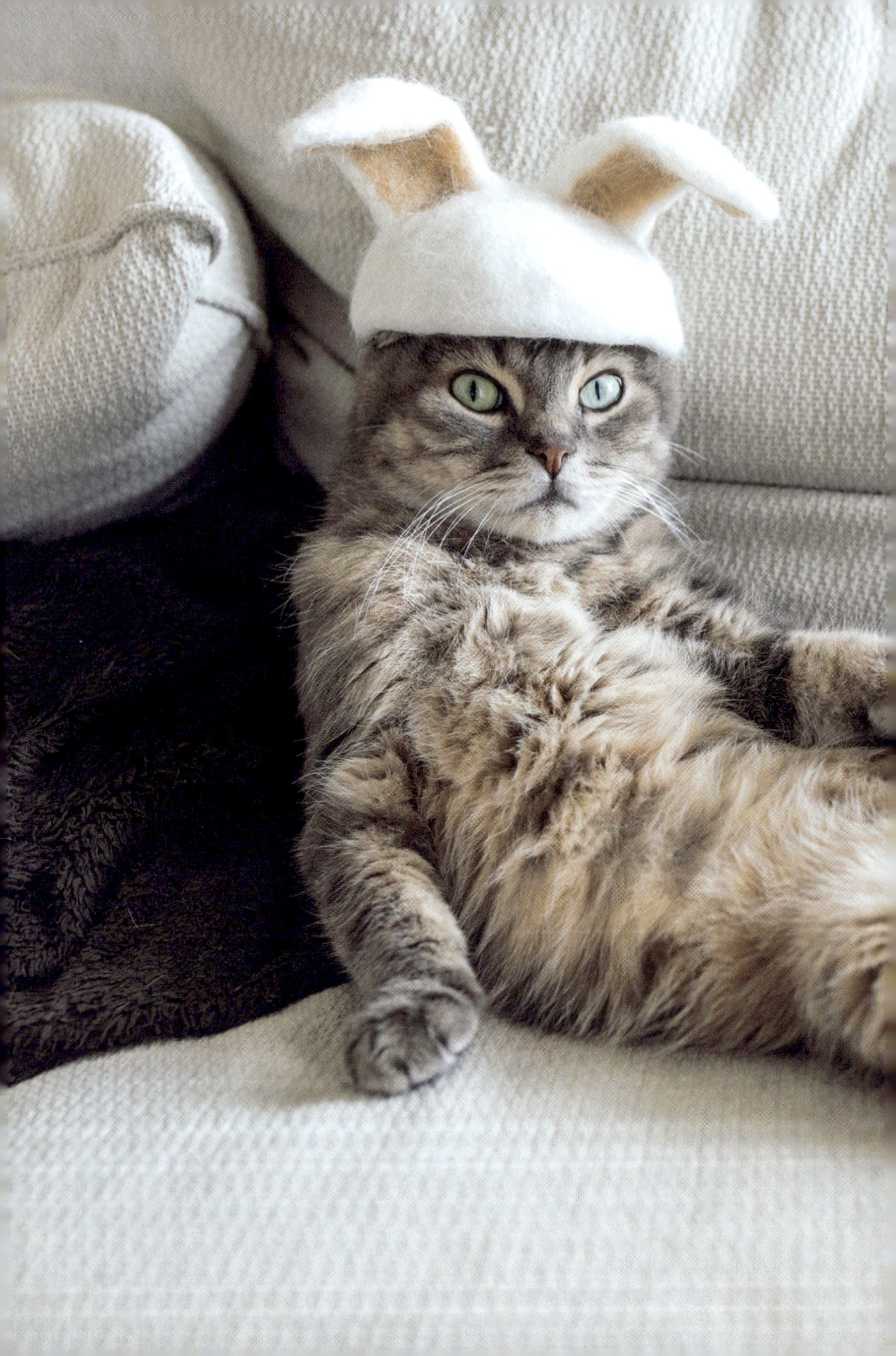

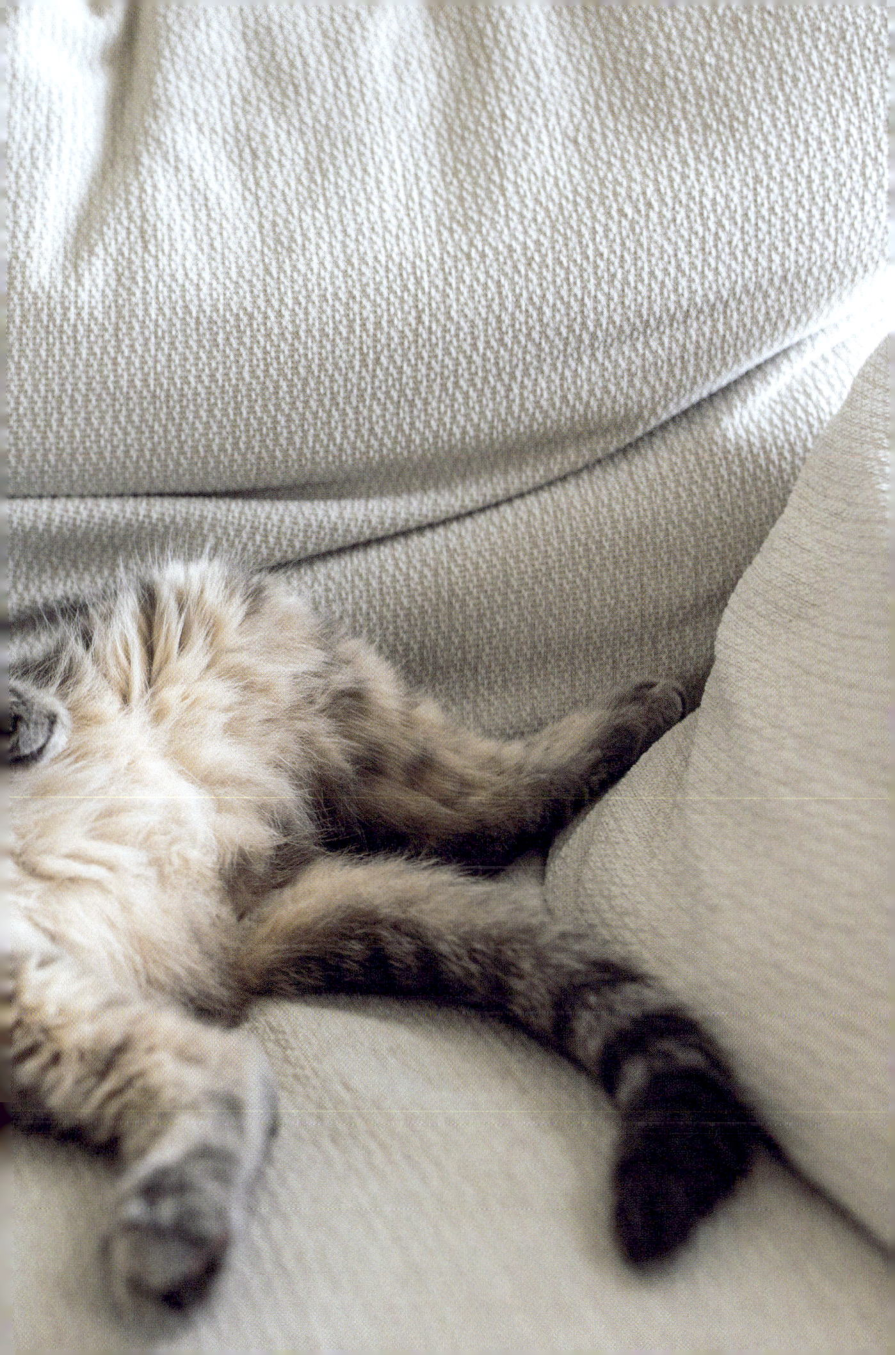

AMELIA & THE ANIMALS

Robin Schwartz

When her daughter Amelia was three, Robin Schwartz's mother and a beloved cat died within a year of each other. Taking pictures of Amelia with the family pets was initially a way to process her grief but turned quickly into a collaboration between mother and daughter that included dogs, llamas, tigers, monkeys and a whole lot more besides.

Robin Schwartz was born an animal person. As a child, she often dressed her cat in doll clothes and took pictures of him with her Kodak Instamatic. 'I considered him my brother,' she says. She and Amelia share a special affinity with the animal kingdom, and as Amelia matured, her input has enriched and expanded the project. The world they explore together is one 'where the line between human and animal overlaps or is blurred. Animals are not represented as beastly, noble or as props. Each is seen and experienced as an individual, part of our everyday world.'

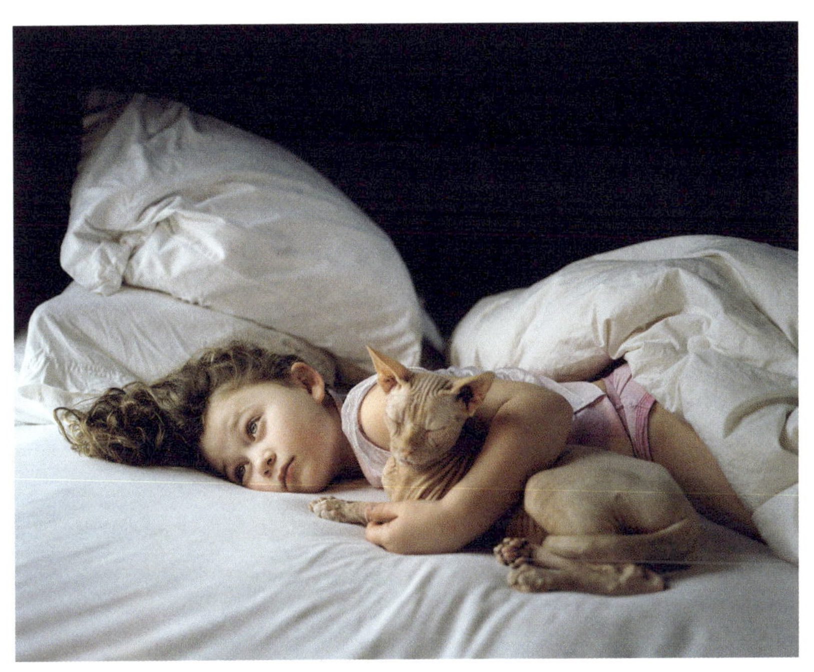

Tower, Amelia and Jacob, 2006

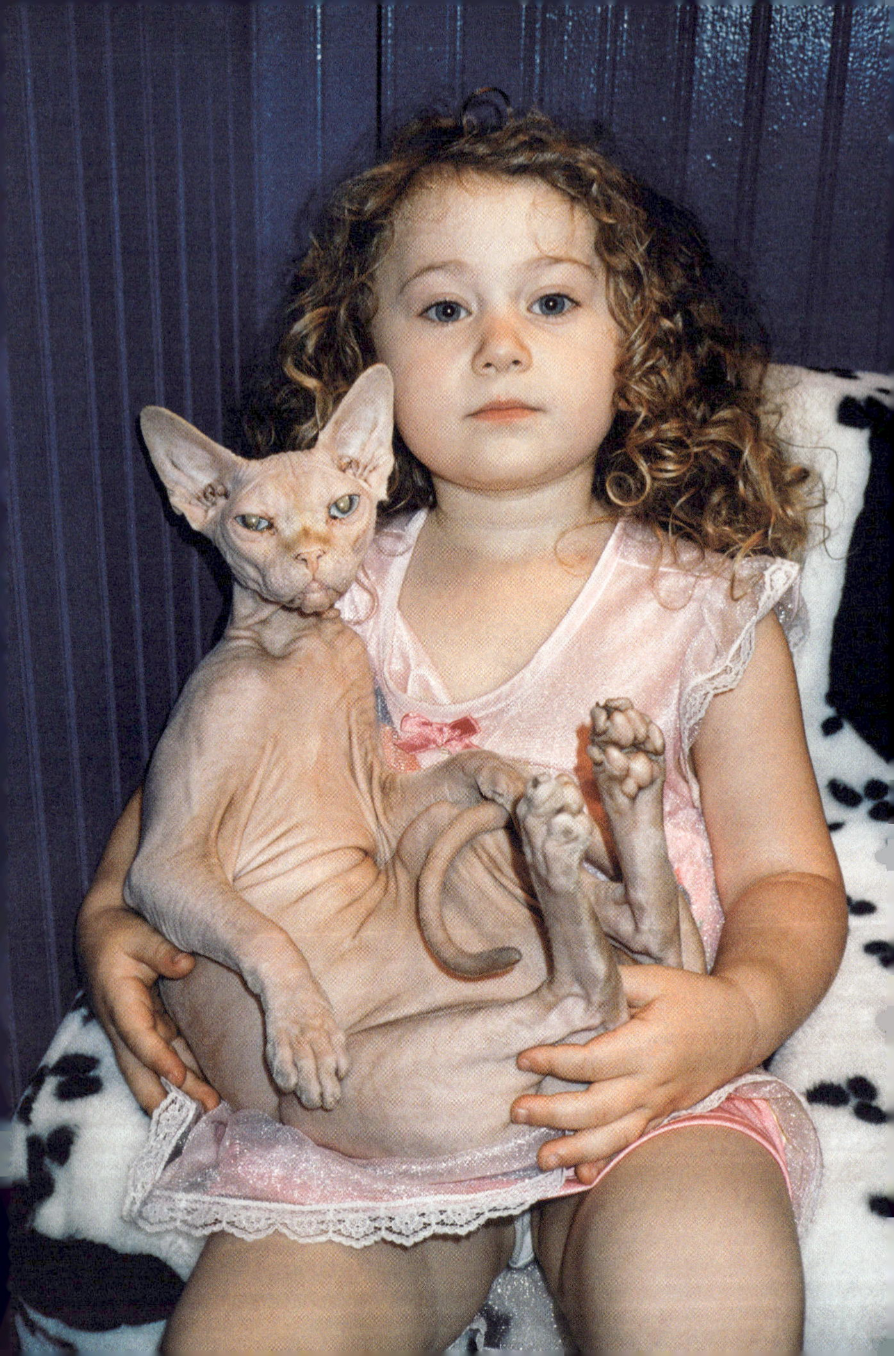

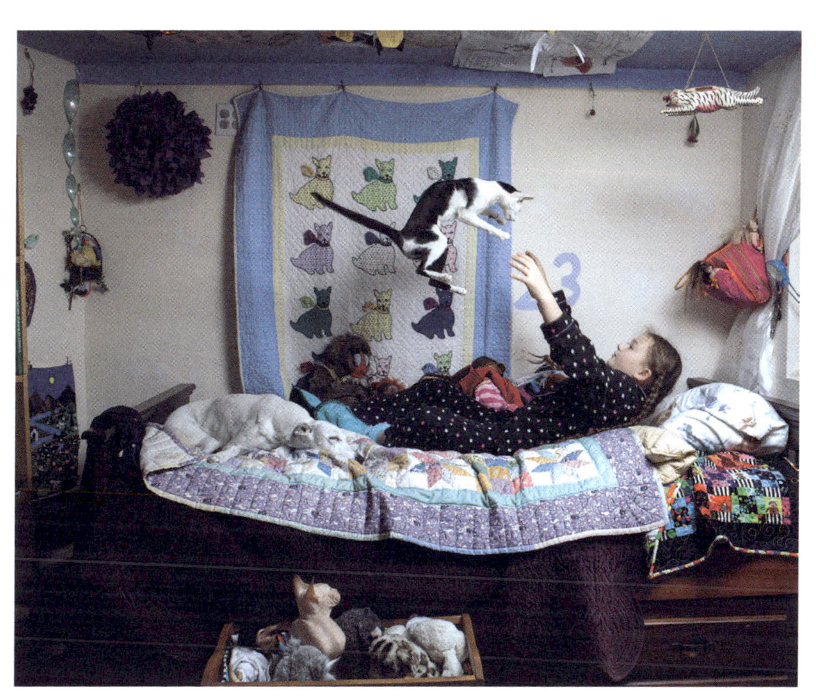

Above: *Flying Hannah, Amelia, Becky and Jacob*, 2010
Opposite: *Amelia and Jacob*, 2003

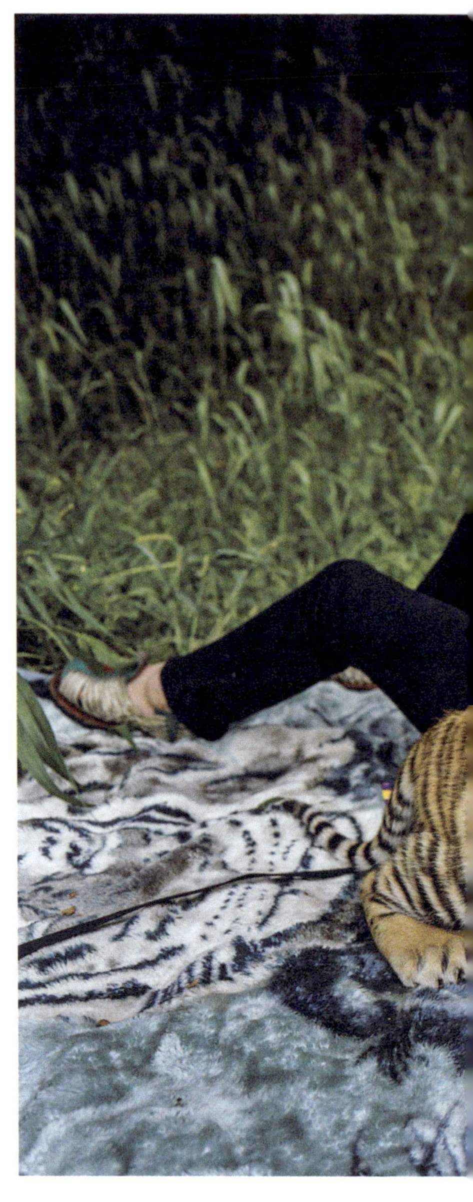

Lorenzo, Amelia bottle feeding, 2011

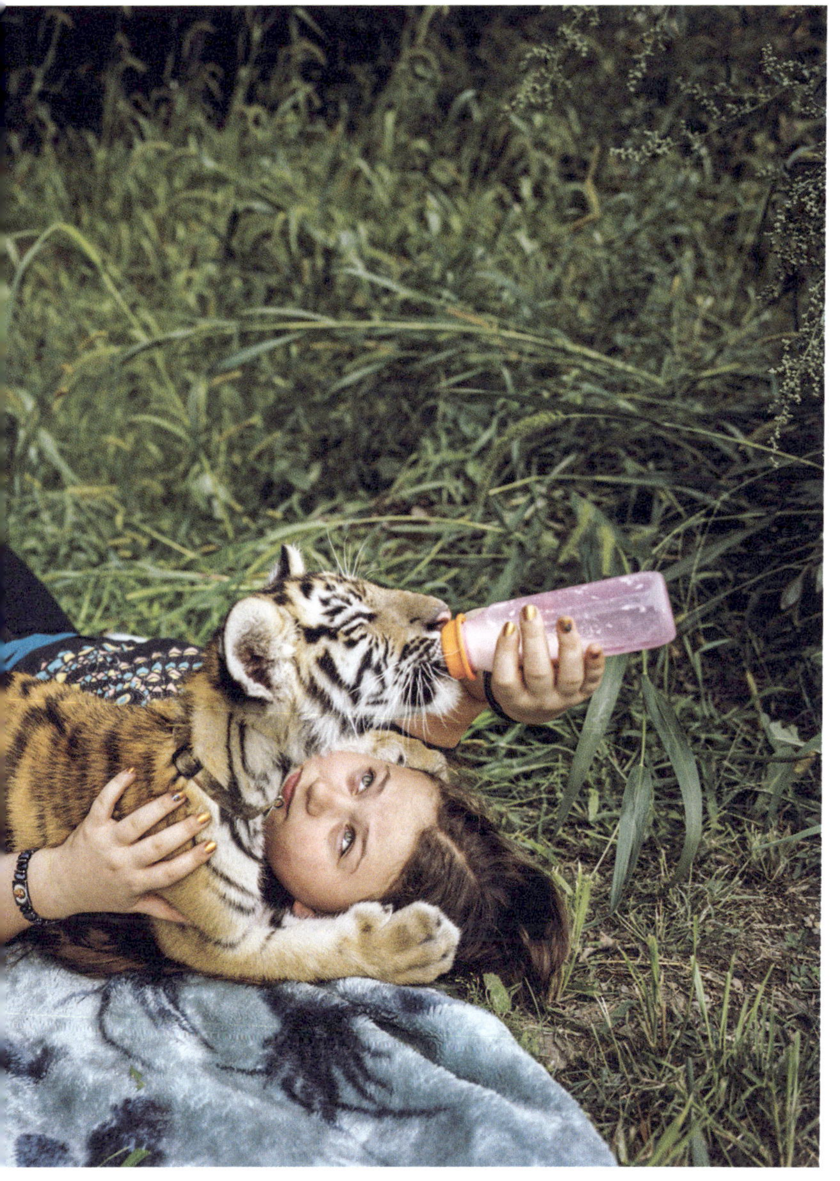

KATT PEOPLE
Julia Lindemalm

Julia Lindemalm is a self-confessed 'dog person', but also intrigued by the strong feelings that cats provoke. 'The love for cats seems more intense than for other pets,' the Swedish photographer says, 'they have become the internet's sweethearts.'

In search of answers to the phenomenon, she began photographing the enigma from the position of 'an outsider looking in'. The result is *Katt People* (*katt* is Swedish for cat), and above all it confirms that the relationship between a cat and a human is as capricious and frequently unrequited (on the cat's part) as it is intense and heartfelt. From indolent passengers in their owner's arms to determined guests at the dinner table, there's a slavish quality to these situations. Without doubt, the cats are the ones in charge.

Vera & Mittens, 2015

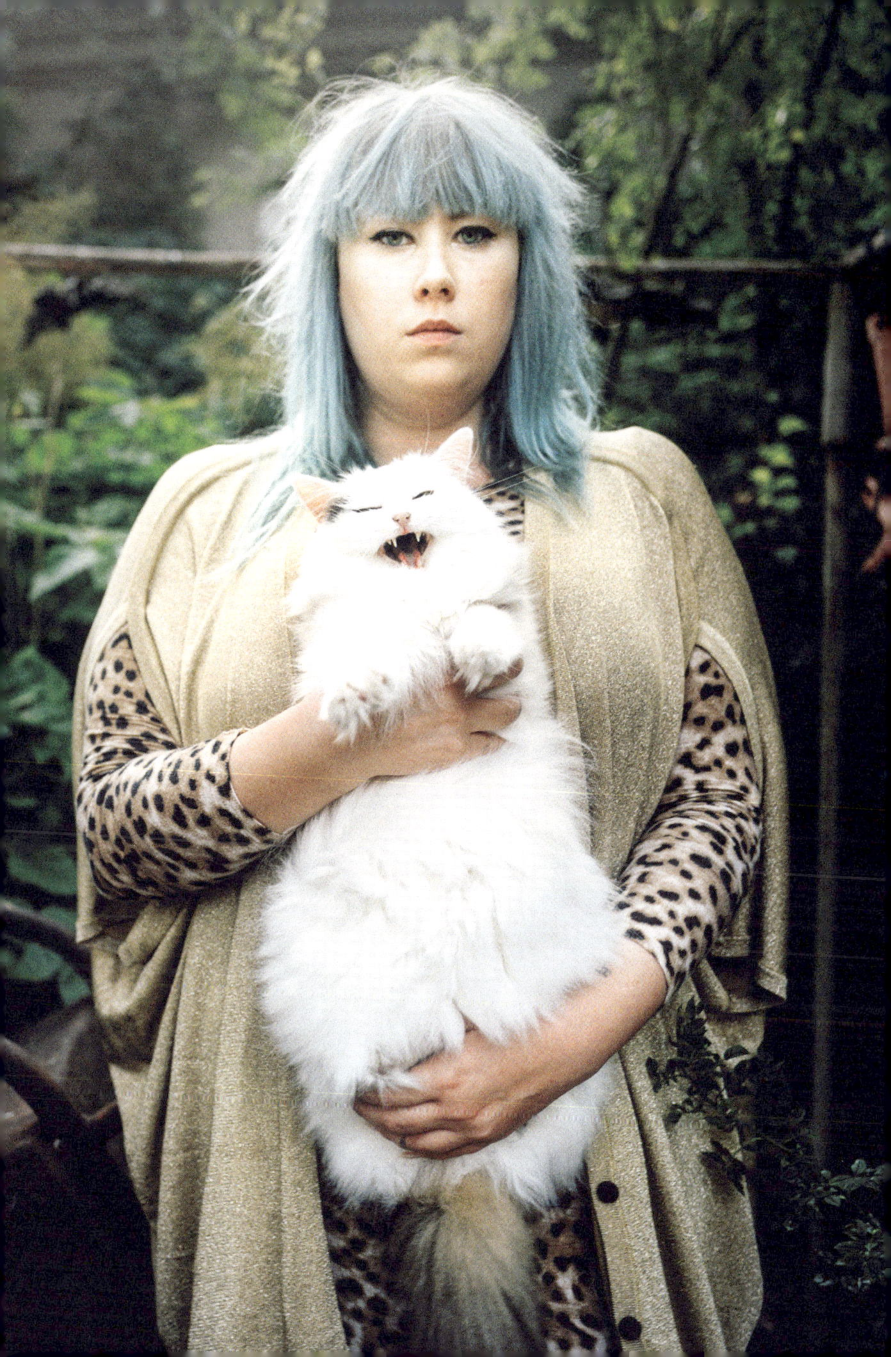

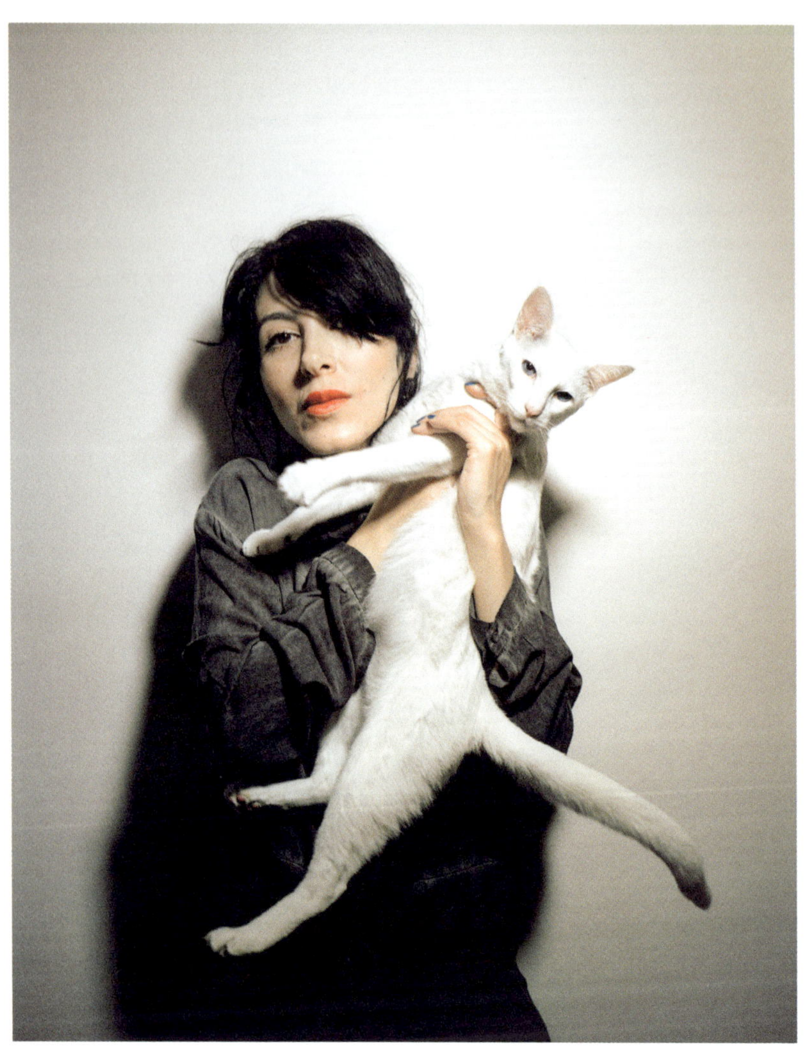

Sarah & Yoshi, 2015

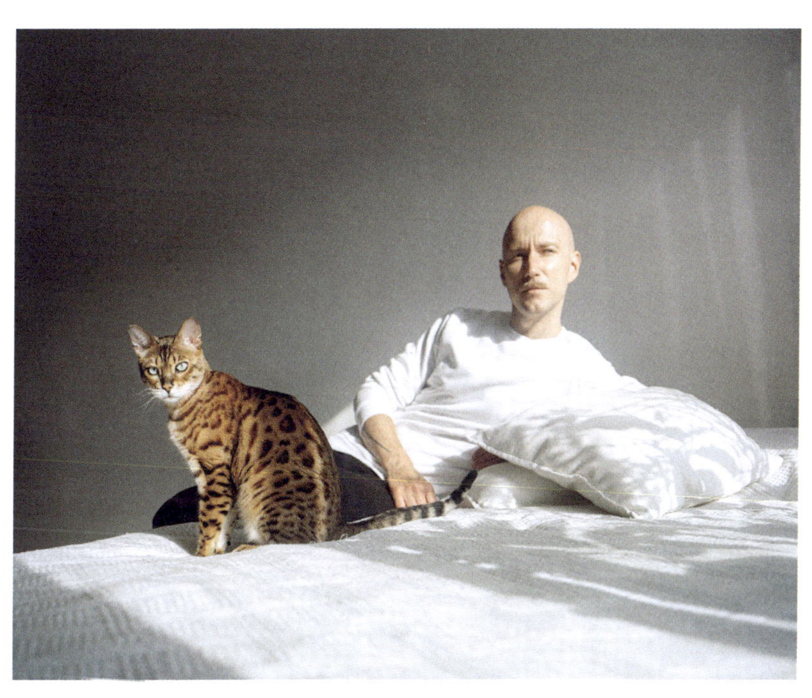

Above: *Par & Alonzo*, 2015
Overleaf: *Margareta & Lisebackes Fedra*, 2016

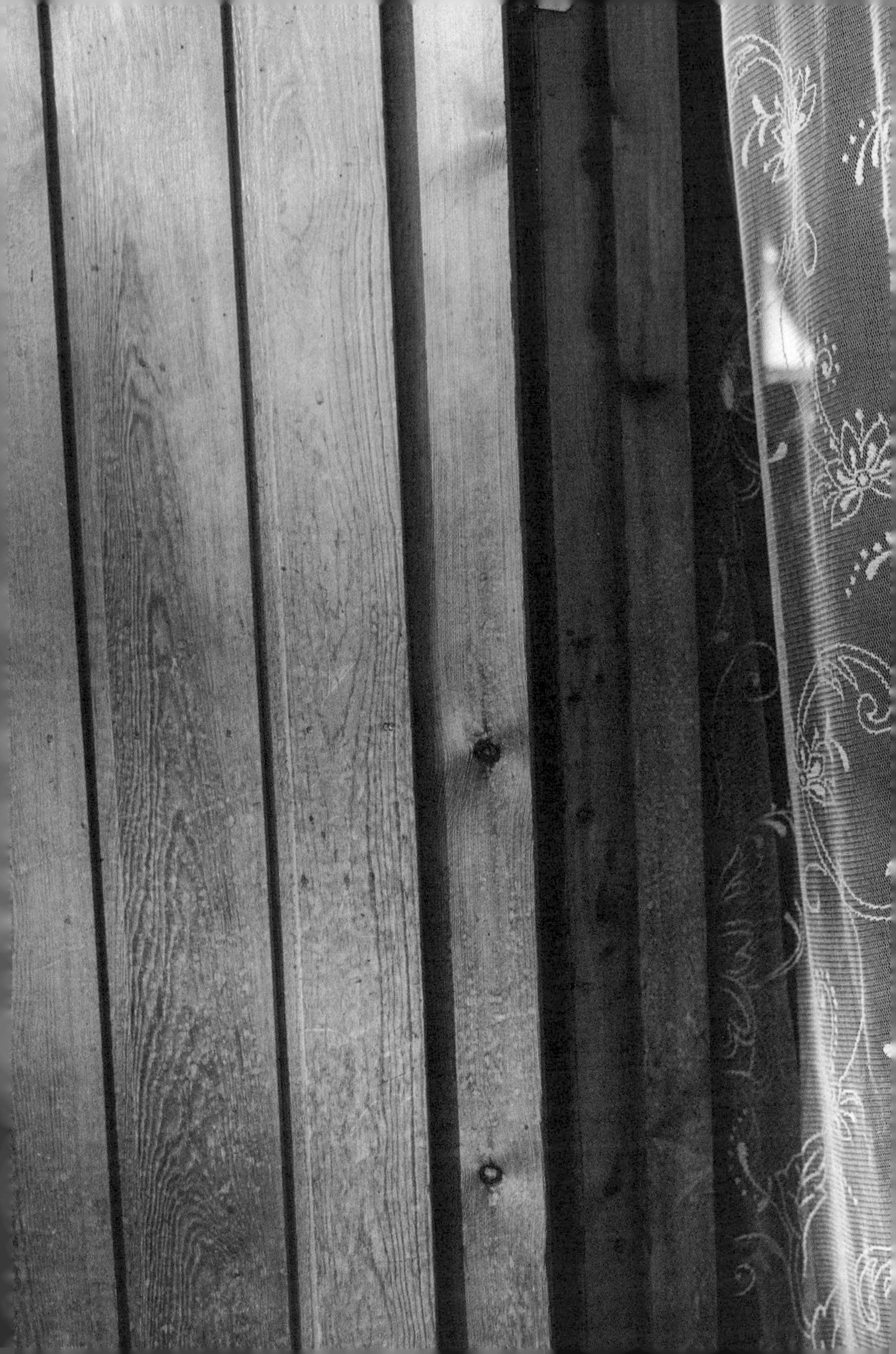

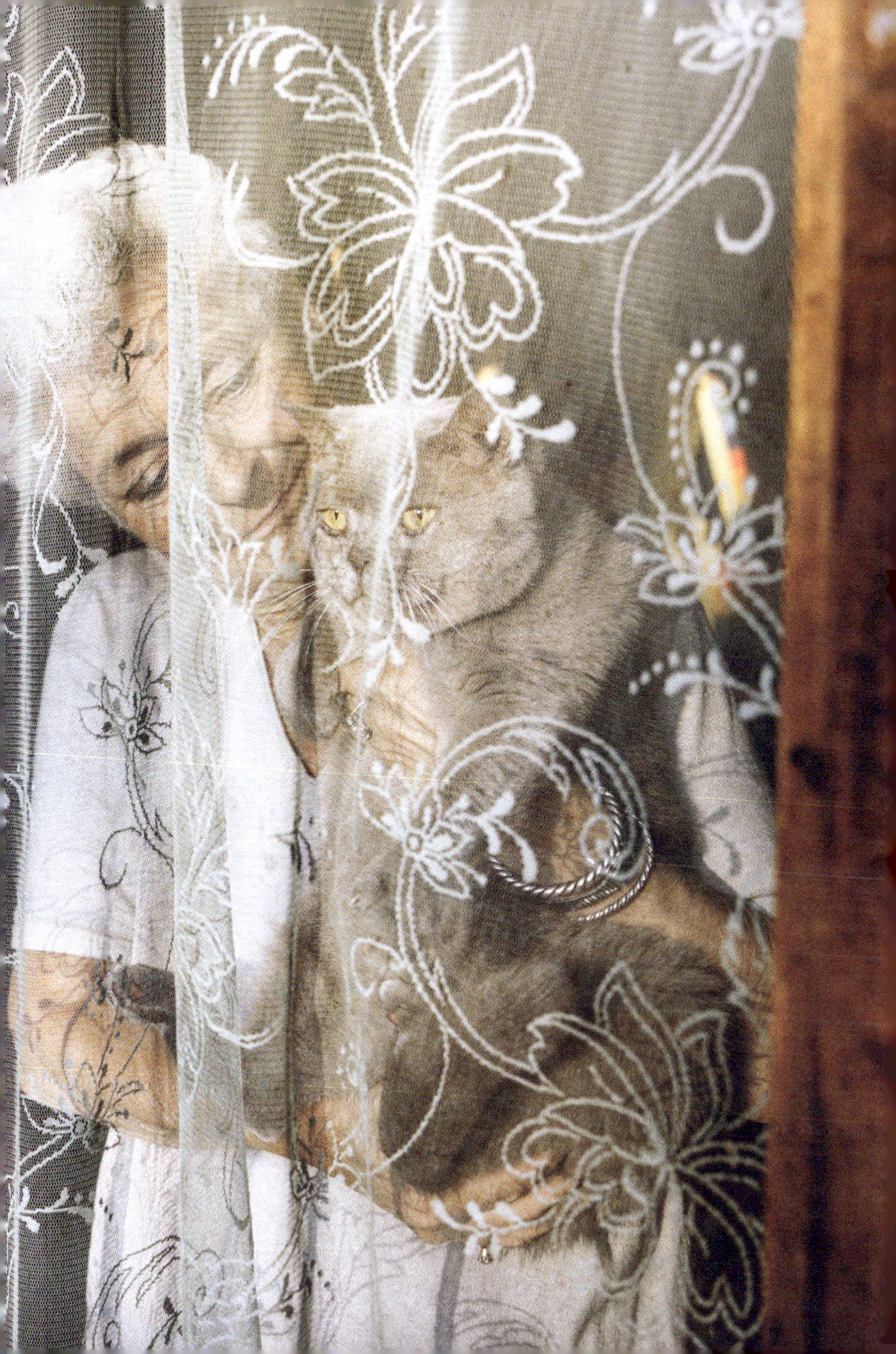

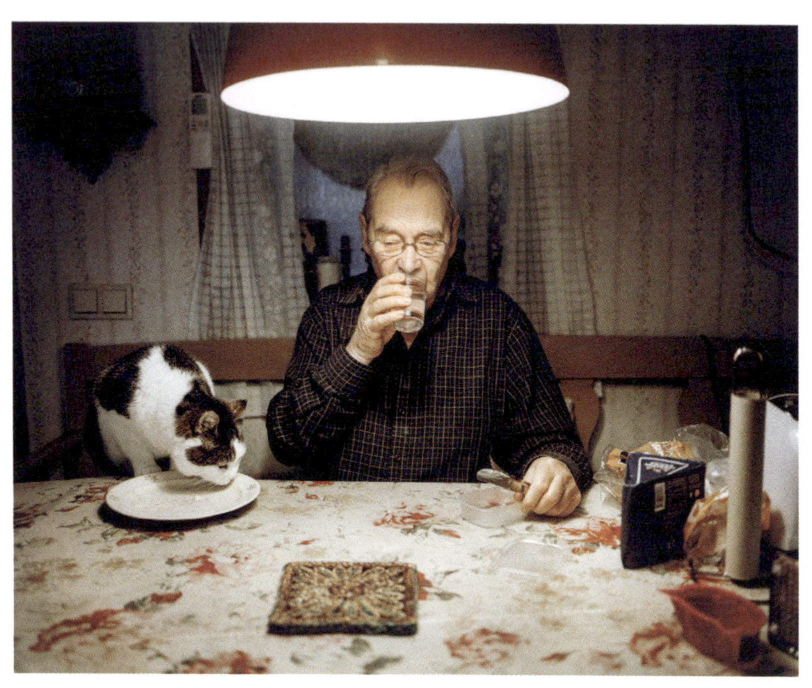

Lars & Baloo, 2016

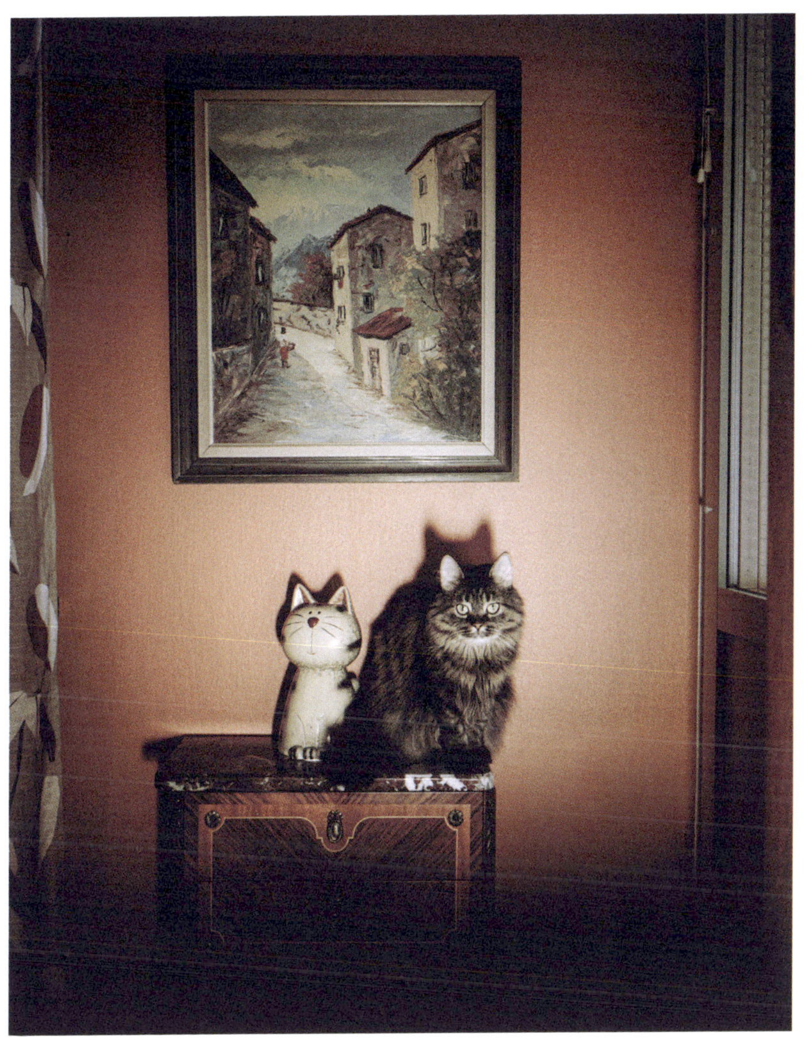

Doris, 2015

CATOGRAPHY

Nils Jacobi

With millions of followers on his socials, plus an archive of more than 10,000 cat photographs and 100 cat videos, it's little wonder Nils Jacobi calls himself 'The Catographer'.

Since he took up the pursuit in 2011, he has developed a special talent for capturing cats making human-esque expressions. Cranky, surprised, a 'seriously?' face – even a lopsided, Humphrey Bogart-style smile. The portraits that he and his fans love most, however, describe a kitten's first few months, combining a sequence of still images into a time-lapse film. He dryly describes it as '50+ hours of work for a few seconds of video', though one of them accrued more than 21 million views on TikTok. The secret ingredient to his shots is a cat's appetite and its instinct for play. 'You can't force cats to do anything,' he says, surprising precisely zero cat owners anywhere.

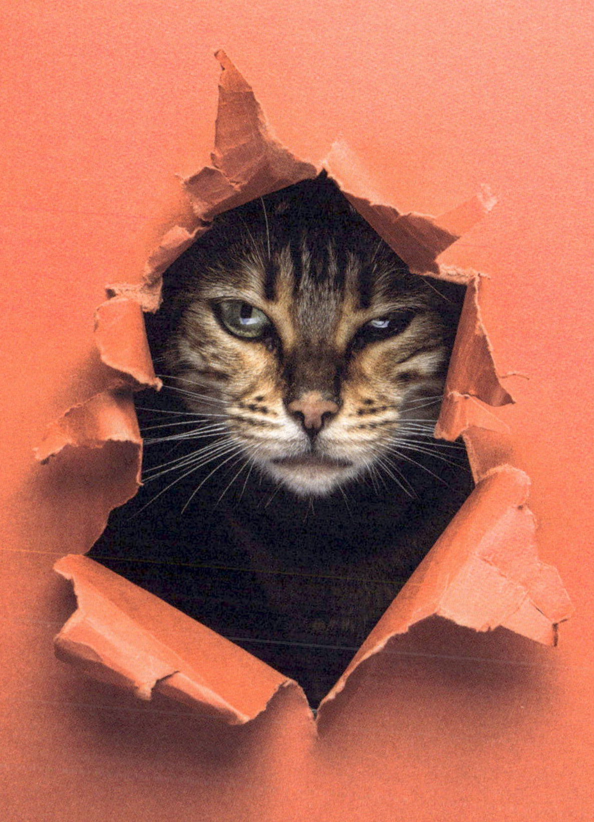

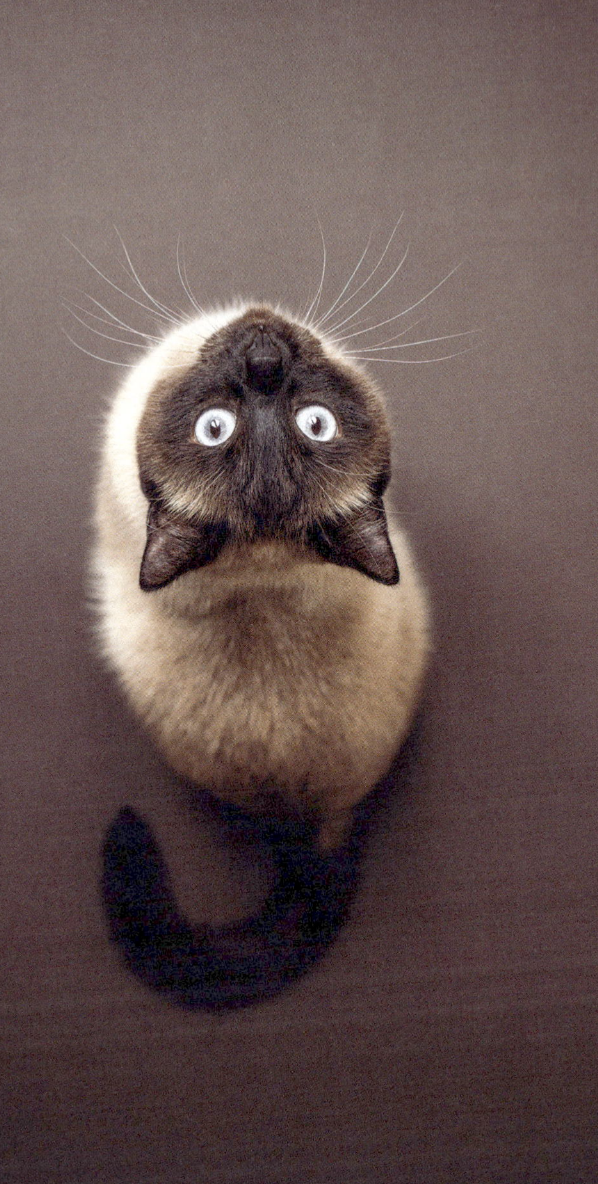

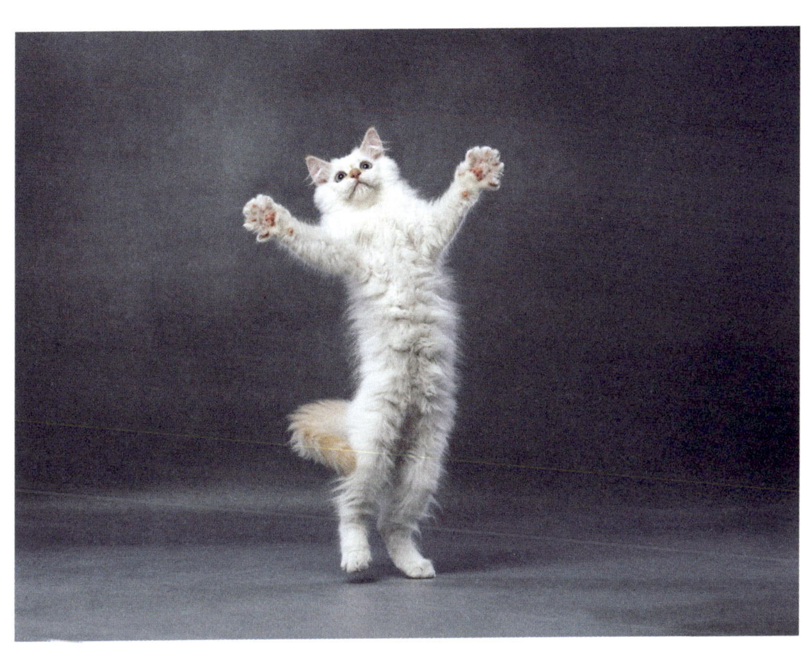

Above: *White Siberian Kitten*
Opposite: *Siamese Cat*

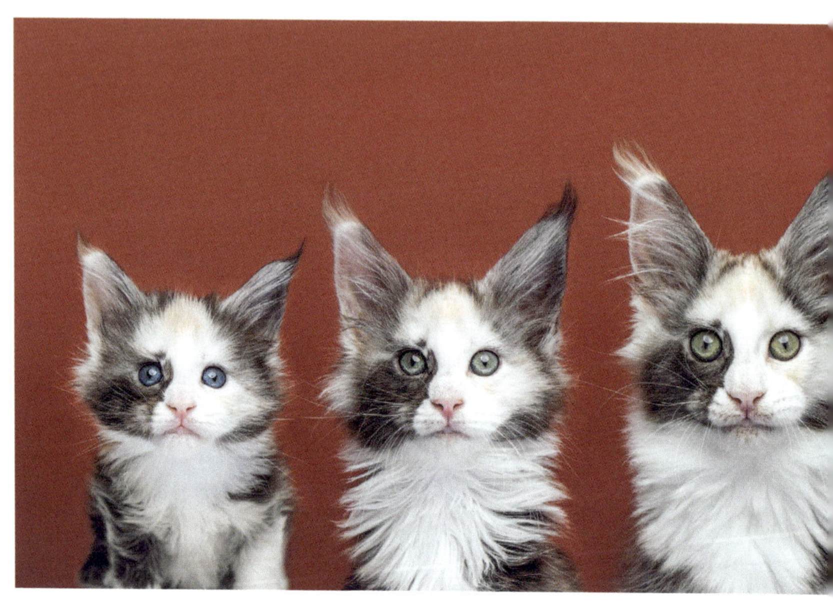

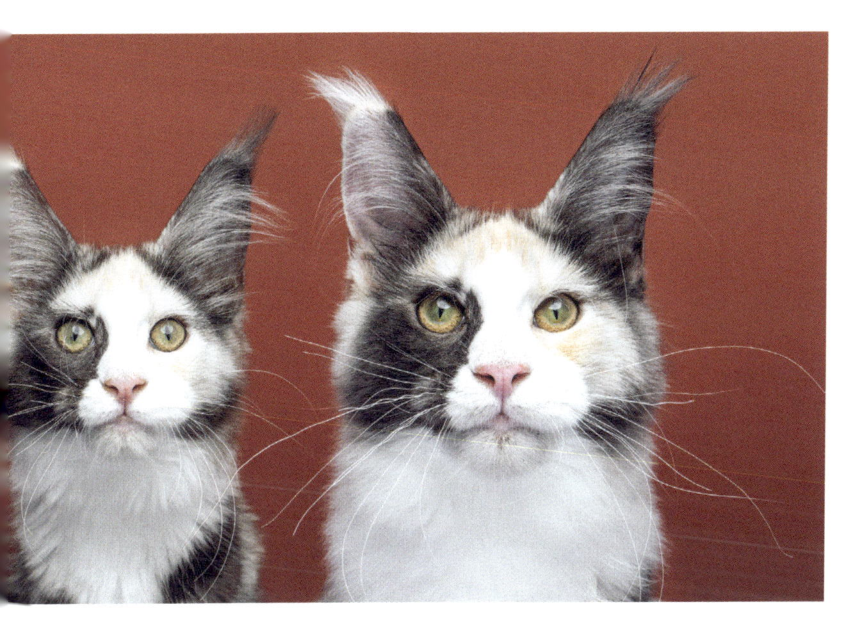

Five stages of a Calico Maine Coon growing up and changing its eye colour from blue to green to yellow

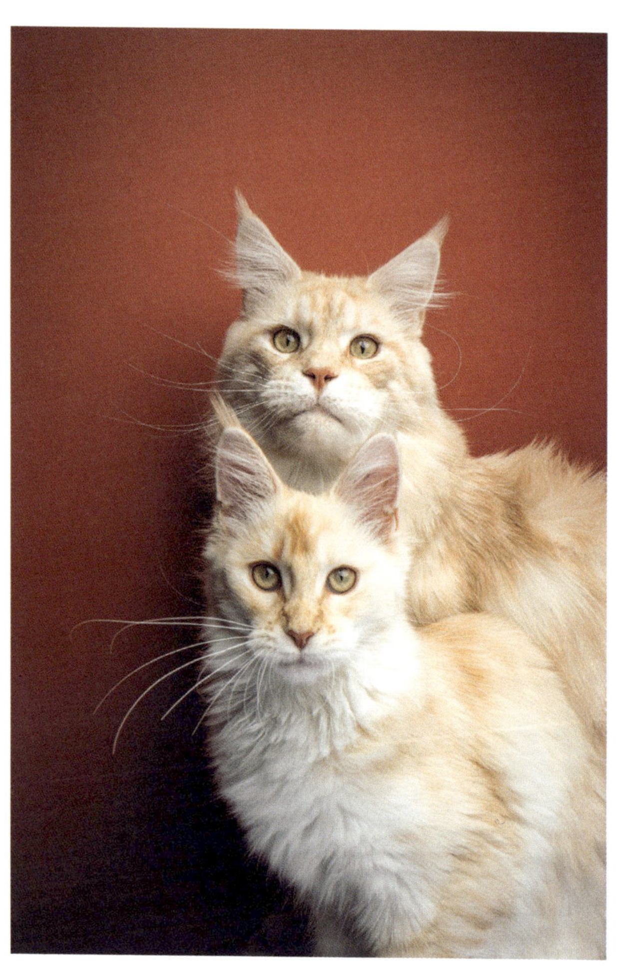

Above: *Two Maine Coons*
Opposite: *Two Black Kittens*

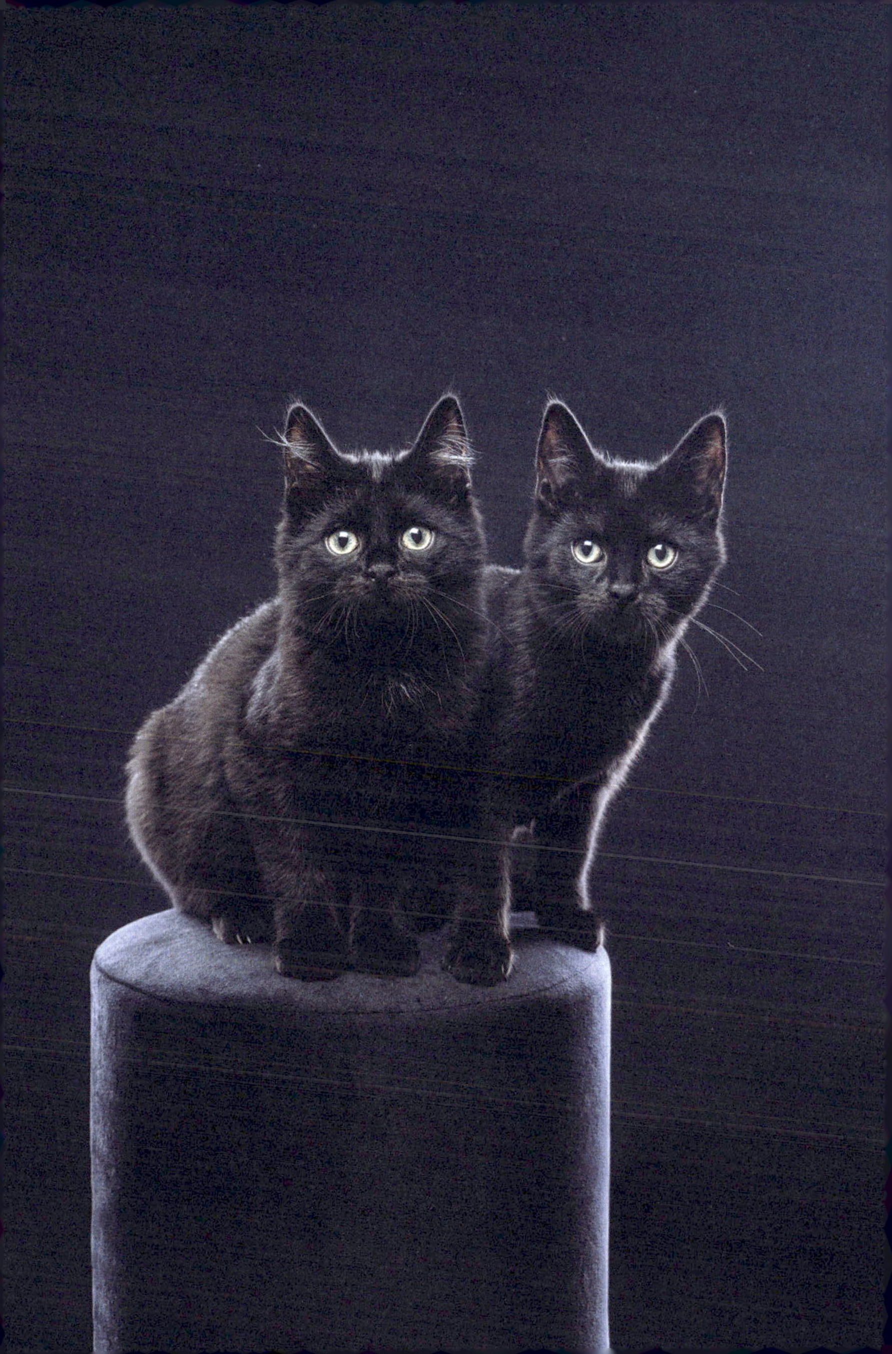

CATS IN WINDOWS
Max Knight

What is it with cats and windows? Admiring their reflection, perhaps, or covertly awaiting their human's homecoming? Feasibly, the birds outside, hopping and chirruping away on the lawn, are a kind of cat-Netflix.

Since he first noticed the phenomenon in Los Angeles in 2009, Max Knight has captured hundreds of cats in the act. His project has since expanded across the USA, and into Belgium, South Africa, Iceland and Britain. Officially, it's complete now, though he can never resist just one more photograph if he sees one. He keeps a map of those spotted while out driving, but every time he returns with a camera, the cat has outwitted him – and vanished.

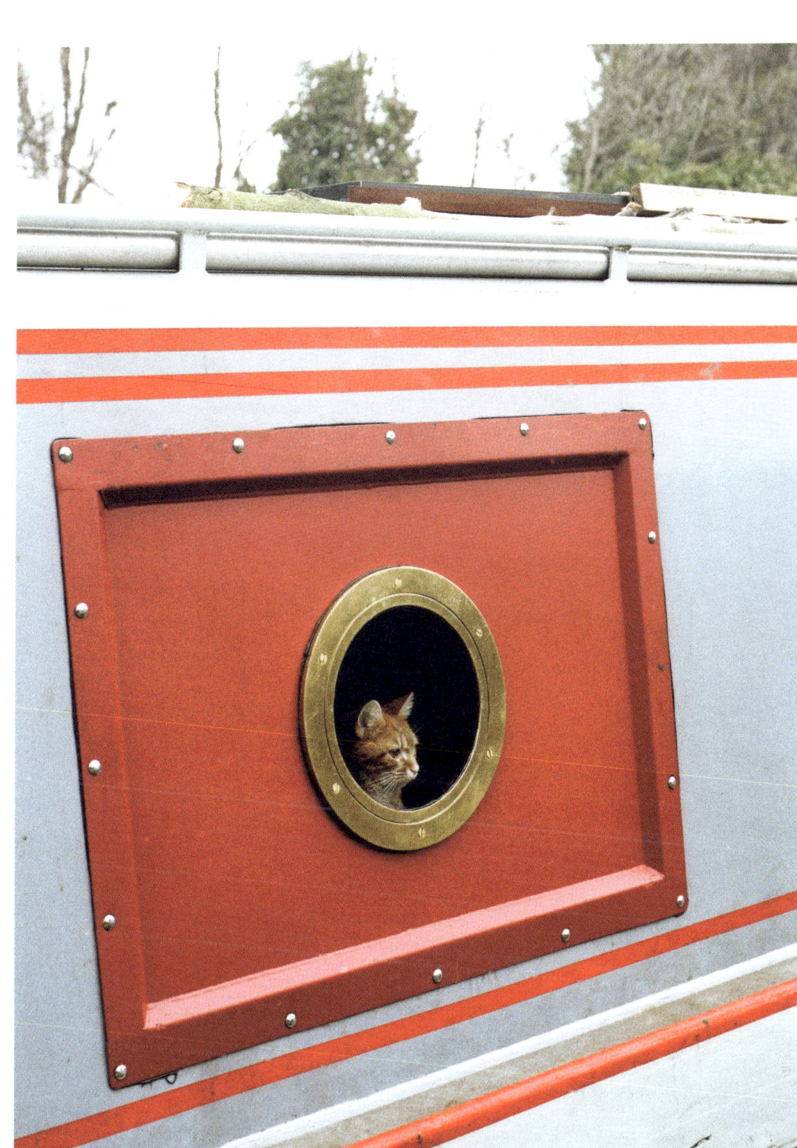

Ladbroke Grove, London, UK, 2010

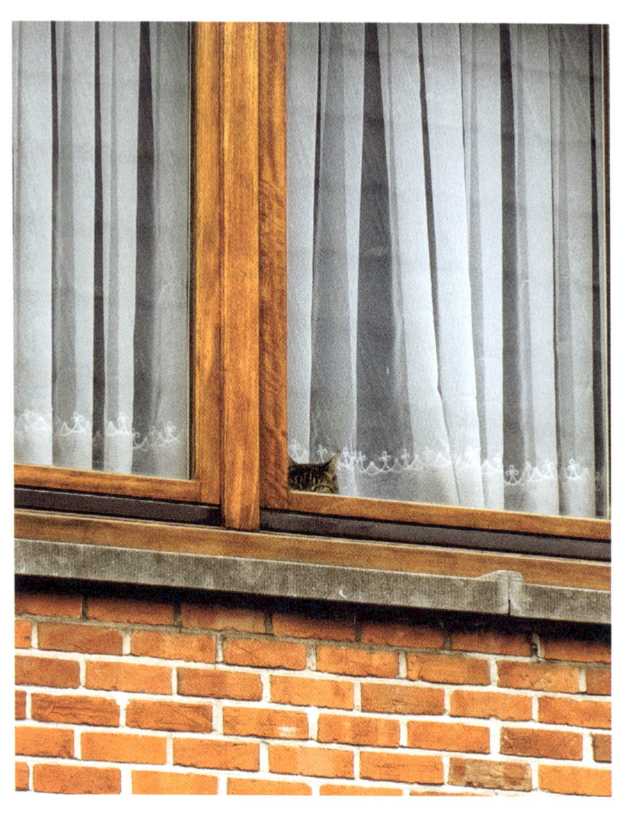

Above: *Preekeke, Belgium*, 2017
Opposite: *Stonington, Maine*, 2023

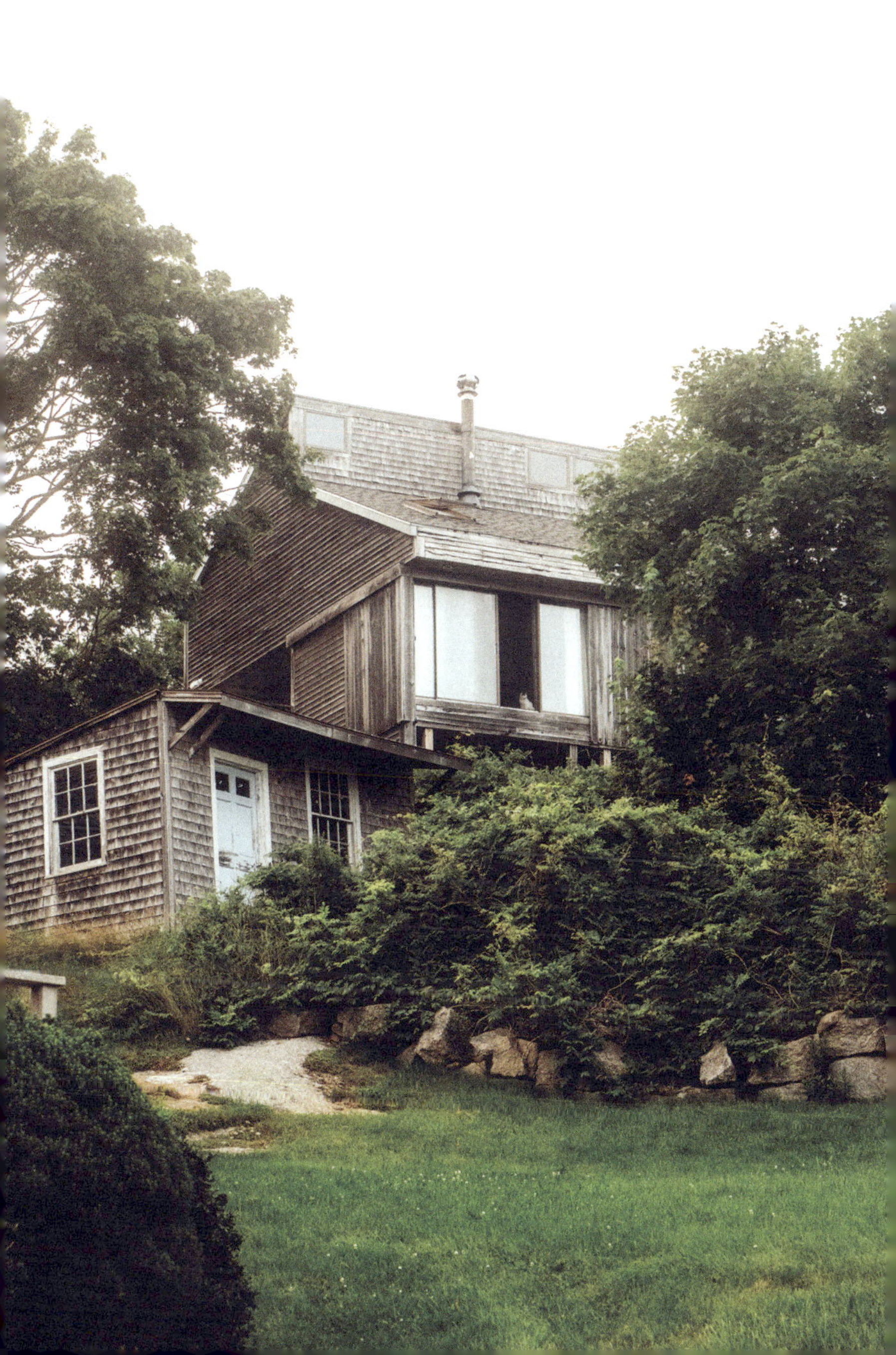

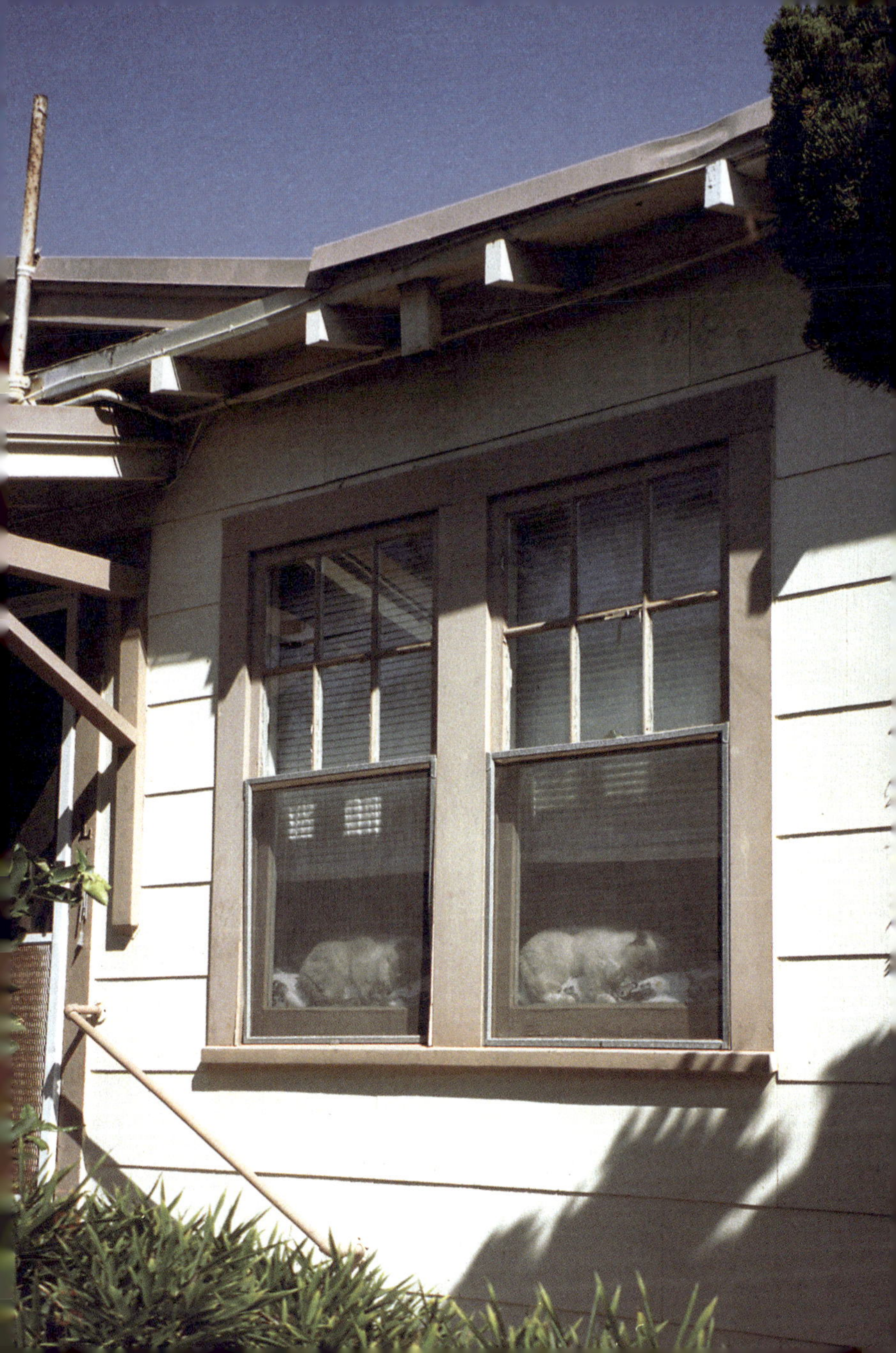

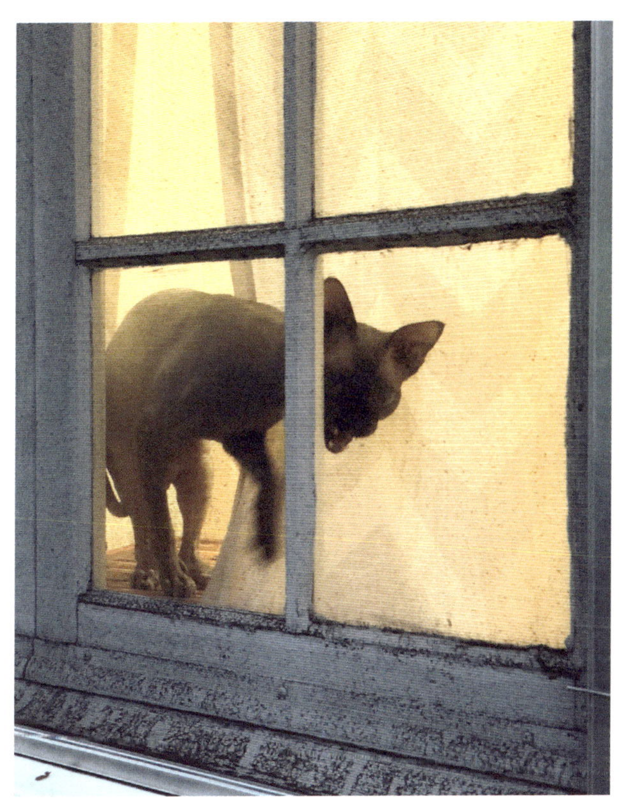

Above: *Los Feliz, California, USA*, 2018
Opposite: *Venice, California, USA*, 2019
Overleaf: *Yosemite National Park, California, USA*, 2018

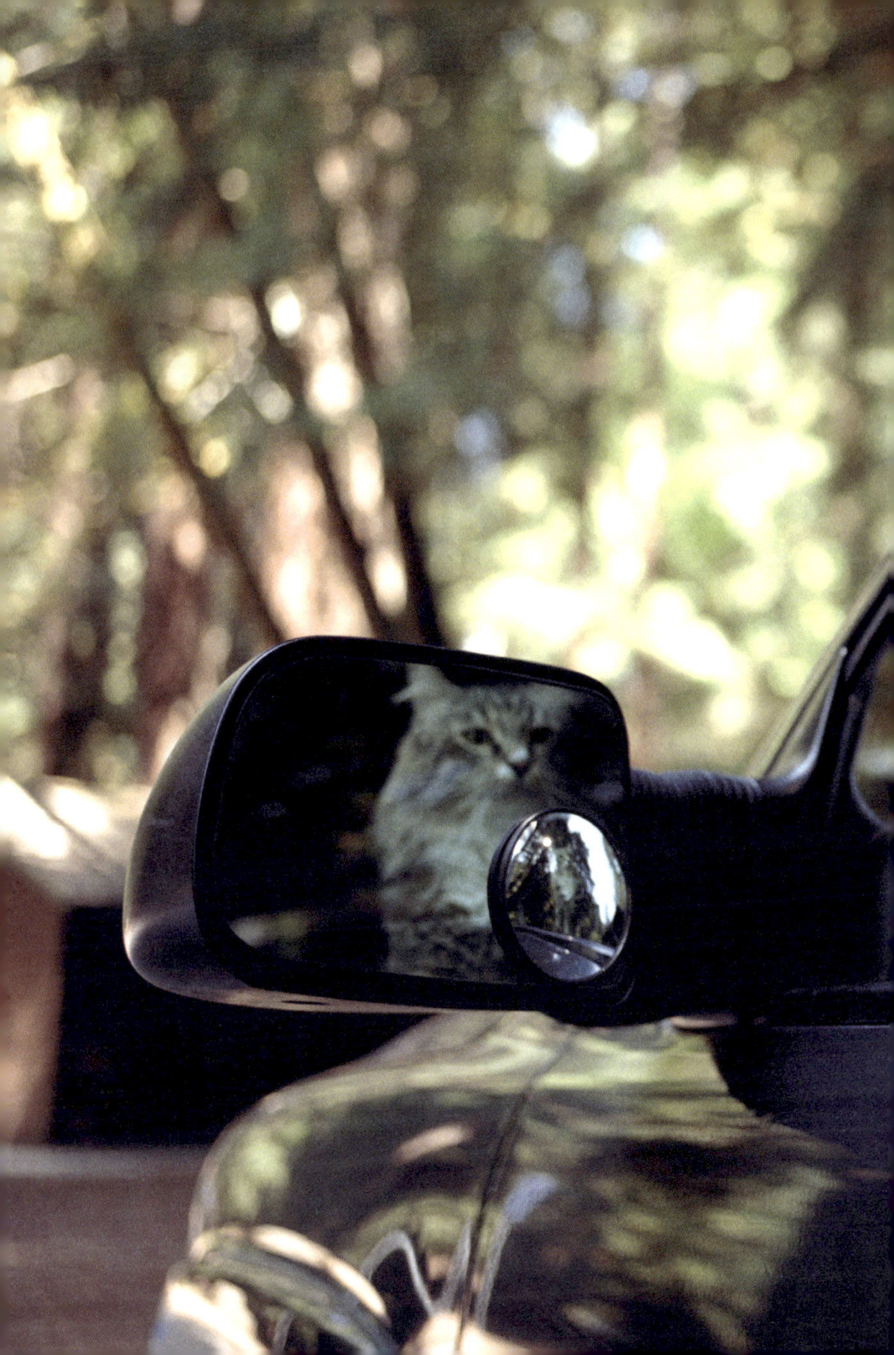

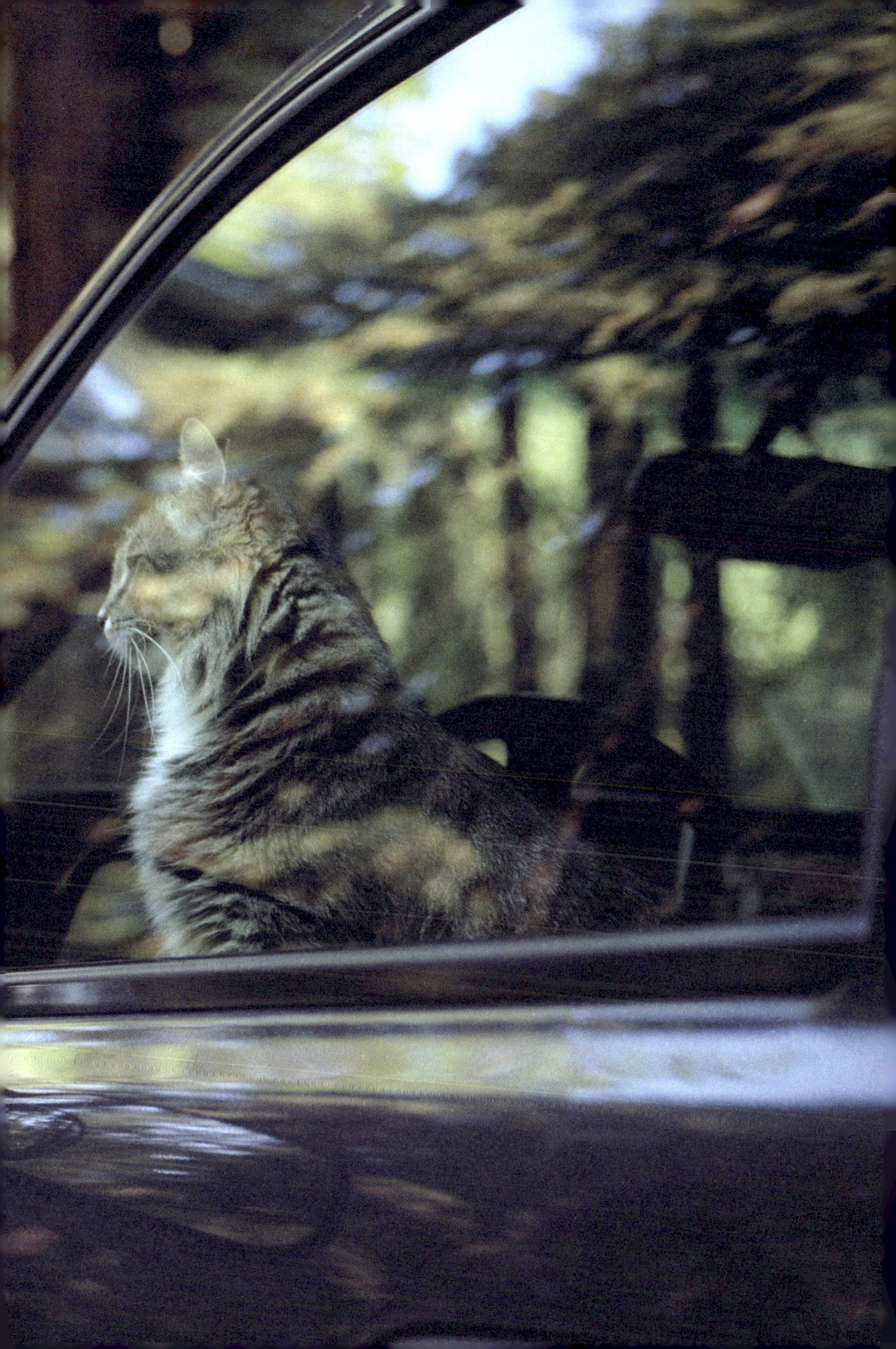

ERNIE

Tony Mendoza

When he moved from Boston to Manhattan in 1980 to make it in the art world, Tony Mendoza had few connections and very little money. Finding an inexpensive loft with a darkroom on his second day, then, was 'very lucky'.

He had answered an ad from Nancy, a painter who wanted to share her place with another artist, and luckier still, she owned a cat – Ernie. 'I looked at the cat and thought: that cat is my next photo project.'

Mendoza had already made a series of photographs of his girlfriend's dog, 'all done from the dog's eye level and focused on the dog in action, doing dog things, as opposed to the dog posing for the camera. I thought, OK. I seem to have a way of photographing animals, so why not photograph Ernie, and for the next four years I did just that.'

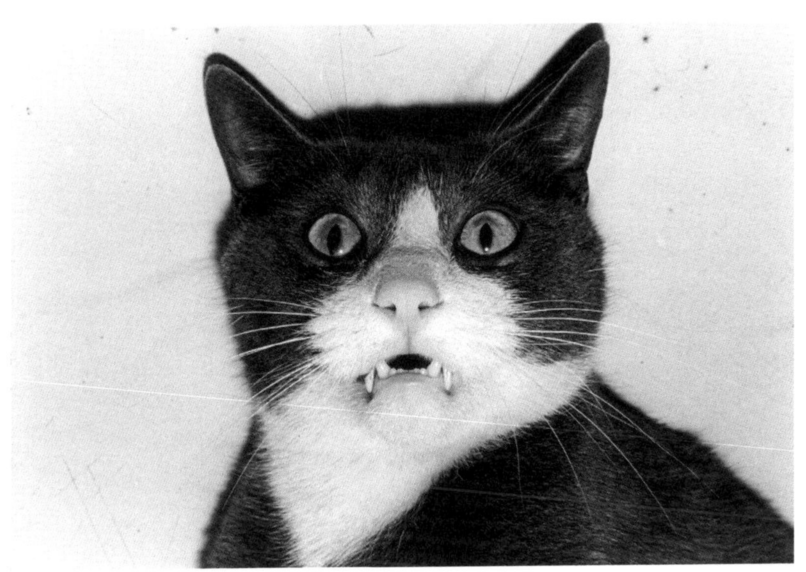

Above and overleaf: *From the Ernie Series*, 1980–1984

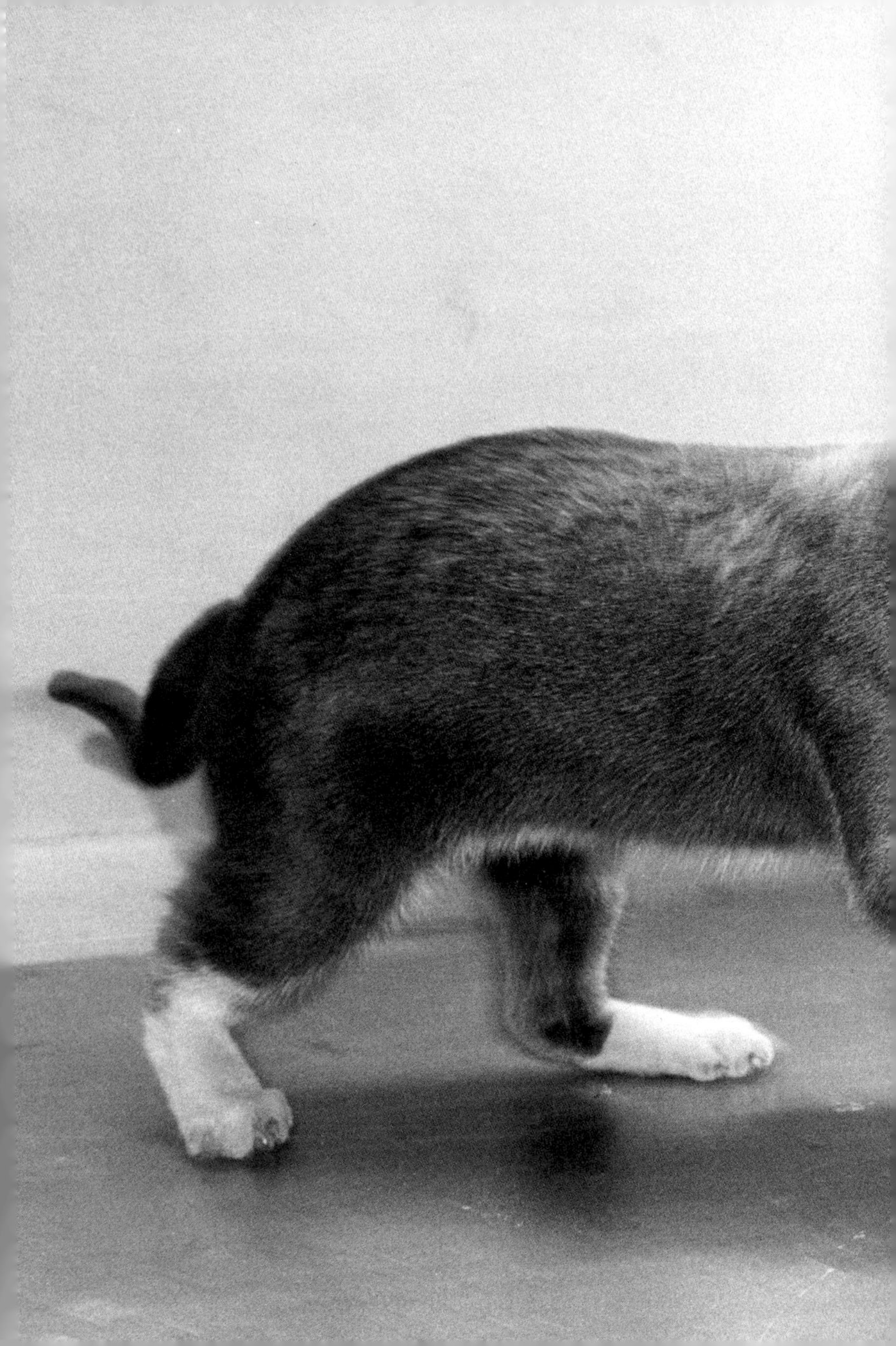

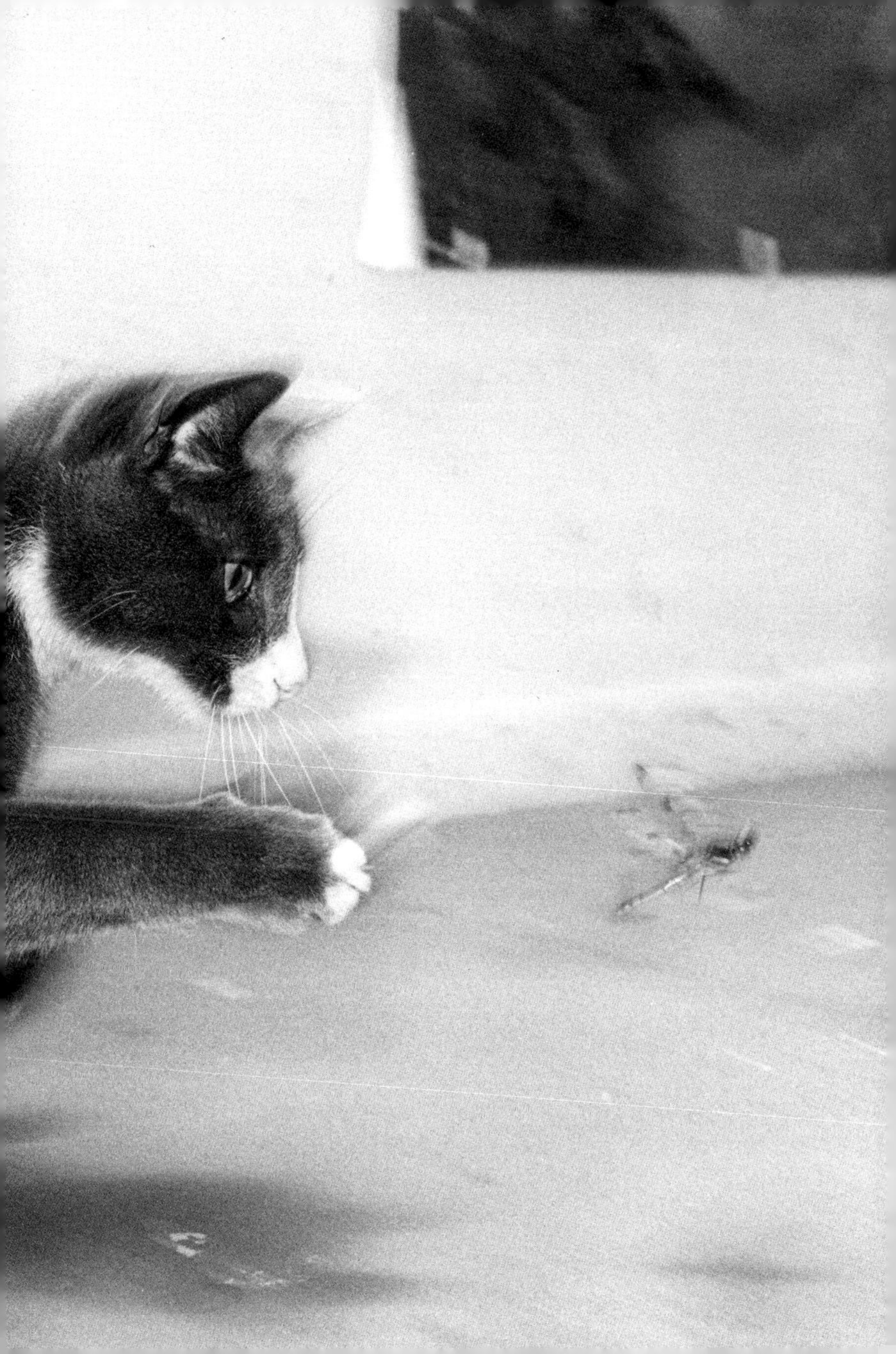

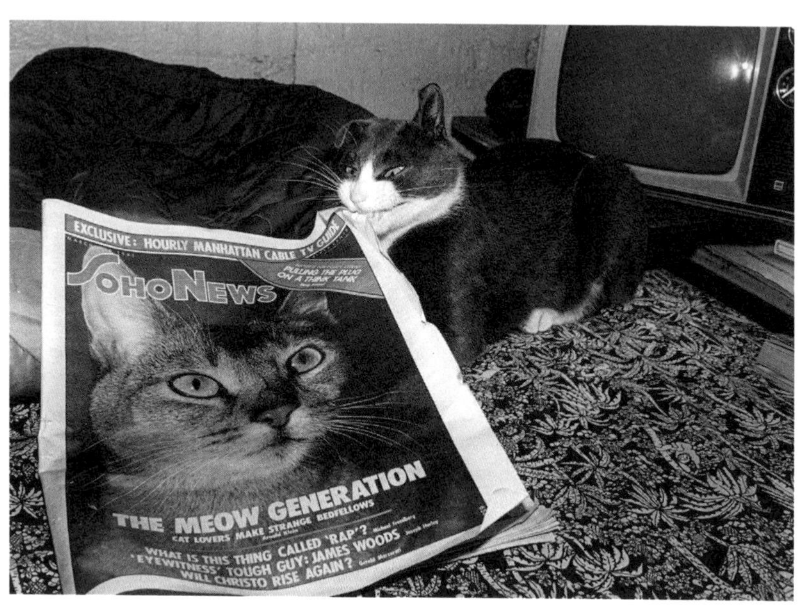

From the Ernie Series, 1980–1984

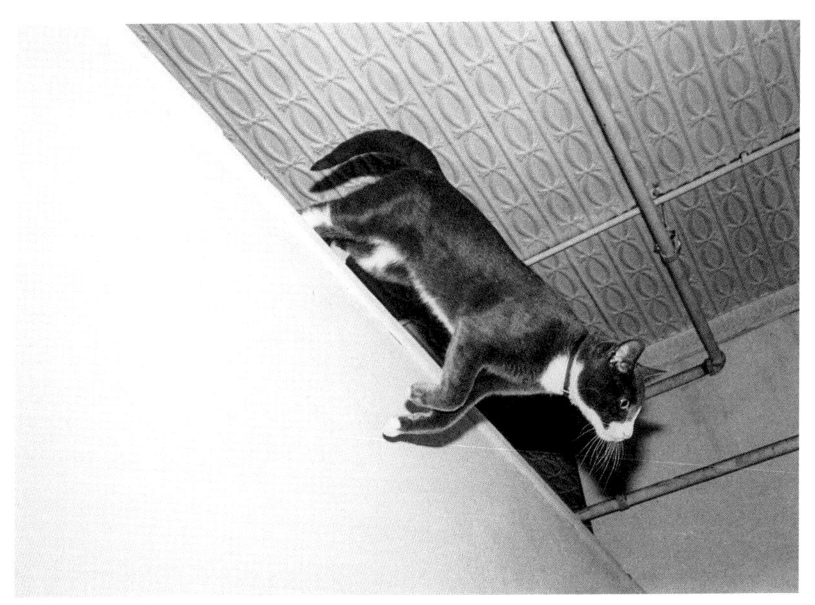

Above and overleaf: *From the Ernie Series,* 1980–1984

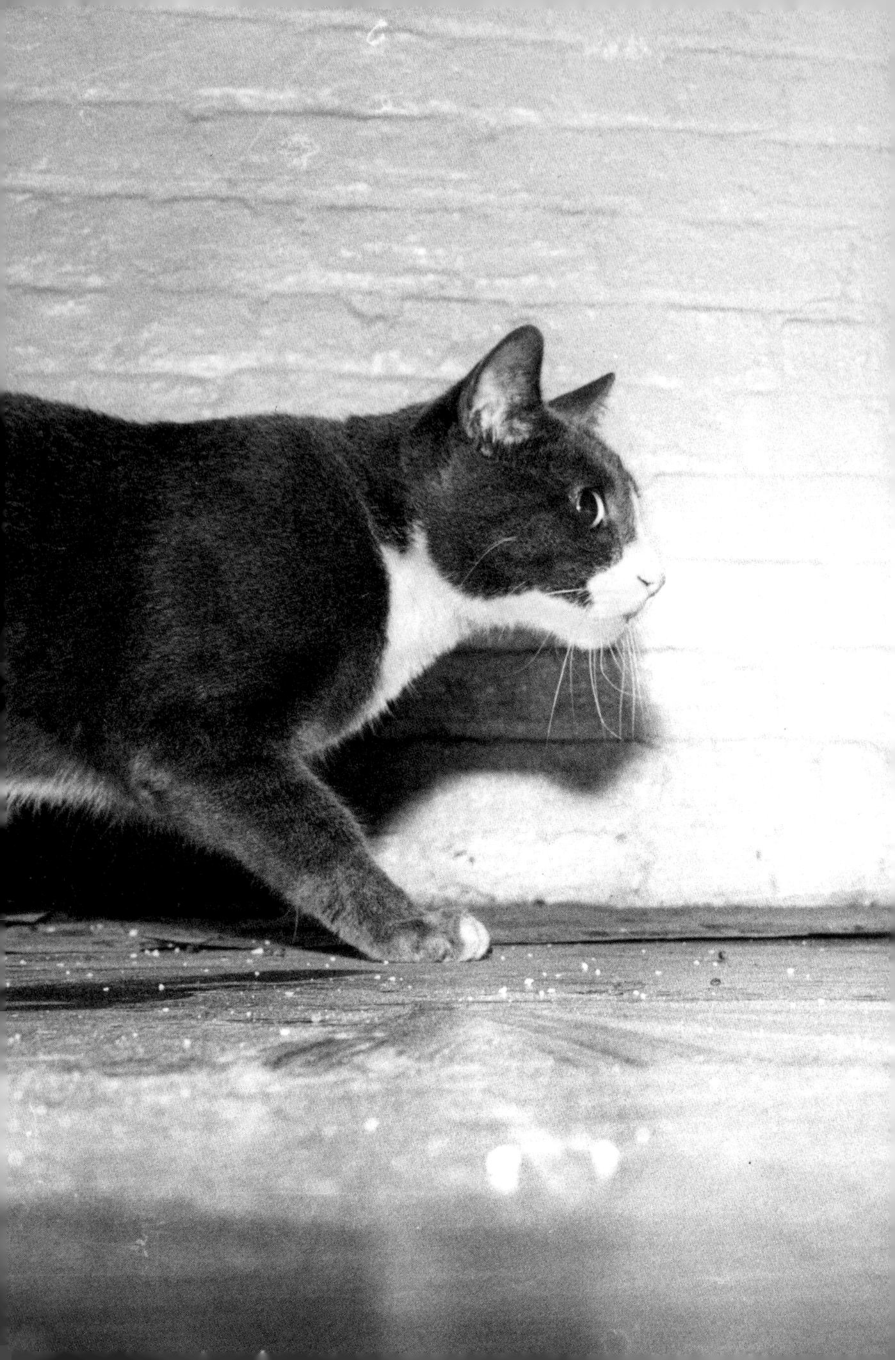

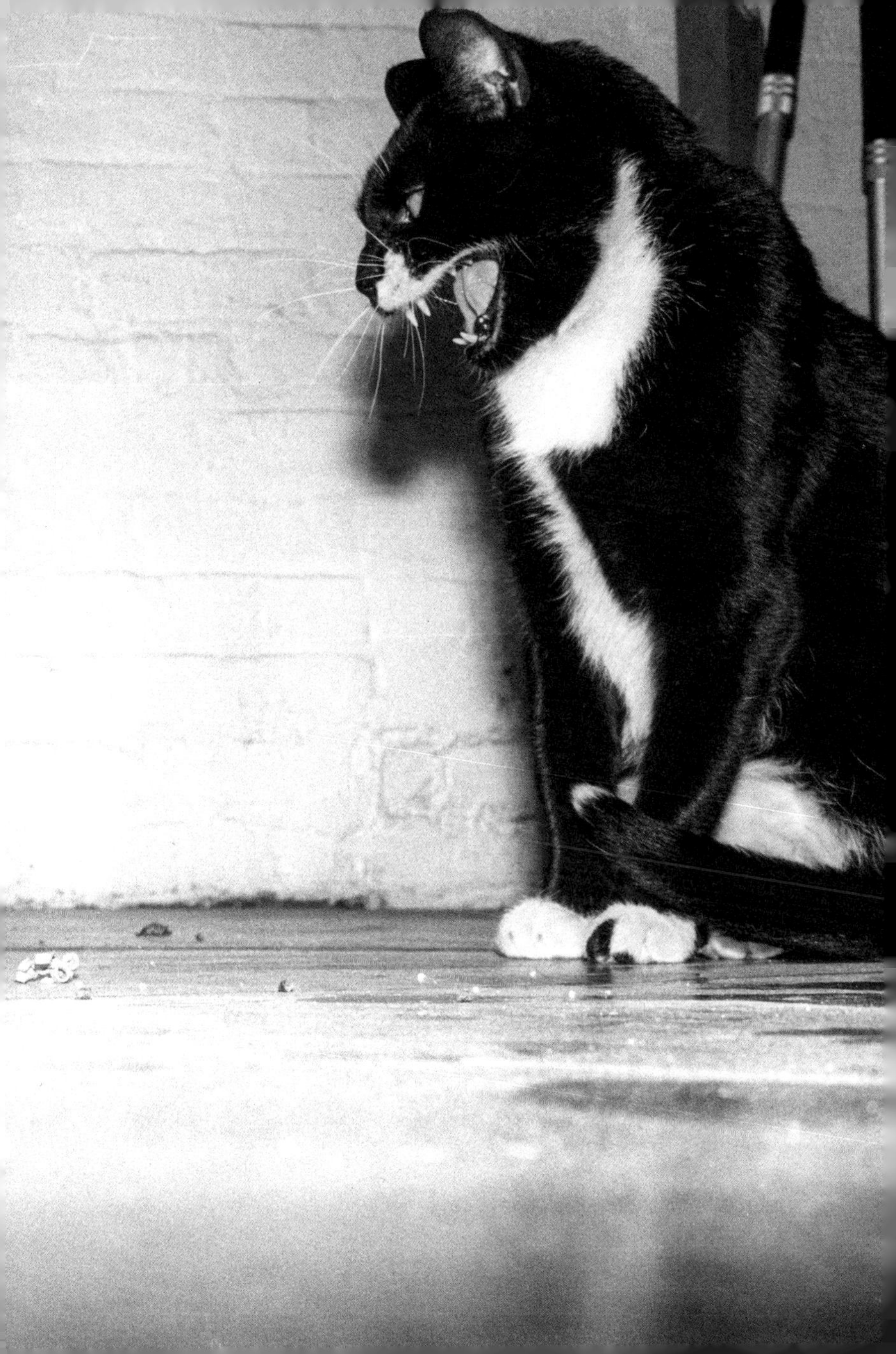

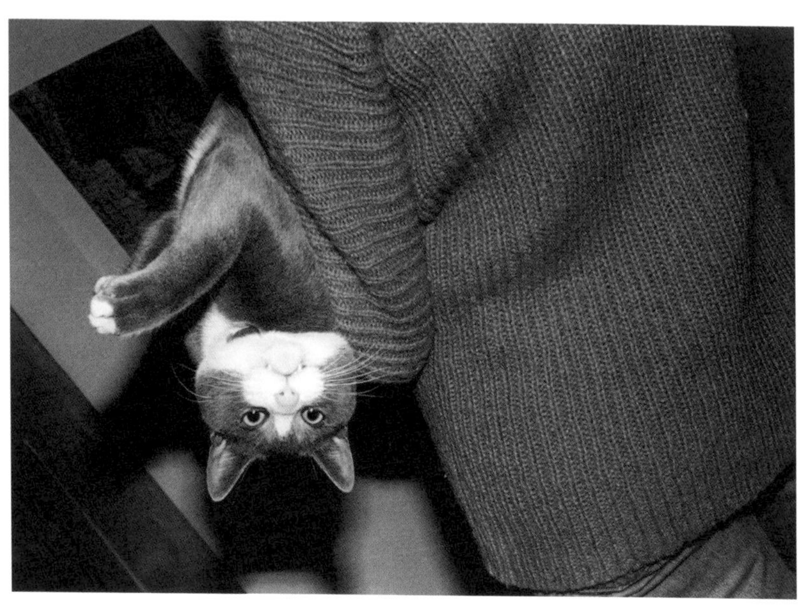

From the Ernie Series, 1980–1984

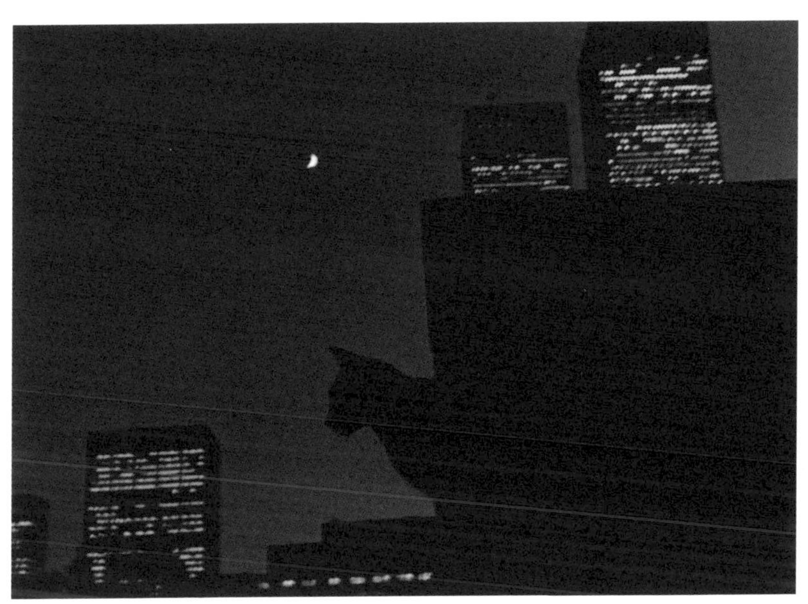

STRAY CAT
Sami Uçan

After moving to Istanbul in 2012, Sami Uçan took great delight in photographing the ancient city walls and its magnificent mosques. At first, he was particularly drawn to the Ottoman tombstones which he saw as 'witnesses to a past time'. Looking afterwards at the photographs he had taken, however, he noticed the 'cute guests' slinking around the town. 'It seemed as if the cats were waiting for a person to be friends with them,' he says.

The more time Uçan spent in the city, the more he felt that the cats had become his photographic partners. 'It was as if I had tapped into a special communication network or frequency that the cats all shared, and suddenly everywhere I went to photograph, I found them,' he says. Now, he can't think of Istanbul without cats. 'Without even looking, you find cats appearing all around you. They come out onto the road to greet us. In many ways, they are the true residents of the city. They reflect Istanbul's spirit.'

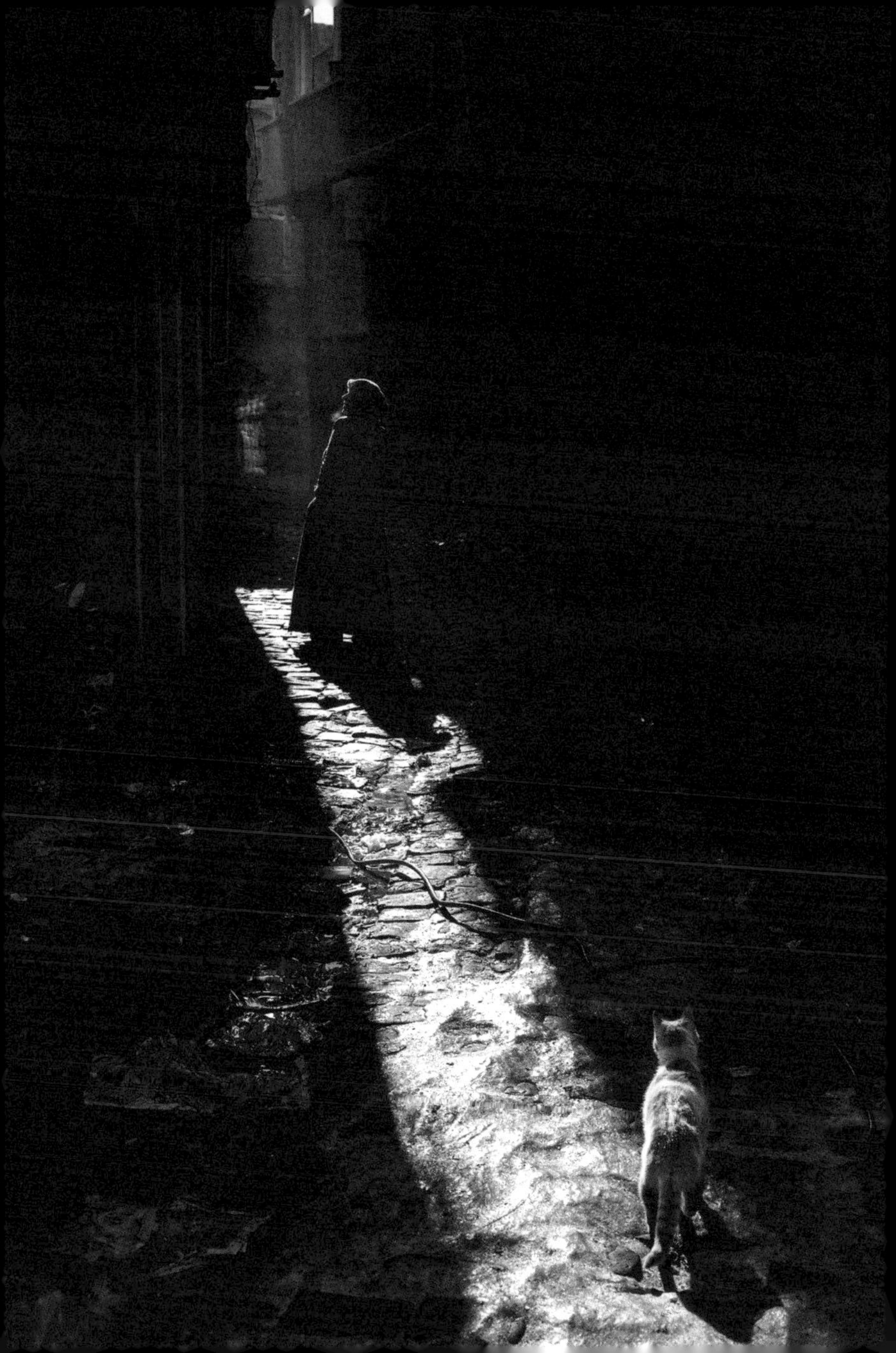

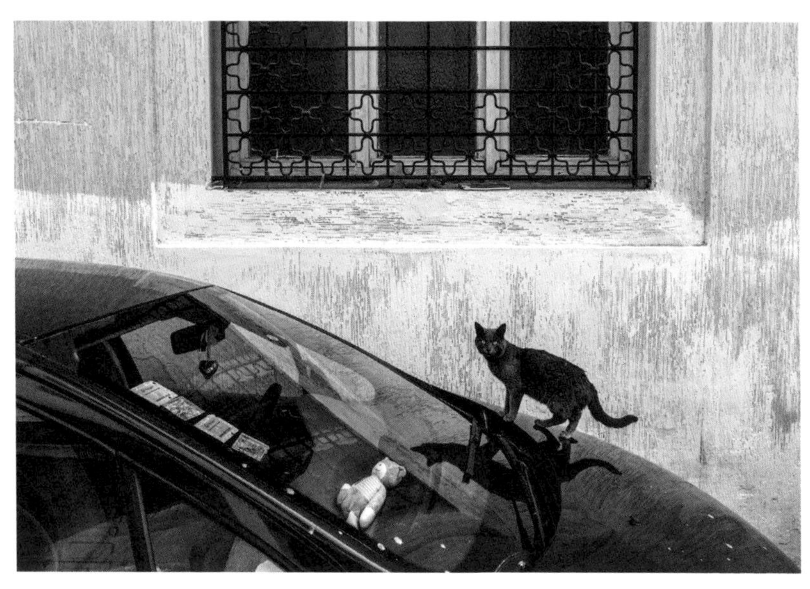

Stray Cat, 2013

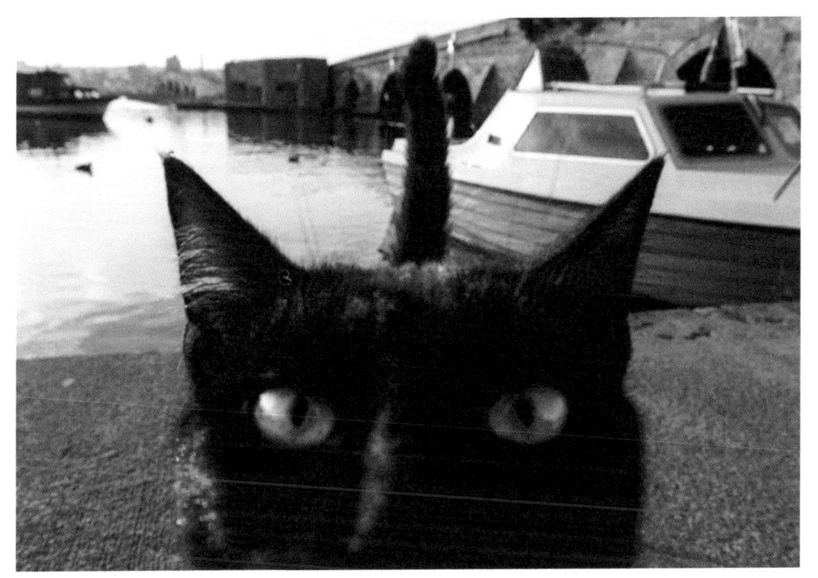

Teddy, 2015

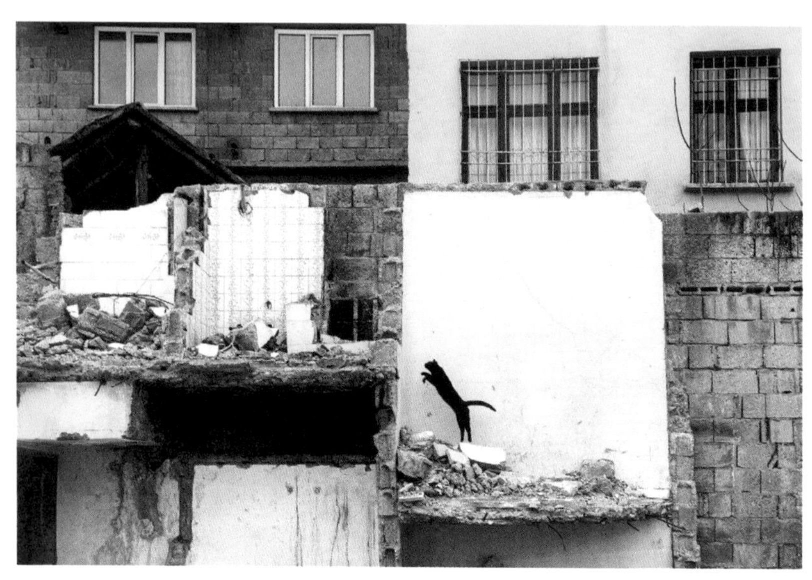

Above: *Puma*, 2018
Opposite: *Friendship*, 2013

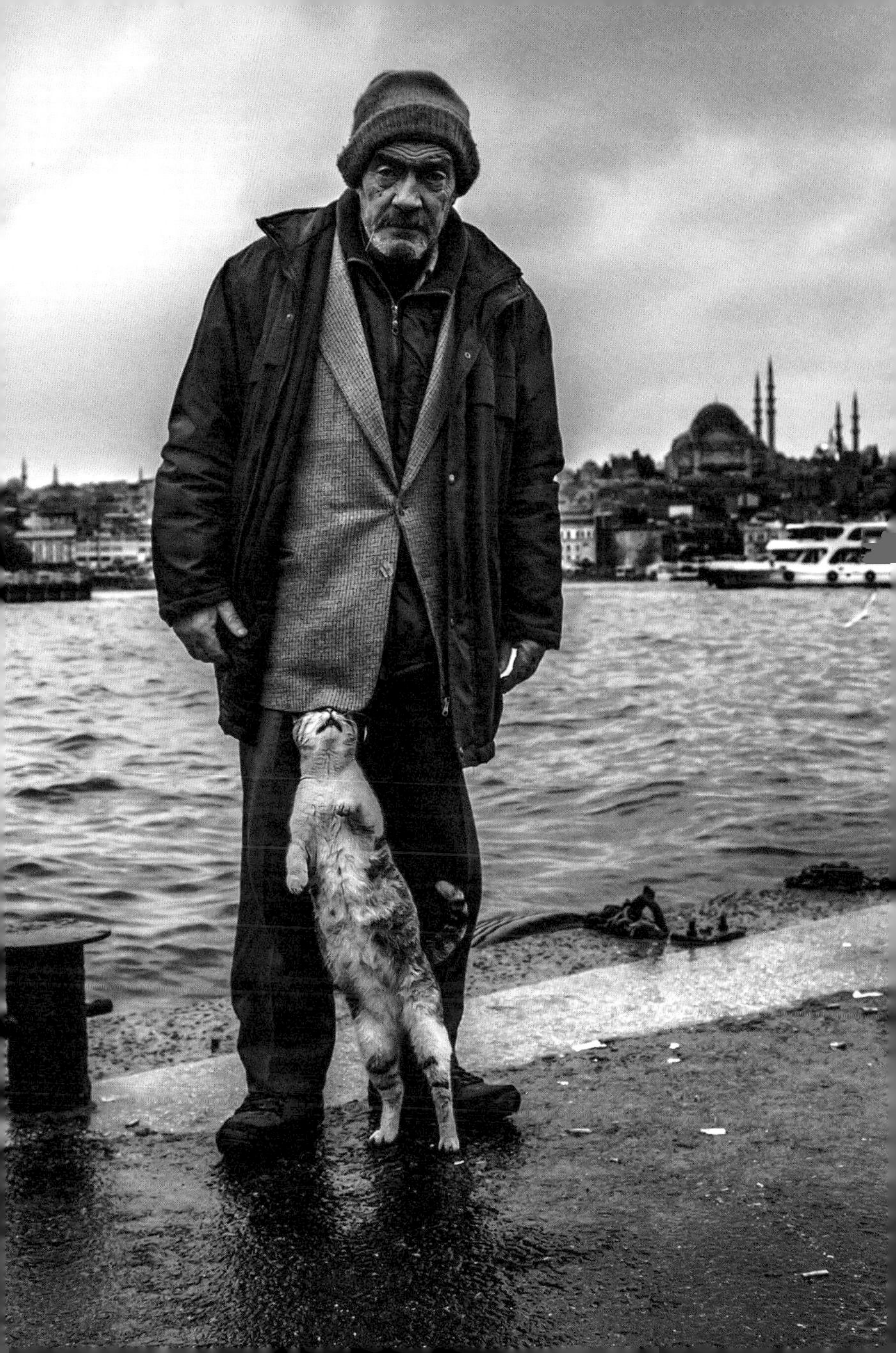

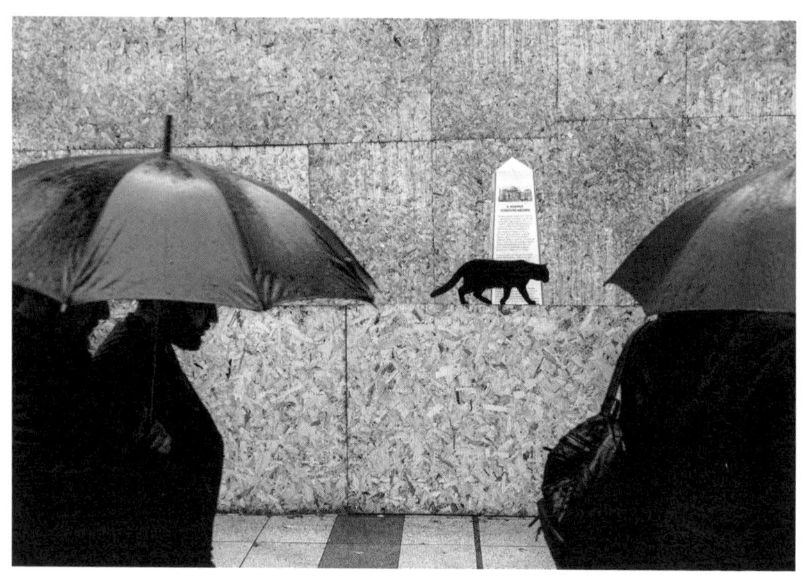

One of Us, 2015

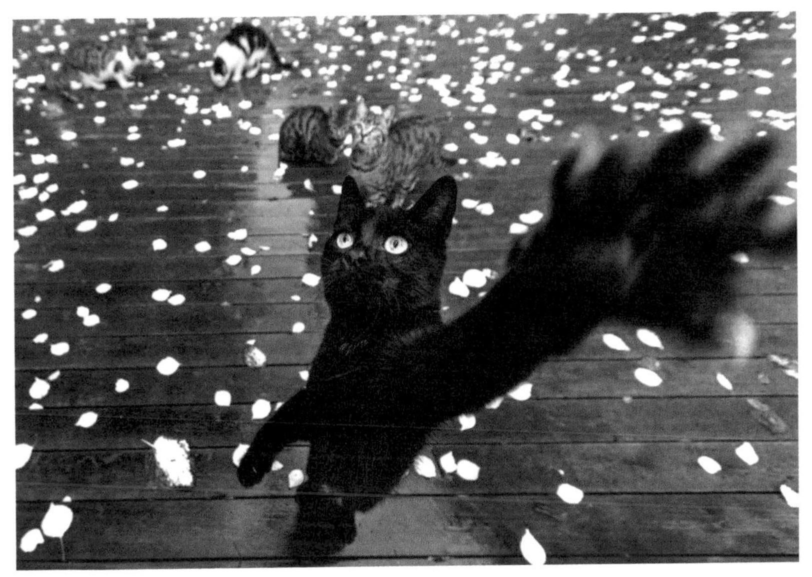

Naughty, 2014

ODEY & BEBE

Jamie Campbell

Stool, blanket, backdrop – the ingredients for his cat photographs are minimal, but Jamie Campbell's images are anything but simple. It comes down to the 'messiness' of the transaction: the cats, he says, 'don't act on command, or care for cues. They scurry, scamper, look away, hiss, groom themselves, hide, yawn. They aren't participating, but they seem to enjoy watching me watching them. It is a weird exchange, but an amicable one.'

Patience is vital – 'I almost have to bore them. Cats give you the best things when you don't expect it.' His photographs lean towards still lifes rather than portraits. 'In slowing things down,' he says, 'in treating them as pure subject, the real-ness is stripped away. They become less cat-like; less alive. I've lost count of how many people have asked me if the cats are taxidermy.'

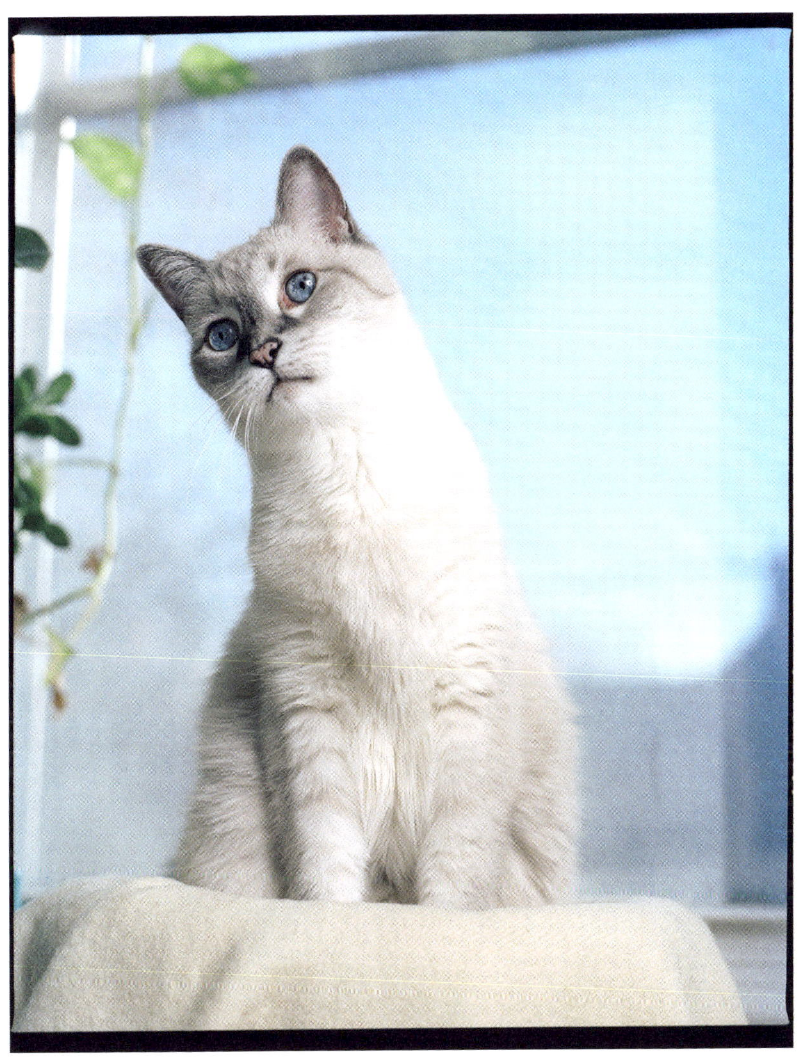

Odey & Bebe, 2008–2024

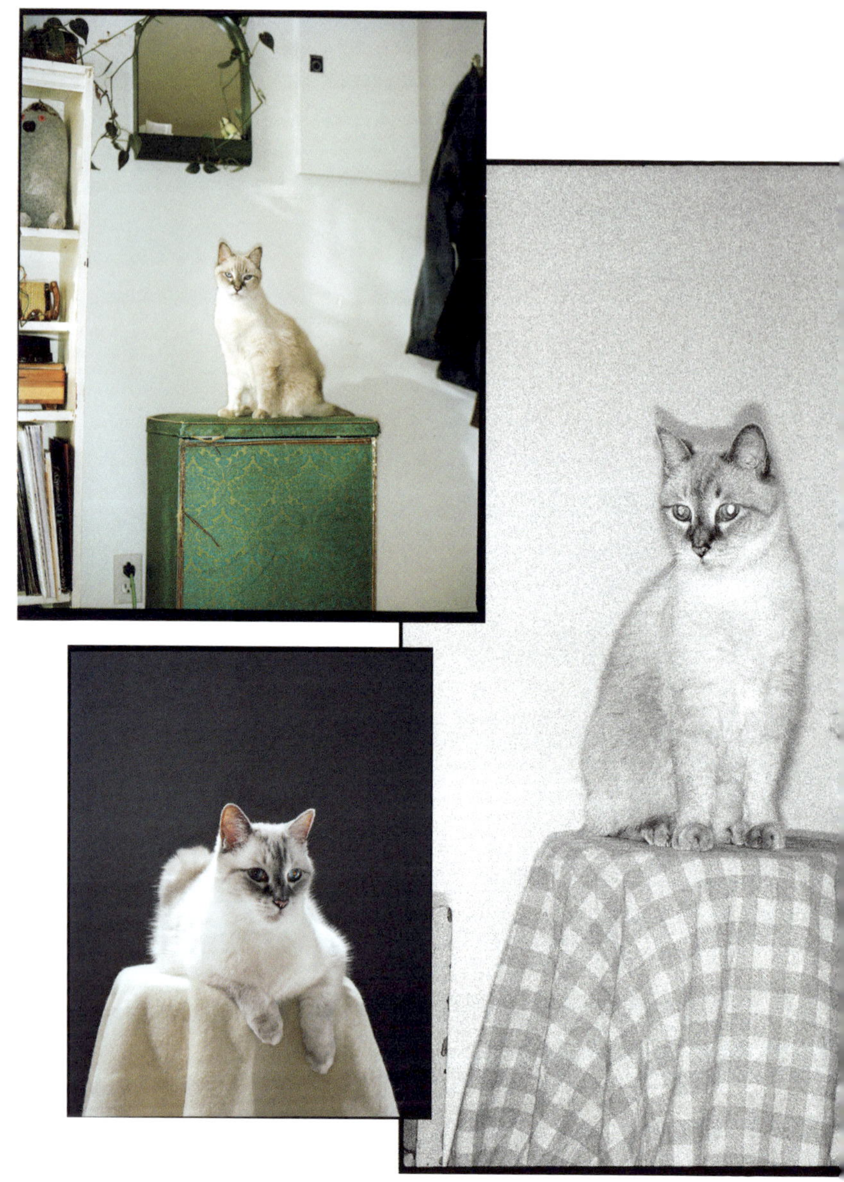

Odey & Bebe, 2008–2024

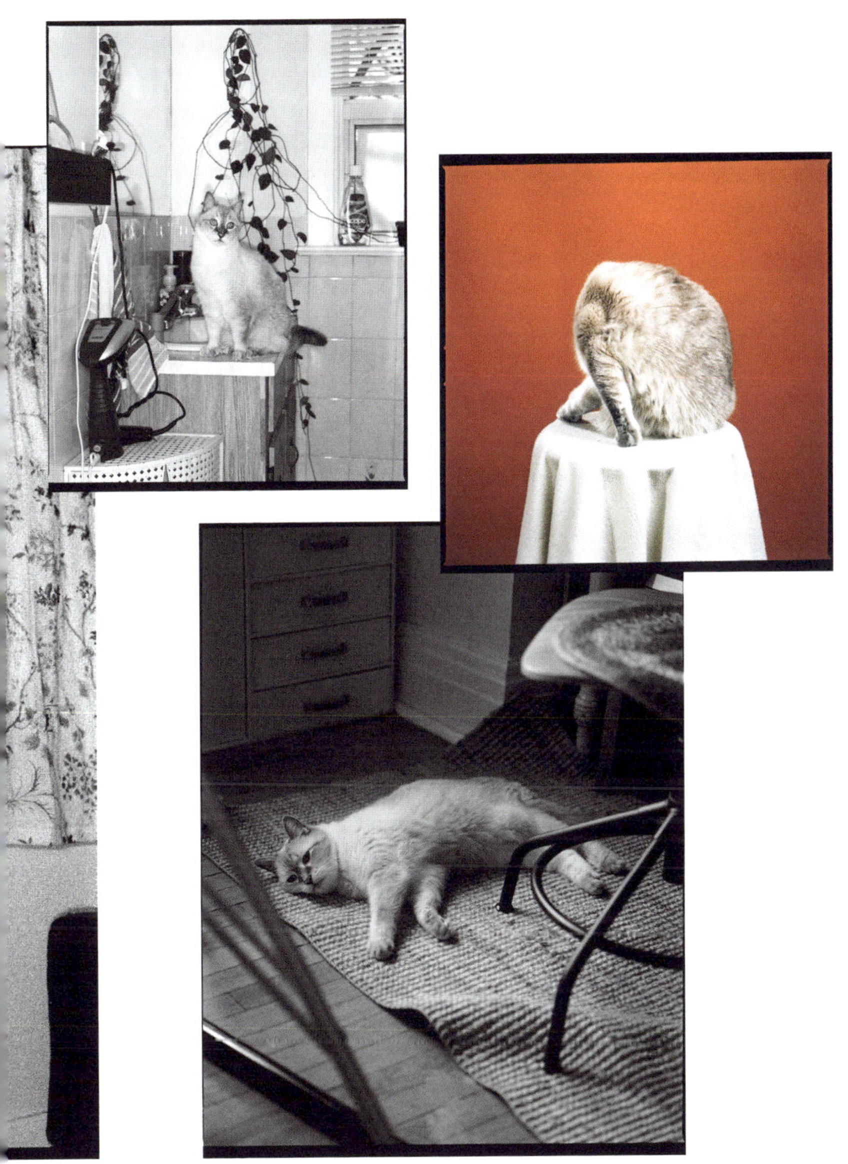

Odey & Bebe, 2008–2024

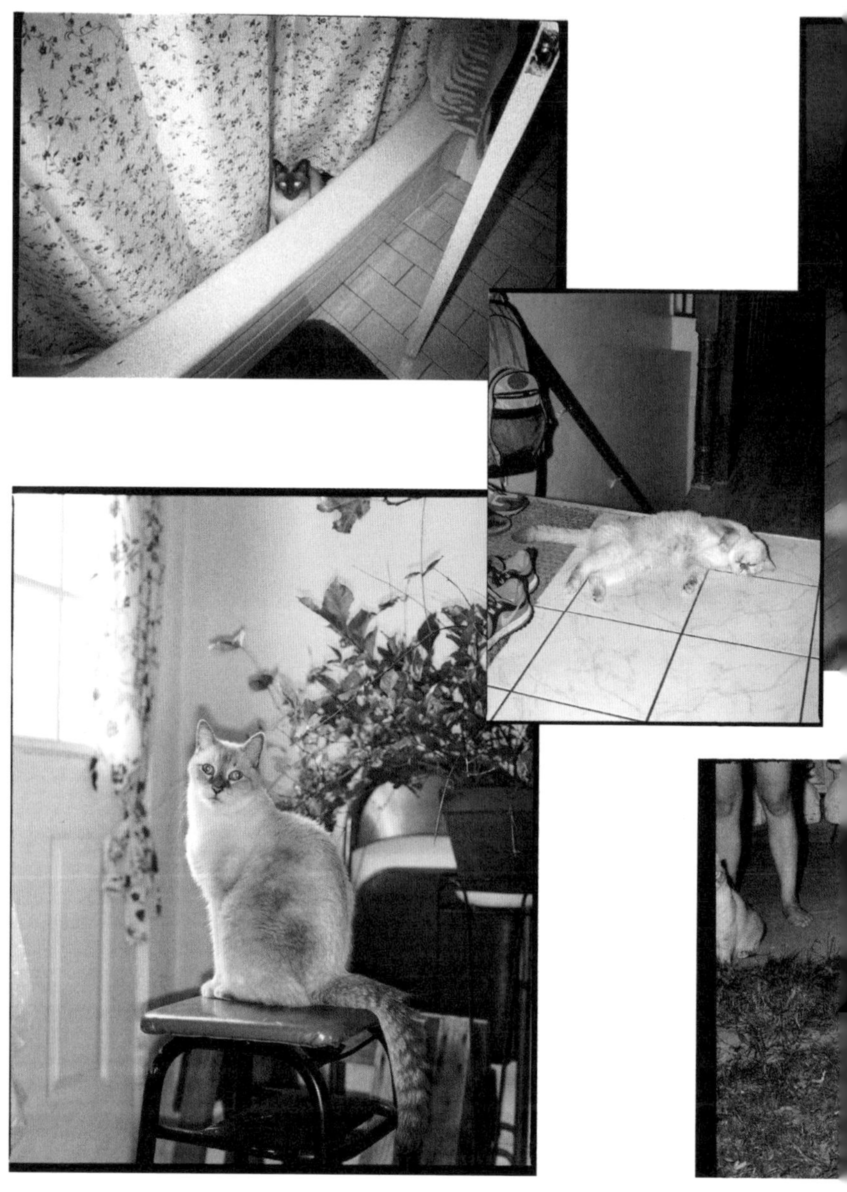

Odey & Bebe, 2008–2024

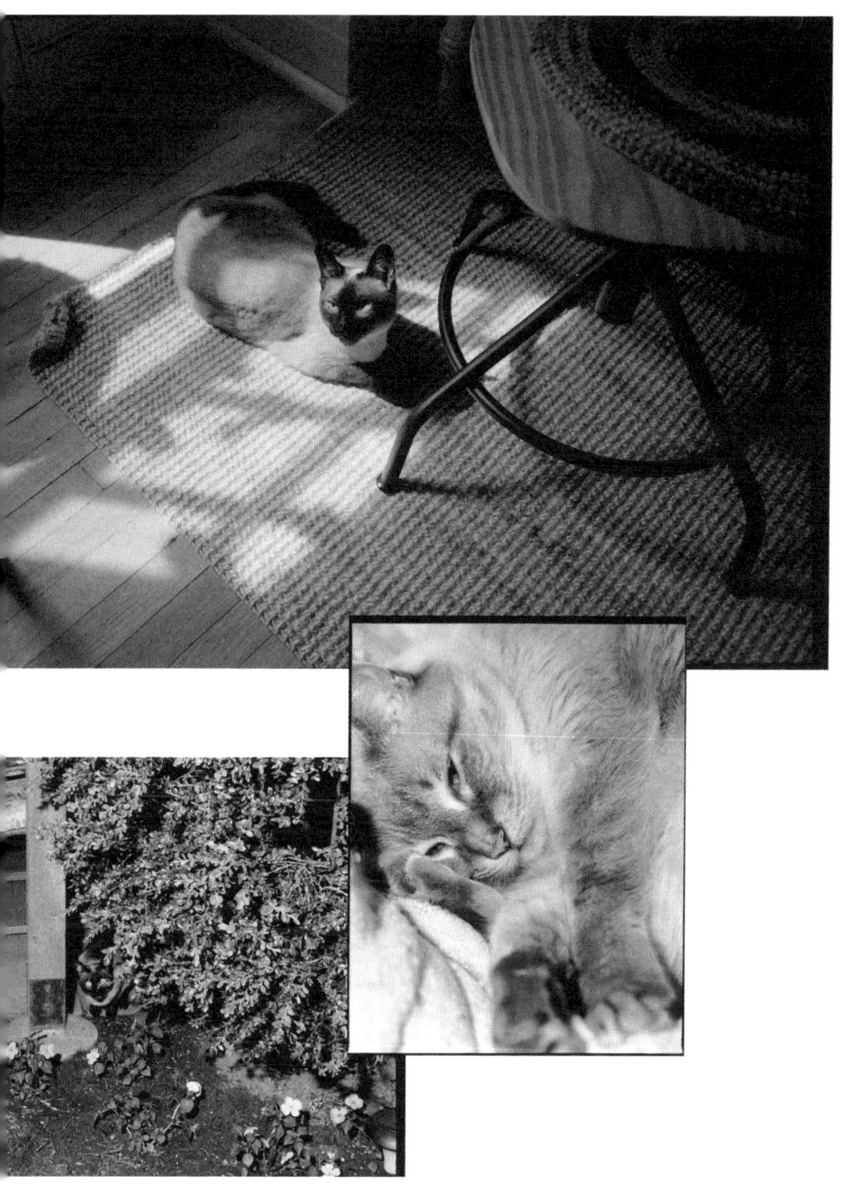

Odey & Bebe, 2008–2024

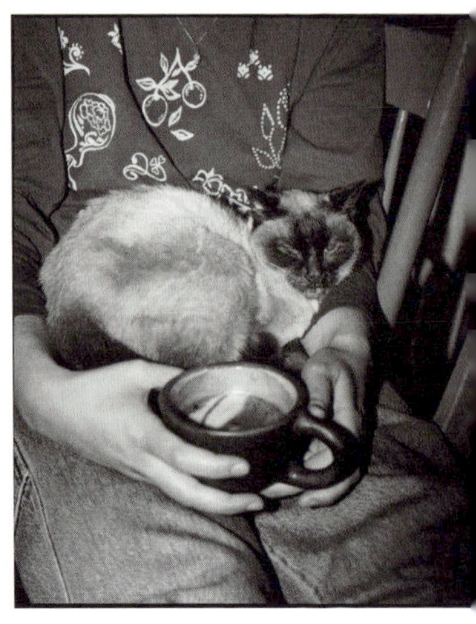

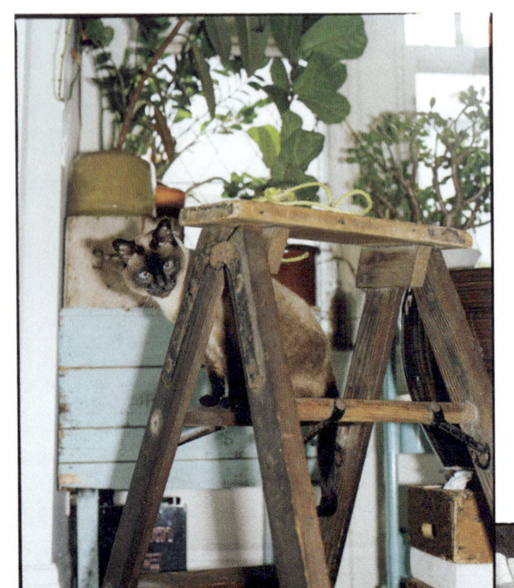

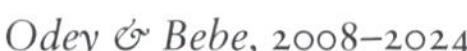

Odey & Bebe, 2008–2024

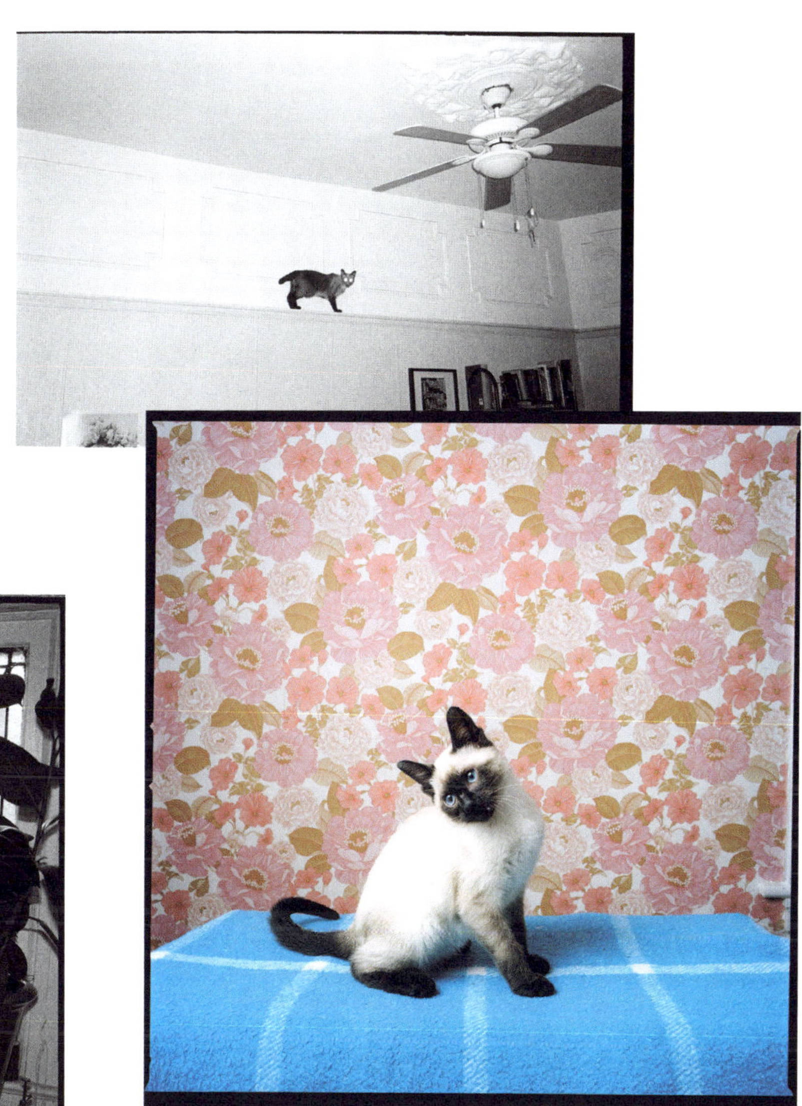

Odey & Bebe, 2008–2024

MAGNUS CATTUS
Matt McCarthy

While observing his pet cats playing with a bug, Matt McCarthy began to wonder how they might react 'if my wife and I were that small. They're so sweet and cuddly that we tend to forget they're apex predators.'

With the aid of Photoshop, he brought that absurd idea to life: a world in which giant felines walk among us. In his surreal collages, cats cling to skyscrapers, curl up and stretch out on a street or beach, climb bridges or slink through tunnels. Many of the scenes are recognisably New York, including Brooklyn, where McCarthy used to live. 'There's an evocative timelessness to New York City that makes it a compelling background,' he says. 'I want to make pictures that feel very familiar to the viewer, yet are slightly off.'

Surrealist and Pop Art are a fertile source of inspiration, though biggest 'by far' is cats themselves, whose way of thinking McCarthy finds 'similar to my own, but in a completely unabashed way that I envy'.

Rosa Always Manages to Find the Best Spot at the Beach, 2024

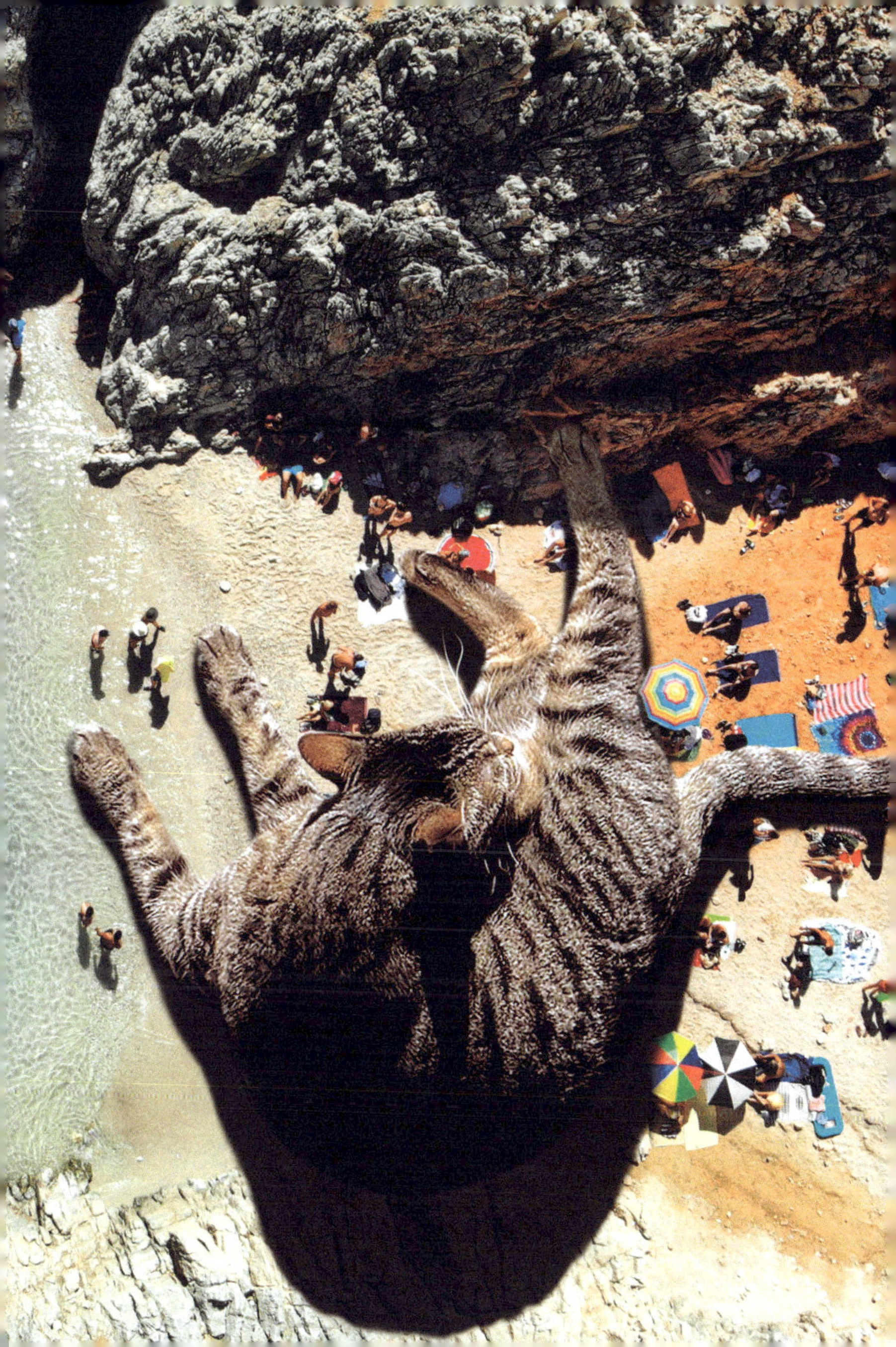

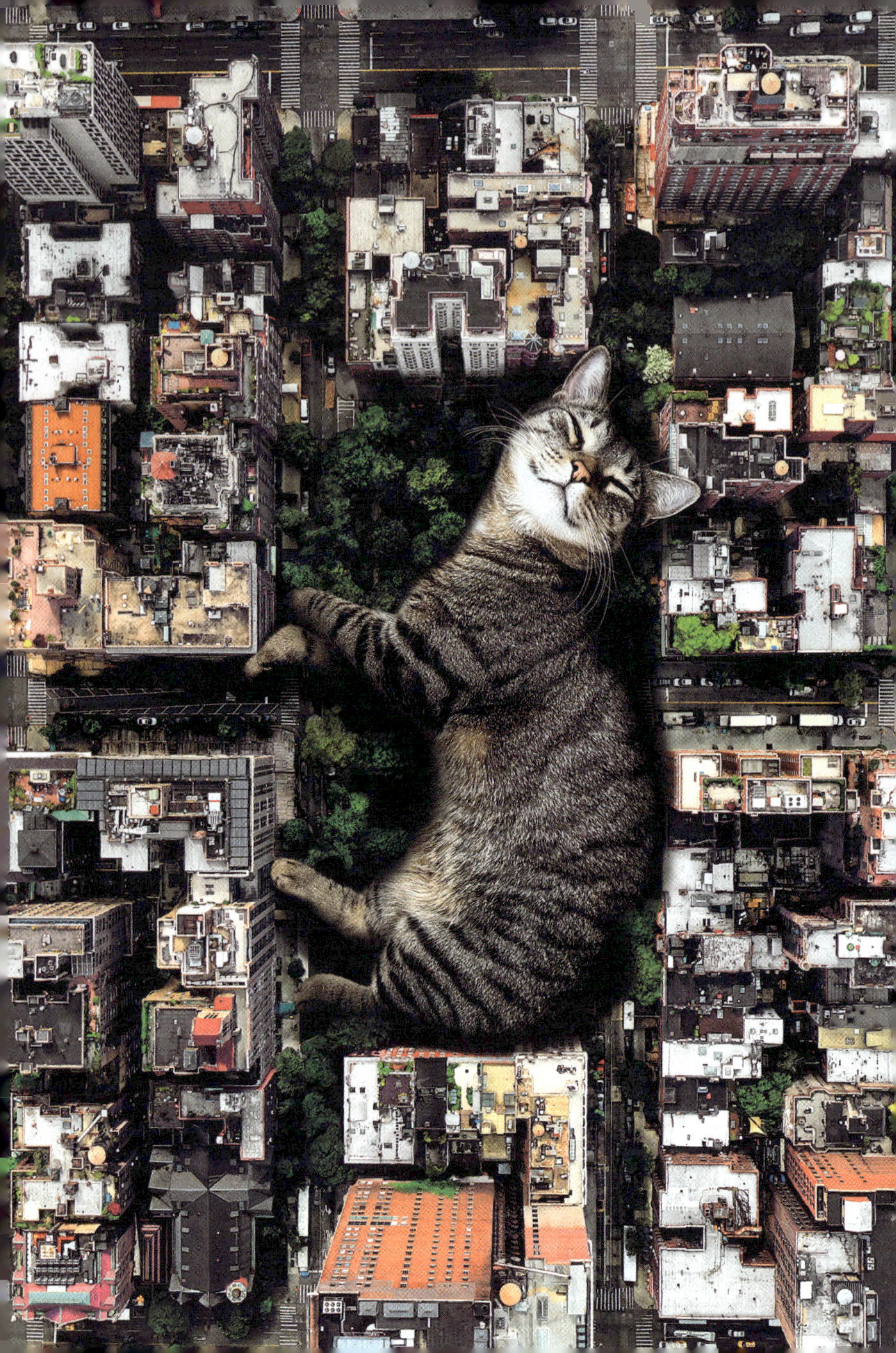

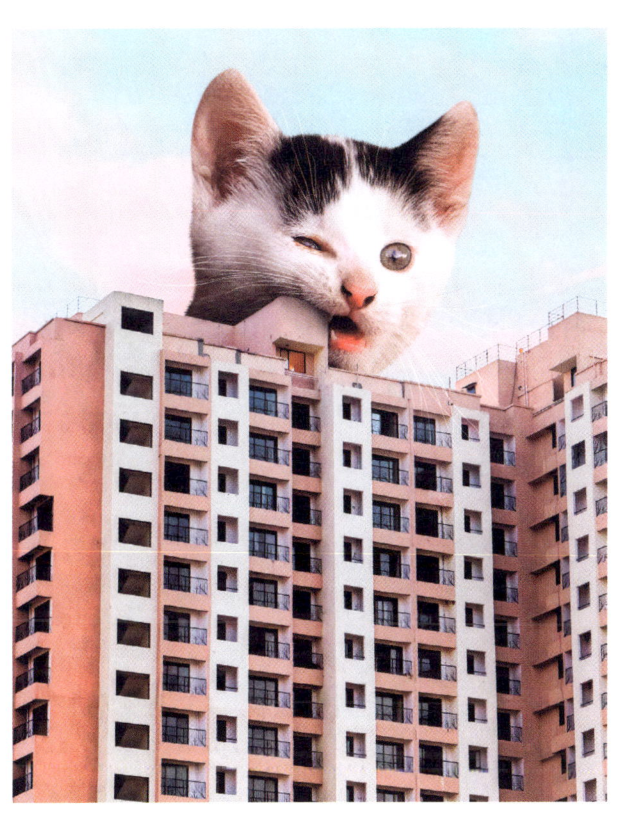

Above: *That's One Way to Floss*, 2021
Opposite: *The Bahamut's Day Out*, 2025

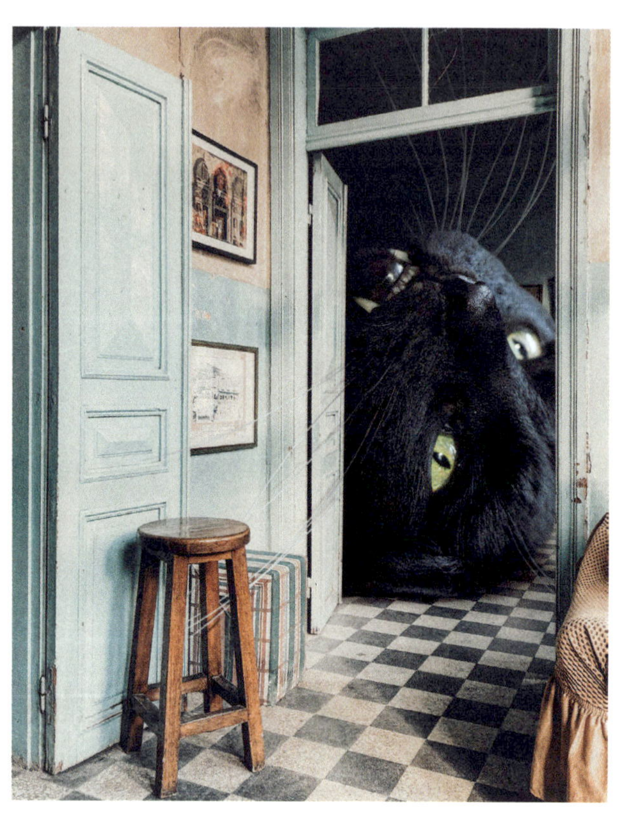

Above: *Najah and the Week That Just Wouldn't End*, 2022
Opposite: *Car Trouble is the Least of Mr Devlin's Problems*, 2024

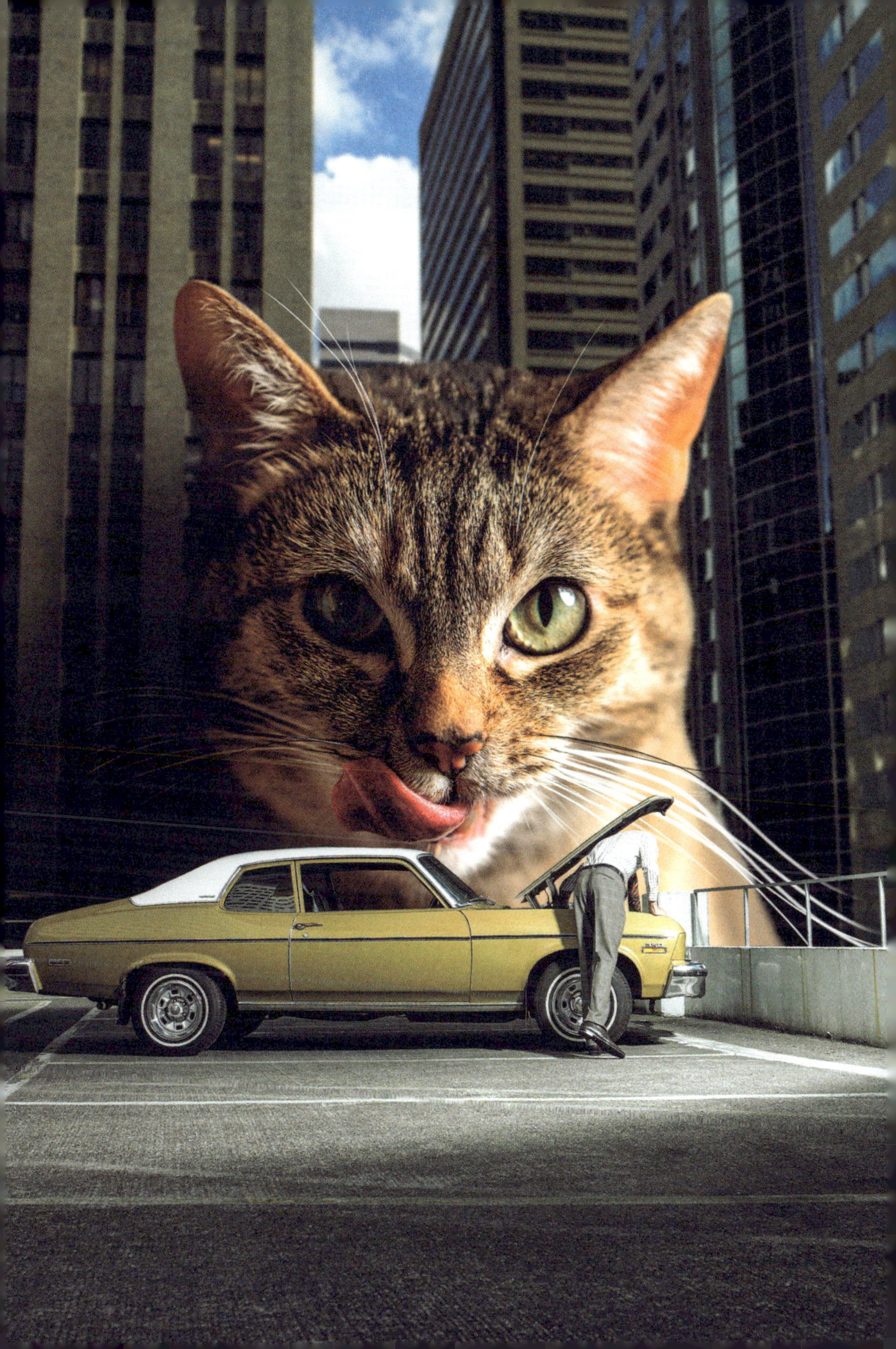

PLAYING DRESS UP WITH AI
Graphic Thought Facility

For an exhibition exploring the force of 'Cute' on contemporary culture at London's Somerset House in 2024, design studio Graphic Thought Facility created a litter of AI-generated cat portraits.

To text prompts such as 'cute and adorable extra fluffy white kitten with unicorn horn', AI began gamely adding its own ideas: dewy doe eyes, big heads, teeny mouths, squishable textures and diffused lighting. The result was a mish-mash of AI's feeding ground, the internet – land of 'lolcat' memes, hilarious cat videos and cat-face filters.

Spend time with these kittens, however, and the cuteness turns creepy; the kitties somewhat menacing. That was always the curator's intention, but still. Six legs, blank eyes and that long hair – shudder. Furry Frankenstein's creatures with invisible stitches.

Playing Dress Up With AI, 2023

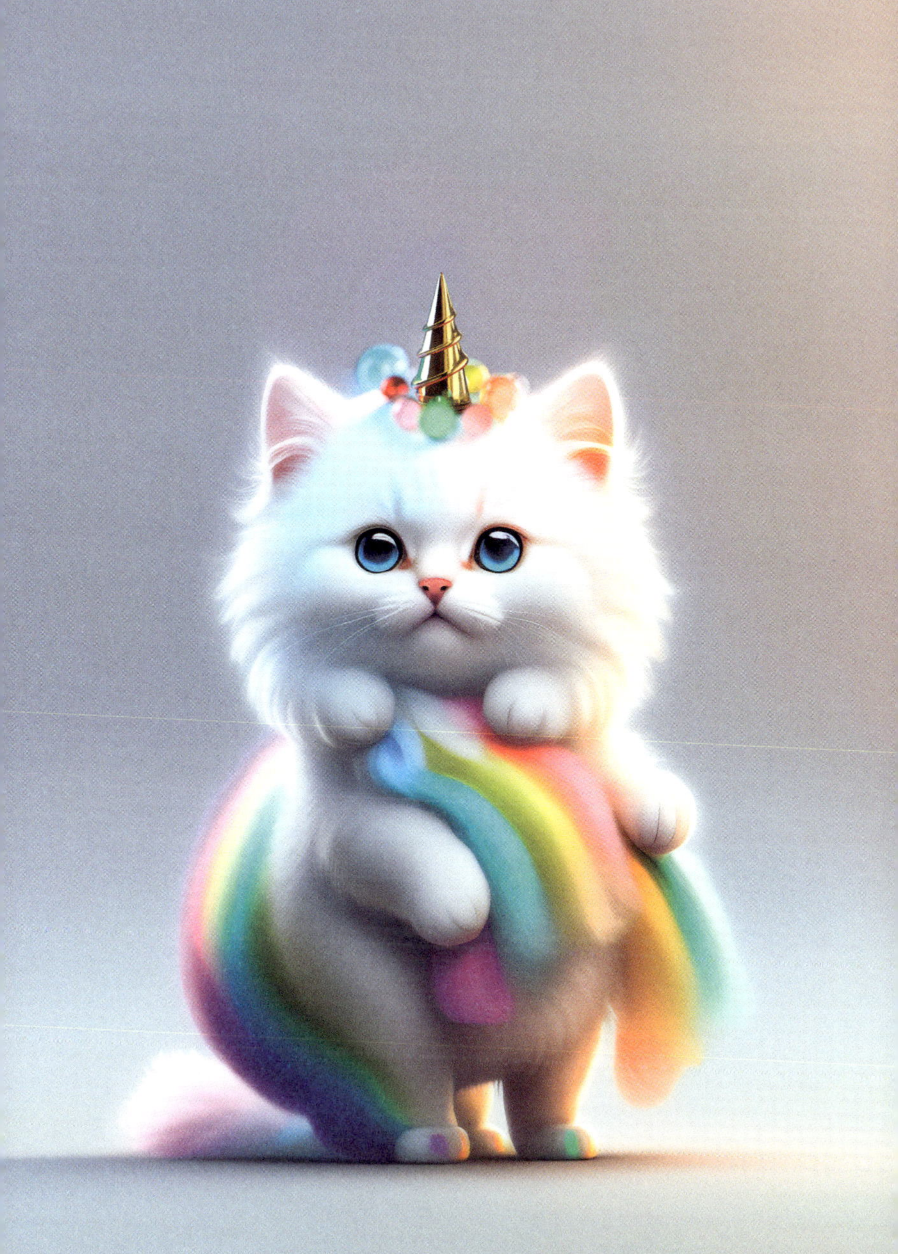

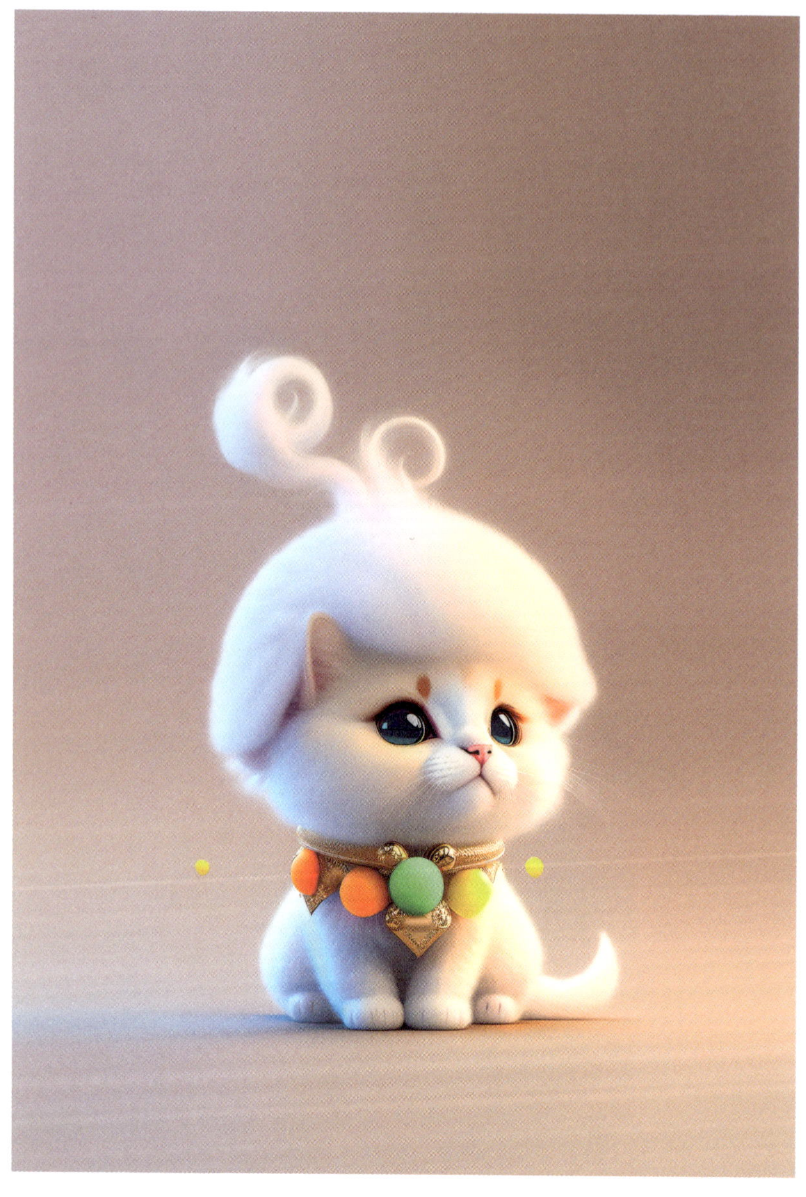

Playing Dress Up With AI, 2023

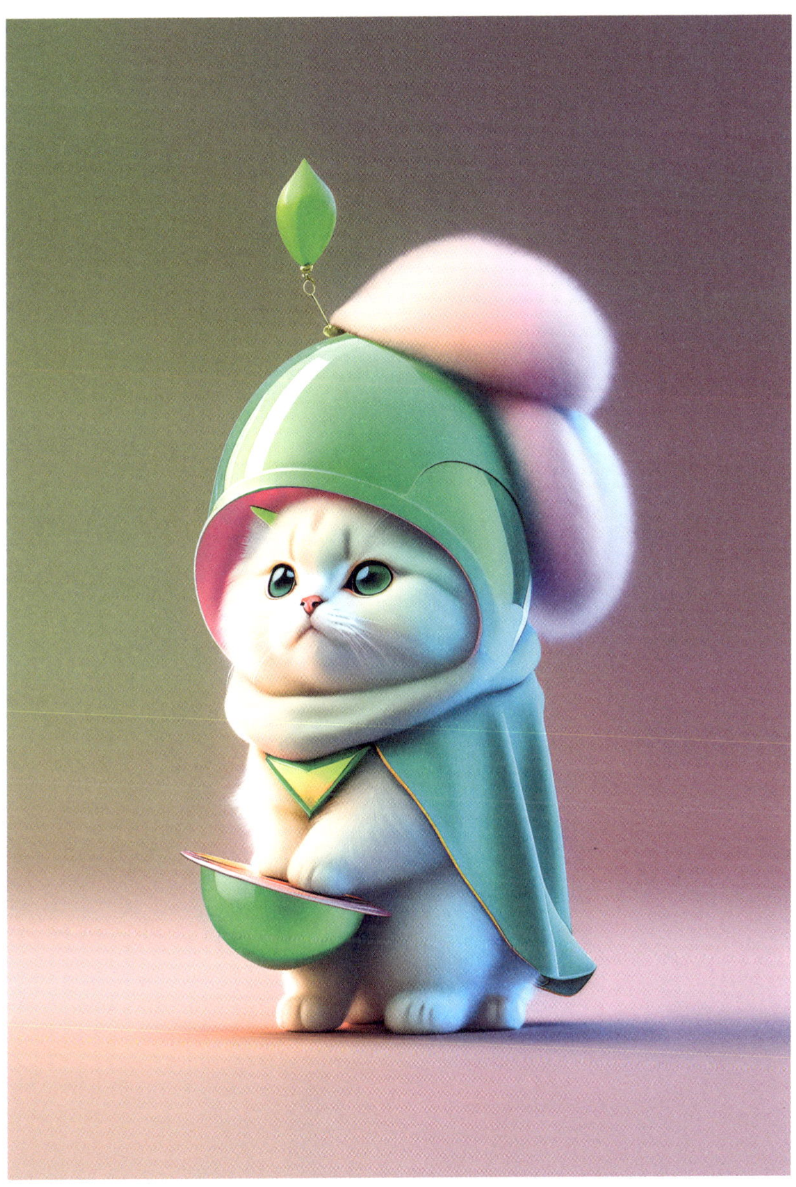

Playing Dress Up With AI, 2023

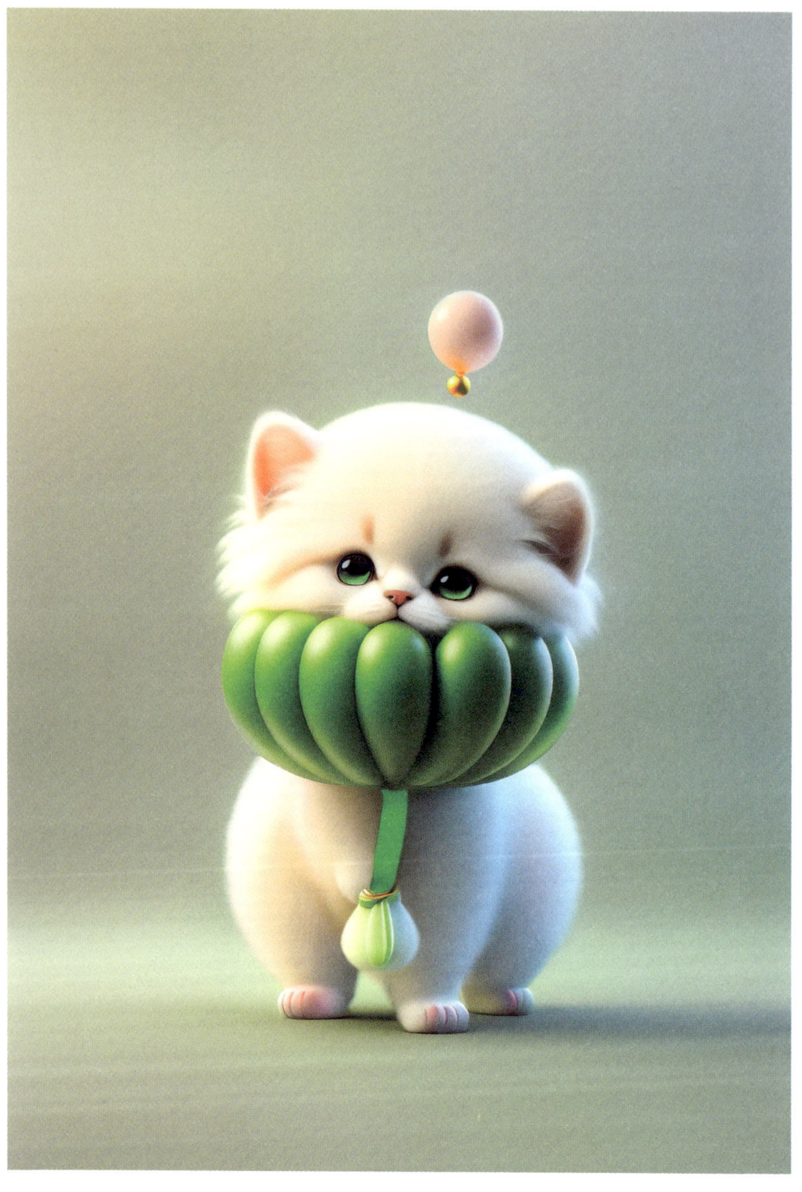

Playing Dress Up With AI, 2023

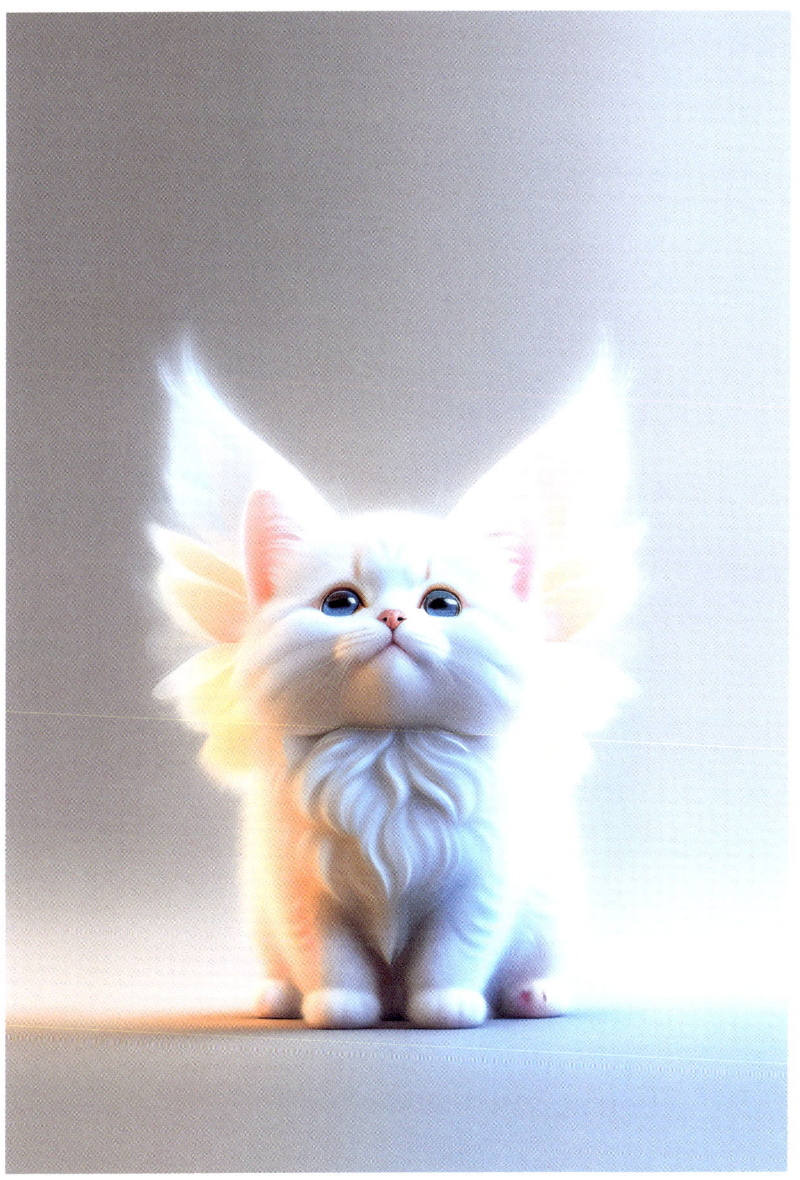

Playing Dress Up With AI, 2023

New Photography of the Cat.
First edition, first printing

Published in 2025 by Hoxton Mini Press, London

Cover image by Robert Bahou
Diesel, 2015

Text by Lucy Davies
Editing by Kate Overy
Production design by Dom Grant
Production control by David Brimble
Proofreading by Florence Ward
Editorial support by Richard Enright

Thank you to all of the individuals and institutions who have provided images and arranged permissions. While every effort has been made to trace the present copyright holders we apologise in advance for any unintentional omission or error, and would be pleased to insert the appropriate acknowledgement in any subsequent edition.

A CIP catalogue record for this book is available from the British Library.

ISBN: 978-1-914314-94-0

Printed and bound by OZGraf, Poland

Manufacturer: Hoxton Mini Press, 104 Northside Studios, 16–29 Andrews Road, London E8 4QF, UK.
www.hoxtonminipress.com

Represented by: Authorised Rep Compliance Ltd., Ground Floor, 71 Lower Baggot Street, Dublin D02 P593, Ireland.
www.arccompliance.com

Photography credits by project:
Chinese Whiskers © Marcel Heijnen; *Animal Soul* © Robert Bahou; *Sphynx Cats* © Alicia Rius; *Charlie* © Lola Dupre; *Fur* © Gerrard Gethings; *Under-Cats Colour* © Andrius Burba; *Girls and Their Cats* © BriAnne Wills; *Writers' Cats* © Jouk Oosterhof; *Community Cats* © Nguan; *Cat Fever* © Ekin Küçük; *Shake Cats* © Carli Davidson; *Symmetricat* © Dag Knudsen; *Cat Worship* © Jack Kenyon; *Backyard Diaries* © Nikita Teryoshin; *Cats and Plants* © Stephen Eichhorn; *For Cats Only* © Pascale Weber; *Cats in Hats* © Rojiman & Umatan Yamazaki; *Amelia & the Animals* © Robin Schwartz; *Katt People* © Julia Lindemalm; *Catography* © Nils Jacobi; *Cats in Windows* © Max Knight; *Ernie* © Tony Mendoza; *Stray Cat* © Sami Uçan; *Odey & Bebe* © Jamie Campbell; *Magnus Cattus* © Matt McCarthy; *Playing Dress Up With AI* 2023 © Graphic Thought Facility. Commissioned by Somerset House, London, for *CUTE* exhibition 25 January–14 April 2024

Hoxton Mini Press is an environmentally conscious publisher, committed to offsetting our carbon footprint. This book is 100 per cent carbon compensated, with offset purchased from Stand For Trees.

Every time you order from our website, we plant a tree: www.hoxtonminipress.com

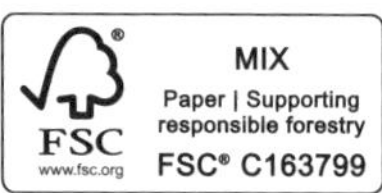